CAPITALISM AS OLIGARCHY

CAPITALISM AS OLIGARCHY

5,000 years of diversion and suppression

Jim O'Reilly

JOR
Boulder

JOR, Boulder, CO
capitalismasoligarchy.com

ISBN 978–0692514269

Cover design: Arantxa Gallastegui

TO ARANTXA

Contents

Figures & Tables

Preface

Many books have been written on capitalism and inequality and it's reasonable to wonder if we need yet another. I believe we do, of course, and this is because most of us are still confused about the system in which we live. I argue that the root problem is our failure to recognize its foundational simplicity. We too easily accept the notion our world is a complex capitalism despite the fact most of us can't explain what that means. It's a black box that somehow burst upon the scene just a few centuries ago and is so intricate even economists who've devoted years to advanced mathematical training don't seem to understand it.

The mainstream account holds we're in something like an evolutionary end state offering the heights of economic efficiency, social justice, and natural liberty. Massive inequality is a mere side-effect. Critics on the left reject the premise it promotes social justice and insist that power be added to the equation, but they still almost universally go along with the idea the system is capitalism and that it's deeply complex and paradoxical. Regardless of whether we accept the mainstream or critical view, we still end up in a thick forest of confusion.

While the details can be complex, they're of little relevance to understanding our social system. The basic pattern is what's important and that, I argue, is extraordinarily simple. This book is about the pattern and makes two inter-related claims. The first is that the notion our system is capitalism is a harmful distortion of reality. It's an intellectual dead end; a wrong turn made over the eighteenth and nineteenth centuries that has brought us into a dark cul-de-sac from which we've no choice but to exit. It limits understanding by imposing unneeded complexity, wrongly insists on being new and unique and thereby severs links with the past, and functions as a cloak that hides the core hostility that's the essence of power.

The second is that inequality can't ever be a mere side-effect of a broader system; whenever and wherever it exists, it *is* the system. It's but another word for concentrated power and as such has ruled mankind throughout the entire span of civilization. Herein lies the crucial defect of capitalism—it distracts us from the existential centrality of inequality. We can't know our social world through its clouded lens for it gets the core motives and dynamics wrong. The system isn't complex capitalism, it's simple inequality.

This book isn't an academic treatise; it's an essay arising from a personal quest to better understand our situation. My argument applies globally but I admit to a parochial focus on the United States and the West for that's what I know best. I hope the worldwide relevance will nevertheless be clear. I also caution that the subtitle doesn't mean this is a history of the past 5,000 years. It isn't; it's an assertion the system today is that old and is best understood in that light.

Finally, very warm thanks go to my wife Arantxa for her excellent critiques and consistent encouragement.

Jim O'Reilly
Boulder 2016

States and governments intrigue and go to war for property: for the banks of the Rhine and territories of Africa, China, or the Balkan Peninsula. Bankers, traders, manufacturers, and landowners work, scheme, and torment themselves and others for property; officials and artisans struggle, cheat, oppress and suffer for the sake of property; our Law Courts and police defend property; our penal settlements and prisons and all the horrors of our so-called repression of crime, exist on account of property.

Property is the root of all evil, and the division and safeguarding of property occupies the whole world.

Leo Tolstoy, 1886[1]

---

[1] Tolstoy (1942: 161)

Introduction

This is an essay on wealth inequality. It addresses what I see as a gigantic problem in our understanding, namely that so many of us fail to recognize its central place in our world. Inequality isn't, I argue, a side-effect, an 'economic' means to allocate resources, a harmless reward for merit, or a sterile statistic; it's the core of what the system is. By placing it front and center in this work, I hope to show that our system is far simpler and far more hostile than we realize.

Massive inequality in the ownership or control of productive resources has dominated mankind throughout the entire 5,000 year span of civilization and current levels are indicative of the norm. Conservative estimates have it that the top one percent of the global population today possesses half of all wealth while the bottom 90 percent just 12. Similar concentrations are found within all nations.

The data is unambiguous; the crucial question is how it should be interpreted. Interpretation, however, leads to the swamp of ideology for we're not dealing with a run of the mill policy issue, we're touching the nucleus of power and the way it justifies itself to the majority. We can bypass the swamp, though, by rejecting interpretation altogether and accepting the data at face value—the system then is seen to be exactly what the data says it is, one of concentrated minority power. The system *is*, in other words, inequality.

This may seem a banal abstraction of a far more complicated world but it turns out it opens the door to a great deal of clarity that otherwise wouldn't be had. By taking this perspective, the most basic logic of the system—its core motives, key risks, and operating dynamics—becomes plain and self-evident. If the system is inequality, then it's reasonable to assume the core motives of the minority in power are nothing other than to aggressively defend its high position and to live luxuriously. To suggest differently seems patently at odds with both history and common sense. The key risks against which the propertied minority must defend itself become equally obvious—they arise from rival competitors and the propertyless majority. Finally, given these motives and risks we can derive two key operating dynamics that must always be present in unequal systems. They're the action processes by which the motives of the minority are achieved and through which wealth gets its meaning. I call them *diversion* and *suppression*.

Diversion is the dynamic whereby the minority *costlessly* diverts human effort into satisfying its motives. Its ability to do so by one means or another is implicit in the definition of wealth. It must be costless because otherwise the power of the minority would flow downward to the majority and inequality as a system would cease to exist.

While diversion is integral to its meaning, wealth ultimately is an expression of minority power over the majority and this requires, above all else, subservience. A differential must be maintained and the dynamic that enforces it is suppression. It's the ongoing imposition of suboptimal living standards, dependence, insecurity, and poverty in service to the vital wealth defense need of sustaining the structural hierarchy. The importance of suppression flows from the fact the majority is the existential risk. Diversion is a form of suppression but I see the latter going much further. It's grounded in the fear that population prosperity is a two-fold threat; first it reduces the minority's differential power over the majority and, second, it creates a 'slippery slope' that encourages ever rising expectations for even greater prosperity.

The immense productive capacity of today is in this way particularly dangerous. Diversion alone doesn't come close to exhausting it and its full *sustainable* use in service to real human needs[1] would generate a widespread prosperity that would threaten the entire edifice. The system demands a servile dependent population and that means our productive potential must forever be suppressed.

The dynamic of suppression is an essential aspect of inequality and it retrodicts[2] what seems otherwise to be one of the great paradoxes of our time—massive poverty and insecurity in the face of extraordinarily high productive capacity. There's no real mystery, though. Inequality requires, causes, and *is* poverty. For the few, it's power, unbridled luxury, and freedom; for the many, it's poverty, insecurity, and subservience. They're two sides of a coin.

This book argues, then, that our modern system is but a phase of the civilization spanning rule of concentrated minority power. The system's logic is simple and flows out of this foundational fact. The prime systemic motives are the aggressive defense of wealth and luxury consumption, the main risks arise from others competing for power and, existentially, from the population below, and the key dynamics are diversion and suppression. I call this ancient system *oligarchy*.

Oligarchy is best thought of in terms of a socioeconomic whole rather than specific individuals or groups. It's a 5,000 year[3] structure of rule comprising an ever shifting yet deeply fortified set of laws, norms, ideologies, and habits of thought that enable and sustain relations of material inequality. Historian Fernand Braudel refers to the structural totality as the "power apparatus," "the sum of the political, social, economic, and cultural hierarchies. . . a collection of means of coercion."[4] Sociologist Michael Mann visualizes it as an "organization chart" by which the rulers have continuously "trapped" the masses.[5]

Ideology in a democratic age can't admit to such a stark state of affairs and presents us instead with a vision in which the system is "capitalism" and

---

[1] I emphasize that I'm referring to *sustainable* capacity in service to true human needs and am not arguing in favor of mindless growth for growth's sake.

[2] "Predicting" an existing fact.

[3] As will be discussed in chapter three, inequality has existed for more than 5,000 years given it was in place at the dawn of civilization. For simplicity, though, I'll often refer to it as a 5,000 year system coterminous with recorded civilization.

[4] Braudel (1982: 554-555)

[5] Mann (1997: 296)

inequality a mere side-effect. Needless complexity bombards us at every turn—here an obsession with obtuse mathematics, there an excessive focus on monetary tokens (even in the name itself, *capital*-ism), and everywhere a concentration on detail. Because it minimizes the fact of massively unequal power and complicates what's inherently simple, capitalism is a false conception and this entire book is an implicit argument against it. The system isn't a capitalism of which inequality is a side-effect; it's inequality (oligarchy) of which capitalism is an ideology.

Sadly, there's no academic discipline called "oligarchy" to help fight this damaging ideology and we'll therefore be forced to cast a wide net across the social sciences. We aren't completely isolated, though, for there's a broad and eclectic tradition which does exactly that; it's the one of *political economy*.[6] As the name implies, political economy rejects the proposition the 'economic' could ever be detached from the 'political.' It thus denies capitalism's central claim of being an 'economic' system somehow floating on a separate plane. The 'economy' is political through and through and doesn't independently exist; there's only the political economy.

The discipline of economics is therefore deeply problematic for it's founded on the idea of an independent sphere. As a 'science' of the non-existent, its main function can only be ideological.[7] Many economists themselves admit to the essential emptiness of their chosen profession. Keynes, for instance, observed in 1936 that "Too large a proportion of recent 'mathematical' economics are mere concoctions, as imprecise as the initial assumptions they rest on, which allows the author to lose sight of the complexities and interdependencies of the real world in a maze of pretentious and unhelpful symbols."[8] Nobel Memorial Prize winner Wassily Leontief noted in 1982 that the mathematical models produced by economic theorists have not been able "to advance, in any perceptible way, a systematic understanding of the structure and the operations of a real economic system."[9] According to a late 1980s survey of US graduate students in

---

[6] I make reference to the definition of *Global Political Economy* offered by political scientist Kees van der Pijl— "those approaches to analyzing world society which seek to overcome the disciplinary divisions of social science." van der Pijl (2009: 1).

[7] I use the term "economics" as applying to mainstream economics. The heterodox and Marxian economic traditions have provided a great deal of insight.

[8] Keynes (1964: 298)

[9] As quoted in Wade (2009: 113).

economics, just 3 percent thought that "having a thorough knowledge of the economy" was "very important" for achieving success in the profession, and 68 percent thought it "unimportant."[10] Economist Thomas Piketty has rather bravely admitted that even after finishing his doctorate, he "knew nothing at all about the world's economic problems."[11] "To put it bluntly," he wrote, "the discipline of economics has yet to get over its childish passion for mathematics and for purely theoretical and often highly ideological speculation."[12] Economist Steve Keen sums it up this way—"the so-called science of economics is a mélange of myths that make the ancient Ptolemaic earth-centered view of the solar system look positively sophisticated in comparison."[13]

This indictment of economics is made even stronger when we take into account the unending series of draconian policy positions put forth by the various national and international economic agencies.[14] The extraordinary puzzle is how it can be we live so poorly in the face of plenty, yet the prescriptions these agencies write are always of the kind that keep our potential far out of reach. The doctors seem set on keeping the patient sick.

We need to expose the debilitating ideologies of capitalism and my working premise is that an effective way of doing so is via a process of radical simplification by which we eschew as much detail as possible and instead focus on the system's broad logic. The entire book is an exercise in simplification. Some may criticize it for this reason but simplicity is widely recognized as a bedrock of the scientific method. The Stanford Encyclopedia of Philosophy asserts that it, not complexity, is held to be a philosophical virtue and that most philosophers "believe that, other things being equal, simpler theories are better."[15] Occam's razor argues in its favor, as does the KISS principle (keep it simple stupid) in engineering. Thomas Aquinas says that even God Himself is "absolutely simple."[16] And the great physicist

---

[10] As quoted in Wade (2009: 114).

[11] Piketty (2014: 31)

[12] Piketty (2014: 32)

[13] Keen (2011,xiii)

[14] These include the national central banks and treasuries, the IMF, World Bank, WTO, BIS, OECD, G7, etc.

[15] Stanford Encyclopedia of Philosophy article on Simplicity. www.plato.stanford.edu/entries/simplicity, accessed November 3, 2014

[16] Aquinas (2006 : 31)

Richard Feynman observed that gravity and nature are simple and thus beautiful.

> But the most impressive fact is that gravity is simple. It is simple to state the principles completely and not have left any vagueness for anybody to change the ideas of the law. It is simple and therefore beautiful. It is simple in its pattern. I do not mean it is simple in its action—the motions of the various planets and the perturbations of one on the other can be quite complicated to work out, and to follow how all those stars in a globular cluster move is quite beyond our ability. It is complicated in its actions, but the basic pattern of the system beneath the whole thing is simple. This is common to all our laws; they all turn out to be simple things, although complex in their actual actions.[17]

The notion our world is well-described by complex capitalism goes against this long philosophic tradition. It's complex only in action, not in its basic pattern. All conclusions in this book derive from radical simplification, abstraction, and exaggeration. This is perfectly acceptable for, as economists Paul Baran and Paul Sweezy have noted, "the function of both science and art is to exaggerate, provided that what is exaggerated is truth and not falsehood."[18]

The book is divided into three sectional headings. The first, *Wealth and Poverty*, contains two chapters. Its purpose is to provide quantitative information on wealth and poverty in our world so we can more intuitively approach the system's logic in the section that follows. Chapter one (*The Wealth Side of Poverty*) examines the extraordinary concentrations of material power that have existed throughout all of civilization right down to the present day. The data speaks for itself and leaves little choice but to conclude the system *is* inequality.

Wealth and poverty are two sides of a coin and chapter two (*The Poverty Side of Wealth*) looks at some poverty statistics. Billions subsist in dehumanizing squalor and majorities everywhere lack secure access to even such basics as a decent home, nutritious food, quality healthcare, sound education, clean environment, safe neighborhood, leisure, and a dignified

---

[17] Feynman (1985: 32-33)
[18] Baran & Sweezy (1966: xiii)

retirement. I argue that a socioeconomic system should be judged by how well it meets these kinds of needs in relation to its productive capabilities. By this metric, modern oligarchy is an abject failure, leaving most of us living far below what's achievable and therefore in a state that's properly termed poverty.

The second section, *The 5,000 Year System*, contains three chapters and devotes itself to the logic of inequality. Chapter three (*The Tyranny of Inequality*) argues that inequality is the root of tyranny and confronts several ideological justifications centered on the Lockean right-libertarian tradition. Chapter four (*Motives, Risks, & Dynamics*) outlines the motives, risks, and dynamics of oligarchy. It focuses on suppression for that's the central dynamic of today given our extraordinary productive capacity. Chapter five (*Capitalism*) takes a brief look at the notion of capitalism and argues it should be dismissed as a useless construct.

The final section, *Modern Oligarchy*, applies what was discussed in the preceding chapters to our system today. Modern oligarchy is a phase of historical oligarchy which, like all past ones, has a few nuances. The most important for our purposes are that wealth is held collectively through ownership claims on a small number of giant oligopolistic firms, there's a tight identity between power and money, productive capacity is immense, and workers are generally free to labor for whomever they choose. There are seven chapters.

Chapter six (*The Global Game*) introduces the approach that will be developed throughout the section. The idea is as simple as inequality itself. Modern oligarchy can be thought of in terms of a global game centered on diversion; its rules are written by the oligarchy as a class and national populations are the pawns. Through this perspective, we'll find that a great deal of confusion about our 'capitalist' system dissolves away. The chapter makes and defends three important simplifying assumptions—that there are just two fundamental classes, that the game is global rather than national, and that in crucial respects the oligarchy is a collective unity. The chapter also presents the two key concepts of *finance* and the *market portfolio*.

Chapter seven (*The Diversion-Profit Loop*) examines how diversion is costlessly sustained in modern oligarchy through what I term the *diversion-profit loop*. We'll find that profit on the macro-scale isn't related to wages but is rather the monetary return flow of oligarchic diversion spending. (There are other sources of profit as well which will be brought out in later chapters.)

We'll also discover that workers are always costless but can never, in and of themselves, be profitable.

In chapter eight (*Suppression*), we begin exploring the dynamic of suppression in modern oligarchy and the ways it's used to control our enormous productive capacity. The essential function of suppression is to prevent widespread prosperity in order to sustain the social hierarchy. It lurks in every single nook and cranny of the system and exhibits a consistent pattern. It almost always presents itself as a duality between collective action and competition; the oligarchy comes together collectively to minimize intra-class competition while it diligently enforces the opposite on workers. This duality captures the game's most basic operating rule—the oligarchy cooperates and populations compete. The chapter concentrates on how this plays out in the 'private' market. It highlights the logic behind preventing price wars via corporate consolidation and the importance of the profit margin as the key monetary metric of suppression.

Chapter nine (*Money & the Oligarchic State*) looks at suppression in the 'public' realm. Its purpose is to deny population access to the collective potential of state spending. The oligarchy accomplishes this through a thick ideological wall serving the essential function of keeping population benefitting state spending low. The chapter examines taxation and public debt and shows that the realities of both are concealed by mythologies that portray them as costly and bad. We'll find that in actuality the oligarchy doesn't incur a tax burden and that so-called public debt can't reasonably be thought of as such.

Chapter ten (*The Transnational Oligarchy*) examines the confusion arising from the dichotomy between the global whole and the national parts. It argues for a global perspective in such matters as trade, production, currencies, taxation, and state debt. The common notion the system is fundamentally inter-national leads to many erroneous conclusions and serves important suppressionary goals. At root, the system isn't inter-national; it's inter-class. The suppressionary duality between collective action and competition plays an important role here as well.

Chapter eleven (*The Grand Casino*) takes a look at inter-oligarchic competition in the grand casino of speculation and fraud. This highly visible power struggle is endemic to the game of oligarchy and grounded in the motive of wealth defense.

The section ends with chapter twelve (*Global Oligarchic Governance*) which argues that we're governed globally by the rules of the game of inequality. The chapter examines some of the key international agencies and practices that enforce these rules. The book then closes with a concluding chapter.

I portray the system as deeply hostile to the majority and therefore illegitimate. While this may generate disagreement in some quarters, I don't think the essential facts are disputable. In the private posh confines of the country club, no oligarch would deny that great inequality has spanned all of civilization or that it's a form of rule. Nor would he[19] refute the proposition that his core motives are the defense of his high position and luxury consumption. He would instead be proud he's part of a grand aristocratic tradition and that his cunning, skill, intelligence, good looks, or family inheritance has put him in the ranks of a nobility going back millennia. His greatest enemy? This he also wouldn't deny—the democratic spirit that rejects his claim to power.

It's to that spirit I dedicate this work. I address it to a wide audience; to the political left as perhaps an aid to thinking about our situation, to those in the middle who may be open to a critical examination of the system, and also to my ideological opponents. Many well-meaning people across the entire spectrum have been misled by harmful ideologies and I believe they'll benefit from the argument presented here.

To those, though, who hold pro-oligarchic opinions despite understanding what that entails, I would point out they carry an immense moral burden. The system they defend has condemned a substantial percentage of mankind to degrading conditions that have robbed them not only of their basic dignity, but often of their lives. Philosopher Thomas Pogge has estimated that 300 million people have died since the end of the Cold War from starvation and preventable disease.[20] This is far more than in all

---

[19] Extreme wealth throughout recorded history has always been patriarchal and remains so today. Among the top 100 global billionaires identified by Forbes, just 9 are women and all are inheritors of their father's or grandfather's fortune. Given the continued masculine dominance of wealth, it seems misleading to use terms like he/her for oligarchs as it falsely implies an equality between the sexes. Even though the class contains a small minority of women, I'll therefore refer to oligarchs as masculine. Forbes website accessed February 24, 2016.

http://www.forbes.com/billionaires/list/#version:static

[20] Pogge (2008: 104)

the wars of the twentieth century and the cause is directly traceable to the logic of oligarchy.

I've of course benefited here from the works of many people, most obviously the ones cited as references. I owe a strong debt to political scientist Jeffrey Winters for his concept of civilization spanning oligarchy and have tried in this book to extend his basic theme into the realm of political economy and capitalism. The economic writings of mid-twentieth century Polish economist Michal Kalecki have been of extraordinary value in developing the links between age-old oligarchy and capitalism. His profit equation is the essential spine of much of the *Modern Oligarchy* section, although I interpret it in a somewhat unconventional way. My goal, after all, isn't to understand capitalism as a stand-alone system but as a phase of a much older one. I also note the key influence of early twentieth century economist Thorstein Veblen. His sharp insights on the consolidating capitalism of his era and his critiques of the "vested interests" and their business methods have been highly influential in developing the concept of suppression.

I hope to have convinced you to join me now in exploring this world of ours that's in such dire need of radical change. The future of our children and grandchildren depends on *you* understanding the nature of our situation.

Wealth and Poverty

1

The Wealth Side of Poverty

This opening chapter examines the extent of inequality both today and throughout the history of civilization. We'll find that our planet and every nation on it has always been owned by a tiny minority while the majority has possessed essentially nothing.

All serious studies support this conclusion despite having differences in their definitions of wealth and sources of data. Some measure the ownership of productive resources and include only *financial wealth* which excludes real estate and other assorted items. The result is a higher concentration ratio since home values, the primary asset of the middle-class, are excluded. Others measure *total wealth*. Financial wealth is probably a better indicator of power but either definition is adequate for our purposes.

A common data source is governmental tax records but its accuracy is affected by the extent of tax evasion. A well-heeled industry has sprung up over the past decades having as its sole goal the sheltering of wealth from taxation. This is done through tax havens, defined by political economists Ronen Palan, Richard Murphy, and Christian Chavagneux as "jurisdictions that deliberately create legislation to ease transactions undertaken by people who are not resident in their domains, with a purpose of avoiding taxation and/or regulations, which they facilitate by providing a legally backed veil of secrecy to obscure the beneficiaries of those transactions." [1] These jurisdictions aren't by any means 'rogue states' operating outside the rules of the system, they're instead integral elements of standardized global business practice.[2] The universally regarded 'best practice' for the management of wealth is the simple stratagem of constructing enormous legal complexity. Assets are placed in tax havens in the name of anonymous off-shore corporations owned by trusts in other jurisdictions whose trustees are scattered in still others.[3] The idea is to create an impenetrable fog through fragmentation.

We don't know how much wealth is holed up in tax havens. Palan, et al. "conservatively" estimate it at $11 to $12 trillion[4] but economist James Henry goes much further, "conservatively" putting the number at $21 to $32 trillion. He notes this is just financial wealth and excludes such assets as real estate, yachts, racehorses, and gold bricks that are also owned in this secret manner.[5] Taking the hidden wealth into account, he concludes that at least a third of global private financial wealth is owned by just 91,000 people, 0.001 percent of the world population, with the next 51 percent being owned by 8.4 million or 0.14 percent.[6] Based on his analysis, a microscopic 0.141 percent of the global population effectively owns the planet, or at least 84 percent of it, with the remaining 99.859 percent being left with a paltry 16 percent.

We shouldn't be fooled by the precision of these numbers for all we really know is that the world is owned by a tiny minority. Thomas Piketty has performed an analysis based on tax data and concludes that the top 0.1, 1, and 10 percent of the global population possess 20, 50, and between 80 to 90 percent of total global wealth with the bottom half owning less than 5 percent.[7] Piketty's numbers include real estate and other wealth forms excluded by Henry and don't account for tax evasion. Credit Suisse is in the same ballpark, reporting that the top 1, 5, and 10 percent own 50, 77, and 88

[1] Palan, et al. (2010: 45)
[2] Palan, et al. (2010: 4)
[3] Henry (2012: 9)
[4] Palan, et al. (2010: 63)
[5] Henry (2012: 5)
[6] Henry (2012: 36)
[7] Piketty (2014: 438)

percent of total global wealth with the bottom half owning less than 1 percent.[8]

The extremity of wealth inequality isn't normally publicized in the mainstream media, but it's well known within the financial industry catering to these lords. A notorious memorandum written in 2005 by Citigroup analysts under the banner "Citigroup Industry Note" is worth quoting in part.

> the world is dividing into two blocs—the plutonomies, where economic growth is powered by and largely consumed by the wealthy few, and the rest. . . . The earth is being held up by the muscular arms of its entrepreneur-plutocrats, like it, or not. . . . In a plutonomy there is no such animal as the 'U.S. consumer' or 'the UK consumer', or indeed the 'Russian consumer'. There are rich consumers, few in number, but disproportionate in the gigantic slice of income and consumption they take. There are the rest, 'the non-rich', the multitudinous many, but only accounting for surprisingly small bites of the national pie.[9]

The report goes on to offer a "Plutonomy Basket" of stocks that provides a "more refined way to play plutonomy" through a focus on companies that "make the toys that the Plutocrats enjoy."[10] The document proudly notes that its basket has outperformed the general stock market since the mid-eighties.

We have no need for exceptional precision to understand we live on a planet we don't own. Well connected former managing director of Kissinger Associates, David Rothkopf, has estimated that the combined net worth of the world's richest thousand or so people is almost twice that of the poorest 2.5 billion.[11] He inescapably concludes that "power on the planet is not only concentrated, it is extraordinarily concentrated."[12] "There is a group of a few thousand people among the corporate elite," he says, "who effectively

---

[8] Credit Suisse Research Institute, Global Wealth Report 2015, October, 2015, Pages 13, 19

[9] Ajay Kapur, Niall Macleod, & Narenda Singh under the banner Industry Note dated October 16, 2005. Taken from pages one and two.
    https://www.scribd.com/doc/131287460/The-Plutonomy-Memo-by-Citigroup, accessed August 22, 2015

[10] Page 25.

[11] Rothkopf (2008: 2)

[12] Rothkopf (2008: 37)

control perhaps $100 trillion, two thirds of the world's total assets."[13] Just a few hundred, according to a former vice-chairman of Merrill Lynch, are the "movers and shakers" in global finance.[14] "The world is pretty small," observes the billionaire chairman and CEO of Wall Street firm Blackstone Group, "In almost every one of the areas in which I'm dealing or in which we at Blackstone are looking at deals, you find just twenty, thirty, or fifty people worldwide who ultimately drive the industry or sector."[15]

Wealth concentrations within individual countries follow the same pattern. Economist Edward Wolff has analyzed the wealth distribution in the United States using data from the Federal Reserve and the Internal Revenue Service. While his analysis excludes the effects of tax havens and thereby underestimates the concentration level, it's a sobering testament to what officially derived statistics tell us. According to Wolff, the top 1, top 10, and bottom 80 percent in the US own respectively 42.7, 82.9, and 7 percent of financial wealth.[16]

I'm throwing out a lot of numbers here and fear their dryness can deaden our senses. Let's therefore take a moment and visualize what Wolff's data is saying. Assume we have 100 chairs lined across a stage with 100 people congregating behind them.[17] Each chair represents 1 percent of total wealth and each person 1 percent of the population. In an equal society, everybody has a chair. A master of ceremonies enters and authoritatively announces he will assign the chairs using Wolff's inequality data. He begins by ordering a full 60 of the people to exit the stage as they'll not get among them even a single chair. That's right, the bottom 60 percent of the population have a combined 0.3 percent of wealth, an insufficient accumulation to warrant a chair. They're escorted to the dark alley behind the theater and asked never to return.

The stage now contains 100 chairs and 40 lucky individuals who are anticipating their prize. The MC announces that 7 chairs will go to 20 of them and the audience laughs as they struggle to fit roughly 3 to a chair. 80 of the 100 have now been assigned their position yet only 7 chairs are occupied. 20

[13] Rothkopf (2008: 121)

[14] As quoted in Rothkopf (2008: 131).

[15] As quoted in Rothkopf (2008: 45).

[16] Wolff (2010: 44)

[17] I make no claim to the originality of portraying inequality via chairs and people. I've seen it somewhere before but haven't been able to locate the source.

are crammed into 7 seats and 60 are roaming the backstage alleys. 93 chairs are empty.

The MC next awards 10 chairs to 10 of the remaining 20 people. Each of these fortunate folks[18] gets a chair and they're quite pleased. There are now only 10 people remaining to fill 83 empty seats. The top 10 percent possess 82.9 percent of financial wealth, the bottom 90 just 17.1 percent.

The MC goes on to announce he will present 11 chairs to the next 5, a bit over 2 per person. Now only 5 people remain and 72 chairs are still empty. The top 5 percent control 72 percent of wealth, the bottom 95 only 28. The next 4 are given 29 chairs or about 7 each. And for the grand finale, the sole remaining person is given 43. The audience erupts in enthusiastic applause; the military guard marches on stage; the National Anthem is played. That, ladies and gentlemen, is the officially derived distribution of financial wealth in the United States. The top 1 percent has far greater wealth than the bottom 95.[19]

If wealth is rule, who in this visualization should we say are the material rulers, what we'll call the oligarchs? It's not the 60 who are roaming the back allies nor the 20 who form a quivering mass surrounding their 7 chairs. The bottom 80 are not members of the oligarchic class; they're the ruled. The 10 who were assigned 1 chair each are doing much better but their wealth is no more than what the average would provide. It's only the top 10 who own disproportionately and they could therefore be considered the broad oligarchic class, owning as they do 83 chairs. But there's a gigantic divergence within this well-heeled group with the bottom five enjoying 11 chairs and the top five 72. The steep gradation continues within the top 5 and, though data isn't provided here, would exist within the top 1 percent as well.

I don't think it's important to get specific; the top 1 percent is clearly in the oligarchic class and I would add to it those within the top 5 and perhaps going somewhat beyond that. But it really doesn't matter where one draws the line or even if it's drawn at all. Little more need be said beyond that the bottom 80 owns just 7 percent of wealth. And we know that Wolff's data is overly conservative because it ignores tax havens; Henry's analysis would give

---

[18] 'Folks' is an increasingly common term in US political discourse, evoking perhaps an illusory sense of equality.

[19] All data was taken from Wolff (2010: 44).

us a global oligarchic class representing a tiny fraction of 1 percent of the population.

Piketty reports that European countries today are somewhat less concentrated than the US with, according to his officially derived tax based figures, 60 percent of total wealth being owned by the top 10 percent versus 72 percent for the US.[20] Piketty's numbers, again, are rock bottom since they exclude the effects of tax evasion. He's in agreement with Wolff's conclusions on the US, stating in a footnote that the upper decile owns 70 to 80 percent or more of financial wealth.[21] European financial concentrations are greater than Piketty's numbers which reflect total wealth.

It's the same theme with only modest local variation outside the US/European core. Extreme inequality is the uniform global situation. "It is true of the oligarchs of Russia, the men and women who run Korea's *chaebol*, the leading family-owned companies of the Philippines and elsewhere in southeast Asia," and it's true in Latin America as well. Chile is "not so much a country as a country club" of just a few families, according to a privileged Chilean.[22] Economist James Cypher and social scientist Raul Wise give us an inkling of country club life in Mexico, observing that the rich "do not, in many ways, live in Mexico so much as they seem to float above it. They live surrounded by a retinue of servants—maids, drivers, gunmen, gardeners, and so on, who curry to their every whim. They have two or more fortified luxury residences and frequently travel abroad—where they ensconce massive financial assets."[23]

Mexico's Carlos Slim Helú was the world's second richest man in 2014 according to Forbes with a reported net worth of $72 billion, $4 billion behind first place Bill Gates.[24] Mexico is a very poor country and the chasm between its poverty and Slim's palatial wealth covers so many orders of magnitude it's beyond easy comprehension. If we represent the country's

[20] Piketty (2014: 257)

[21] Piketty (2014: footnote 20 of chapter 7, p. 237)

[22] For both quotes, see Rothkopf (2008: 55-56) Italics in original.

[23] Cypher & Wise (2010: 25)

[24] See Forbes list of The World's 500 Richest People. www.forbes.com/sites/abrambrown/2014/03/03/forbes-billionaires-full-list-of-the-worlds-500-richest-people/, retrieved April 27, 2014

median annual household income of $4,500 [25] as the 167 miles (269 kilometers) between the mega-slum Neza-Chalco-Izta in Mexico City and Chilpancingo, the capital city of the murderous state of Guerrero, Slim's wealth would be the distance between, say, billionaire Ira Rennert's 65,000 square foot, 29 bedroom mansion on Long Island[26] and the planet Neptune, four light hours or 2,700,000,000 miles.

The concentrations we've been discussing so far represent the essence of oligarchic power but it's not the whole story. The large corporation arose at the turn of the twentieth century and has become today's dominant unit with a small number of them controlling significant portions of the global economy. According to data from Forbes and McKinsey, the sales of the top 250, 500, 1,000, and 8,000 account for 28, 37, 46, and 90 percent of the entire global GDP.[27] Every major industry is consolidated into just a few giant firms and a few examples are presented in Table 1 below.

---

[25] OECD (2014: 86). The OECD terms it median equivalised household disposable income.

[26] See Forbes listing of The Most Expensive Billionaire Homes in the World
www.forbes.com/sites/morganbrennan/2013/03/29/the-most-expensive-billionaire-homes-in-the-world/) , Retrieved April 27, 2014

[27] Data for the top 250 through 1,000 companies was obtained from the Forbes Global 2000 website, sorted by sales. Data for the top 8,000 companies was obtained from McKinsey (2013: 2) for the year 2010.
www.forbes.com/global2000/list/#page:1_sort:3_direction:desc_search:_filter:All%20industries_filter:All%20countries_filter:All%20states, accessed June 23, 2014.

Global 2013 GDP was obtained from the *The World Factbook* produced by the CIA.
www.cia.gov/library/publications/the-world-factbook/geos/xx.html, accessed June 23, 2014.

Table 1: Market Shares in Various Industries

Industry	Firms	Global Market Share
Large Commercial Aircraft	2	100%
Autos	10	77
PC's	4	55
Mobile Handsets	3	65
Pharmaceuticals	10	69
Agricultural Equipment	3	69
Cigarettes (1)	4	75
Aircraft Engines	3	100
Auto Tires	3	75
PC Microprocessors	2	100
PC Operating Systems	1	100
Beer Brewing (2)	2	80
Wine (3)	3	52
Soft Drinks (4)	2	75

Unless otherwise noted, data is from Nolan & Zhang (2010: 99) for the years 2006-2009.

(1) Excluding China.

(2) US only. Taken from Ascher (2012: 5).

(3) US only. Taken from the 2012 online report *Concentration of the US Wine Industry* by Phillip Howard, et al.

www.msu.edu/~howardp/wine.html, accessed August 22, 2015

(4) Nolan, Zhang, & Liu (2008)

Corporate consolidation is an important fact of our era but we need to be careful how we interpret it. Inequality is a system of class power, not corporate. Corporations are mere legal shells that have no power in and of themselves absent the enormous wealth concentrated into them. The real problem of power lies not with the corporation but with concentrated wealth. We'll look closer at the large corporation in chapters six (*The Global Game*) and eight (*Suppression*).

Let's now consider inequality in the past. Quantitative measurements are more difficult here but they all tell the same story. For every country in Europe at the turn of the twentieth century for which we have data, says

Piketty, the richest 10 percent owned "virtually all of the nation's wealth."[28] The orders of magnitude, 90 percent for the top decile and at least 50 percent for the top centile, "were also characteristic of traditional rural societies, whether Ancien Regime France or eighteenth century England."[29] The US around 1900 was only slightly less concentrated, with the top decile owning 80 percent of total wealth.[30] "In all known societies, at all times, the least wealthy half of the population owned virtually nothing."[31]

Archaeologist Bruce Trigger tells us the upper classes in the earliest periods of civilization were never more than a few percent.[32] In classical Athens, according to professor of Greek history Geoffrey Kron, the top 1 and 10 percent of citizens possessed 30.9 and 60.2 percent of total wealth.[33] This excludes slaves, however, and if we estimate a ratio of one slave per citizen, we'd find that the top 0.5 and 5 percent controlled 30.9 and 60.2 percent.

Jeffrey Winters estimates that in the Roman Empire between 100 BC and 100 AD, just ten senatorial families controlled 1.06 percent of total citizen property and the combined families of senators, equities, and municipal senators, accounting for just 2.89 percent of the population in the empire, owned practically all wealth. The bottom 87 percent owned virtually nothing.[34] The vast majority were serfs when Rome collapsed and they continued in that subordinate position for many centuries afterward.

It was little different in the towns and cities that arose in the medieval era. In fourteenth century Nuremburg, the aristocracy was restricted by law to just 43 families or 150 to 200 people out of 40,000. The nobility in Venice before 1575 comprised 5 percent of the population but even some of them were impoverished. And in Genoa the nobility was 700 out of 80,000.[35]

Continuing to more modern times, the ruling aristocracy in seventeenth century Netherlands comprised just 10,000 out of 2 million, while less than 200 wealthy merchants essentially ran 1603 London. In the whole of

---

[28] Piketty (2014: 260)

[29] Piketty (2014: 262)

[30] Piketty (2014: 347)

[31] Piketty (2014 :336)

[32] Trigger (2003: 147)

[33] Kron (2011: 134)

[34] Winters (2011: 92-93)

[35] Braudel (1982: 467)

eighteenth century Lombardy, 1 percent possessed half the land. In England around 1760, "the really rich and powerful" comprised 150 families while in France, the nobility was 1 to 1.5 percent of the population.[36]

The data is conclusive and monotonous. Whether we're speaking of ancient Mesopotamia, classical Greece, the Roman Empire, the feudal manor, medieval Venice, nineteenth century England, or modern day New York, it simply doesn't matter. Massive inequality has always been the dominating reality of civilization.

---

[36] Braudel (1982: 468-470)

2

The Poverty Side of Wealth

Wealth is a relationship between material power and poverty; the two are intertwined with the former depending definitionally on the latter. Great wealth *is* great poverty[1] and in this chapter, we'll explore the extent of today's poverty side of wealth. We'll find it's not only endemic but, when properly measured, is the near universal condition of mankind.

Since we can't measure poverty without first defining it, let's begin by considering how to come up with a reasonable definition. The word derives from the Latin *paupertāt* which can be translated as "small means and moderate circumstances." This is insufficient by itself, however, as these are relative terms that have no meaning absent a standard of reference. The World Bank, by far the most dominant institution in the poverty 'field,' sets that standard at brute survival, a bleak and doubtfully survivable $1.25 per

---

[1] The reasons for this link will be discussed in the next section, *The 5,000 Year System*. Adam Smith offered a worthy summation of the identity between wealth and poverty and it holds as strongly today as it did in the eighteenth century. "Wherever there is a great property, there is great inequality. For one very rich man, there must be at least five hundred poor, and the affluence of the few supposes the indigence of the many." Smith (2011, 271)

day.[2] The US government also defines poverty in relation to a survival standard, one formulated in the sixties using the US Department of Agriculture's derivation of an "economy food plan" times three, the multiplier being based on research at the time that showed food accounted for a third of average income. This one time historical calculation has then been adjusted each year for inflation; in 2014, it was an annual income of $11,670 and $23,850 for a one and four person household. Survival standards are also used by the Economic Commission on Latin America and the Caribbean (ECLAC) and the Asian Development Bank.

Median income is another common standard, based on the view that poverty is a matter of economic and social distance within a society. The Organization for Economic Cooperation and Development (OECD) sets its poverty line at half a country's median income, while Eurostat puts it at 60 percent for the European Union (EU). Finally, some institutions generate so-called "multidimensional" measurements which take into account factors like education, health, and housing in addition to income. Mexico is prominent in this area.

We find, then, that poverty is defined by these various institutions as an income level below a standard determined by a metric of survival need or percentage of median income, perhaps adjusted by "multidimensional" factors. Despite their prominence, though, none are adequate for understanding the true nature of "small means and moderate circumstances" in today's world. This is because the standards are set at absurdly low thresholds for a global civilization having enormous productive capacity.

It's this capacity, I argue, that's the only meaningful standard by which to judge the true extent of poverty in a socioeconomic system. That's what it's capable of achieving and it should be held to that metric. All who live below it are living in a state of poverty since they have small means and moderate circumstances in relation to the know-how and capability of their society. The percentage defined this way will be significantly higher than conventional statistics and it has almost certainly been increasing over time as well, meaning a growing gap between productive capacity and actual living standards.

---

[2] This represents an increase from the previous standard of $1.00 per day. It's based on 2005 prices and translated to the currency of the particular country using a purchasing power parity index.

Our capacity today isn't easily quantifiable but there can be little doubt we've solved the material production problem for everything that's essential for a quality life. Anyone denying this should be asked to identify the specific technologies we lack so we can devote the needed resources to obtain them. It's an embarrassing question for proponents of the status-quo, however, as it's plain no new technologies are required. Economist Joseph Stiglitz has observed that "a small percentage of the people of the world can produce all the food and with productivity in manufacturing, a small percentage can produce all the goods that might be bought."[3] This is certainly the case and we need to draw the appropriate conclusion. As economist John Kenneth Galbraith noted a half century ago, "To have failed to solve the problem of producing goods would have been to continue man in his oldest and most grievous misfortune. But to fail to see that we've solved it, and to fail to proceed thence to the next tasks would be fully as tragic."[4]

We have the knowledge and technology in hand to assure prosperity for everyone and it's expanding every day. MIT researchers Erik Brynjolfsson and Andrew McAfee see it growing at a geometric rate and observe we're at the stage where "exponential growth yields jaw-dropping results" that are "transforming manufacturing, distribution, retailing, media, finance, law, medicine, research, management, marketing, and almost every other sector and business function."[5] The so-called "fundamental economic problem" is not, as mainstream economists tell us, how best to allocate scarce resources; it's rather how best to explain endless struggle in a world of super-abundance.

While it's uncertain how we'd set a poverty standard reflecting this immense productive capacity, perhaps something down the lines of average household income could be a start. The average has a significant advantage over the median as it takes into account the higher incomes at the top. The average household income in the US in 2010 was $92,200[6] yet the median for the same year was just $50,020,[7] the difference being due to income inequality. While far from perfect, a standard set at the average would give us an inkling into the general magnitudes involved. Based on income

---

[3] Stiglitz (2010: 24)

[4] Galbraith (1984: 273)

[5] Brynjolfsson & McAffee (2011: 19-22)

[6] Congressional Budget Office (2013: 8)

[7] US Census Bureau
www.census.gov/prod/2011pubs/acsbr10-02.pdf

distribution data, we'd find that about 75 percent of the US population would be classified as living in poverty.[8]

This may seem high but I ask the reader to keep in mind that the standard isn't brute survival but productive capacity. A poverty rate of 75 percent coincides closely with the wealth distribution data presented in the last chapter which showed that the bottom 80 percent of the US population owned just 7 percent of financial wealth. It's not surprising that a group having such a poverty of wealth would also suffer a poverty of income. If we applied this standard globally, and there's no technical or moral reason that knowledge and capacity shouldn't be shared, then the worldwide poverty rate would reach well into the nineties.

But let's not proceed further in this direction for the whole idea of a monetary poverty line is superfluous. This isn't only because it's obvious huge numbers live far below any semblance of the life quality our productivity could provide, but also because consumption is the wrong metric. Our focus should align itself with what's important for a quality life.

A growing literature is finding that after basic needs are met, rising consumption doesn't add a lasting increment in subjective well-being.[9] What's the purpose of it all? This question is asked by every spiritual tradition and their answers are never an endlessly expanding GDP. Majorities agree according to international surveys which report that only 20 percent in OECD countries say a high income is very important.[10]

The US and other industrialized countries have seen great advances in technological progress and measured GDP in the past half century. You'd expect everyone to be so happy they'd be "dancing in the streets" notes a mockingly confused economist Richard Easterlin,[11] yet a host of studies show no increase in happiness. *Money can't buy happiness* is age-old wisdom that's supported by a great deal of psychological research, yet we seem to accept the naturalness of basing our socioeconomic system on its unending pursuit. Economist Jeffrey Sachs observes that the "western economist's logic of ever higher GNP is built on a vision of humanity completely at

---

[8] This is an estimate based on the Congressional Budget Office (2013: 8) tables which puts the average income in the fourth quintile at $95,500.

[9] See for example Frank (1997: 8).

[10] Layard, Clark, & Senik (2012: 67)

[11] Easterlin, et al. (2010: 5) referring specifically to China, Chile, and South Korea but more broadly to all countries.

variance with the wisdom of the sages, the research of psychologists, and the practice of advertisers."[12]

With all this in mind, let's now turn to some published reports on poverty levels. Productive capacity as it relates to life quality, I emphasize, and not brute survival or percentage of median income, is the proper global standard. That the rates using the measly standards of the poverty institutions can be as high as they are is a testament to the system's brutality.

I turn first to the World Bank's *2014 World Development Report*,[13] a revealing document coming from an institution branding itself as "Working for a World Free of Poverty."[14] I criticized mainstream economics and the major economic institutions in the introduction for being a key part of the problem, and here we have an excellent example. Despite the grisly numbers in their report, the authors choose to frame poverty as an issue of "risk management" and concoct a subtitle worthy of a hedge fund convention—*Risk and Opportunity: Managing Risk for Development*. "Pursuing opportunities requires taking risks,"[15] we're told, as if it were a truism of nature rather than the nature of inequality. The force of nature allusion is a theme hitting us right from the start as the front cover presents a portrait of four rowers in a small boat on rough seas. The entire conception is ludicrous—why should achieving prosperity in a world of plenty ever be risky? In what seems a farcical joke, our premier poverty institution calls on the billions living in excreta filled slums to "move from being 'crisis fighters' to becoming 'proactive and systematic risk managers.'"[16] A few pages later we're provided an example via a full page glossy photo of a mother holding her infant inside a mosquito net. Is she a desperately poor African woman? Who knows, but the soppy caption leads us to think life is just filled with grandeur for this successful risk manager: "Managing risk for a life full of opportunities: a mother protects her child against malaria with a bed net in Ghana."[17] The report mercilessly goes on to hit a number of hot buttons that have nothing to do with the hard realities of malnutrition, sanitation, or poverty, but

---

[12] Sachs (2012: 5)

[13] World Bank (2014)

[14] As displayed on its website. www.worldbank.org/

[15] World Bank (2014: viii)

[16] World Bank (2014: viii)

[17] World Bank (2014: 2)

everything to do with the key concerns of oligarchy—warning against budget deficits, pushing fiscal sustainability, promoting self-reliance, and stressing central bank independence.[18] Within its "five principles of public action for better risk management," it even cautions against what constitutes the most existential danger to wealth—the expropriation of financial assets—an action it says would "end up hampering the ability of the financial system and the enterprise sector to grow, develop, and provide risk management resources to the entire population."[19] What absolute nonsense! The whole report reads like a parody but it's not; it's the voice of power spoken through one of the world's most influential agencies. (I summarize an investigation of IMF and World Bank structural adjustment programs in appendix four.)

The harsh data in the document, though, presents a far less status-quo friendly picture; risk management apparently requires extensive study and the opportunities are well disguised. We're told that more than 20 percent of the population in 'developing' countries, over a billion people, live on less than $1.25 per day, more than 50 percent on less than $2.50 per day, and nearly 75 percent on less than $4.00 per day.[20] The report states that 2.7 billion lack access to sanitation and one billion defecate in the open.[21] One in eight children in sub-Saharan Africa and one in fifteen in South Asia die before their fifth birthday.[22] One and a half billion are employed in informal sector jobs having poor working conditions and no social security benefits.[23] Two and a third billion are infected by zoonotic pathogens because of weak human health systems.[24]

ECLAC provides a similarly depressed picture of Latin America, reporting that 28.2 percent are in poverty[25] and at least 100 million are exposed to air pollution above World Health Organization limits.[26] Mexico's agency CONEVAL[27] estimates that over four in five Mexicans are poor or

---

[18] We'll discuss the oligarchic nature of these items in the *Modern Oligarchy* section.

[19] World Bank (2014: 40-42)

[20] World Bank (2014: 5)

[21] World Bank (2014: 156)

[22] World Bank (2014: 156)

[23] World Bank (2014: 190)

[24] World Bank (2014: 248)

[25] ECLAC (2014: 16)

[26] ECLAC (2014: 30)

[27] Consejo Nacional de Evaluación de la Política de Desarrollo Social

vulnerable and a full 45.5 percent are in poverty.[28] Visit any major city in Latin America and one is immediately struck by the poverty, inequality, and danger of violent crime. In the name of what economists call efficiency and freedom, vast majorities struggle to make ends meet. Poverty is evidenced everywhere, from the dilapidated homes and buildings, to the crumbling streets and sidewalks, to the buses belching soot, and to the horrible air quality. Police form a major presence in the upscale locales, bulked up in bullet-proof vests and bearing military style weapons. They're a stark reminder of the unremitting volatility of wealth and poverty.

Conditions in richer countries look good only in comparison. Within its set of higher income nations, the OECD reports that unemployment has reached 48 million,[29] one in four is experiencing income difficulty,[30] millions are in financial distress,[31] and 11 percent are in poverty.[32]

The US is a country of glaring contrast—gleaming corporate downtown towers and re-gentrified well-to-do neighborhoods surrounded by deteriorated, gloomy places of high crime and run-down housing and infrastructure. Many cities are effectively bankrupt. The official poverty rate for the country is 15 percent with child poverty at 21.8 percent.[33] Americans are burdened by an outlandishly expensive health care system which accounts for 60 percent of bankruptcies. Retirement income is meager. Most Americans don't have pensions and social security is the only significant source of income beyond staying in the workforce. Yet it averages only $1,175 per month, just 21 percent above the official poverty line for a single-person household and almost a third less than the OECD average.[34]

The so-called "northeast corridor" of the US runs between Washington and Boston and is the richest region of the country. Let's take a brief tour of

----

[28] Taken from the CONEVAL website on May 7, 2014.
    www.coneval.gob.mx/Medicion/Paginas/Medici%C3%B3n/Pobreza%20
    2012/Anexo-estad%C3%ADstico-pobreza-2012.aspx

[29] To be considered unemployed by the OECD, one must not have worked even one hour in the survey week and be taking active steps to find employment.

[30] OECD (2014: 9)

[31] OECD (2014: 11)

[32] OECD (2014: 112)

[33] Stanford Center on Poverty & Inequality (2014: 6)

[34] Data for social security is taken from the Center on Budget and Policy Priorities.
    www.cbpp.org/cms/?fa=view&id=3368, accessed May 15, 2014

this gilded domain and consider conditions in its major cities. Beginning in Washington, the nation's and indeed the world's political capital, we find nearly one in five, 18.5 percent are subsisting below the poverty line. Heading north, we quickly arrive in Maryland's capital, Baltimore, and are told it has a poverty rate of 23.4 percent. Our next stop is Wilmington, the capital of the tax haven state of Delaware, and 23.5 percent of its population is poverty stricken. The tour continues with Philadelphia, the birthplace of the US Constitution, and here we find a rate of 26.2 percent. We also visit Pennsylvania's capital city of Harrisburg at 31.2 percent and then move onward to a bit less prosperous Reading sitting at a lofty 37.9 percent. Crossing the Delaware River to New Jersey, we come to Camden with a rate of 38.6 percent, the state capital Trenton at 26.6 percent, and Newark at 28 percent. The glittering financial capital of New York City is next on the trek, poverty rate: 19.9 percent, though its outlying borough of the Bronx, home of the New York Yankees, sits at a grand slam rate of 29.3 percent. Moving now to Connecticut, we pass through its largest city, Bridgeport, at 23.6 percent, New Haven at 26.9 percent, and its capital, Hartford, at 33.9 percent. Providence, Rhode Island is next with 27.9 percent of its population in officially measured dire straits. And finally, with great relief, we reach the northern terminus of our voyage through decrepitude as we enter Boston with 21.2 percent in poverty.[35]

The facts are "quite overwhelming" according to the Stanford Center on Poverty and Inequality. We "ask our health and educational institutions to perform rather the miracle, confronting as they do a population with high levels of poverty and inequality and all the health and educational problems that are thereby generated."[36]

That the US is reported near the top in median income speaks volumes about the miserable state of the global population. As is so often the case, statistics don't capture a reality that's much harsher. The standard of living of most Americans, observes Stiglitz,[37] has declined more than national statistics suggest given the rise in job insecurity, the cost of education, inadequate retirement funds, and the risk of losing the home. The Gallup

---

[35] Poverty data taken from the US Census Bureau website.
   www.quickfacts.census.gov/qfd/index.html. Accessed May 15, 2014
[36] Stanford Center on Poverty & Inequality (2014: 5-7)
[37] Stiglitz (2010: 285-286)

World Poll supports this assessment, reporting that a full 44 percent of Americans say they're struggling or suffering.[38]

Let's return to the northeast corridor theme taking special note that it contains the political, military, financial, cultural, and educational capitals of the country. There are, therefore, some glittering oases of wealth interspersed within the general ruin. They're where a good percentage of oligarchs live or have a spare penthouse or two and they can be thought of as comprising a single interconnected community. Call it Park Avenue in honor of the richest oasis of them all, today's Palatine Hill.[39] The residents of this dazzling interconnected Valhalla have little interest in the great problems besetting so many as their passion focuses on global markets and the grandeur of world power, often code-worded "leadership abroad."[40]

Hillary Clinton wrote an article in *Foreign Policy* a few years back which well captures the cold self-interested logic of power by which Park Avenue and its political representatives in Washington view the world. I quote a few excerpts.

And we are focused on the steps we have to take at home—increasing our savings, reforming our financial systems, relying less on borrowing, overcoming partisan division—to secure and sustain our leadership abroad . . . the future of politics will be decided in Asia, not Afghanistan or Iraq, and the United States will be right at the center of the action . . . From opening new markets for American businesses to curbing nuclear proliferation to keeping the sea lanes free for commerce and navigation, our work abroad holds the key to our prosperity and security at home . . . Our economic recovery at home will depend on exports and the ability of American firms to tap into the vast and growing consumer base of Asia.[41]

---

[38] Gallup World Poll.

www.gallup.com/poll/wellbeing.aspx?ref=b, accessed May 11, 2014

[39] It would actually encompass Manhattan's Upper East Side between Fifth and Park Avenues beginning at 59th Street to the south and most assuredly stopping well short of Harlem.

[40] Andrew Bacevich (2002: 218) has noted that "leadership" is a code word, "one whose use honored the cherished American tradition according to which the United States is not and cannot be an empire." He was referring specifically to its use by Bill Clinton.

[41] Foreign Policy, October 13, 2011, *America's Pacific Century*

Note that her focus on finance is irrelevant to the real concerns of everyday people and the outlandishness of the idea that the best way to help the struggling populations of Baltimore, Harrisburg, Trenton, et al. is by producing more products for Asians. Would it not be far simpler to "tap into" the "vast" "consumer base" in Hartford, the Bronx, and Camden rather than going through all the trouble of exporting to Asia? The question is irrational within the logic of inequality, though—the people in these cities have no money.

We find the same tale when we shift our gaze to Europe. Eurostat reports that in 2012 (the latest available), 125 million people, 24.8 percent of the entire European population, are at risk of poverty or social exclusion.[42] In Greece, the figure is 34.6 percent, Italy 29.9, Ireland 29.4, Spain 28.2, Portugal 25.3, the UK 24.1, and even Germany is at 19.6 percent. Unemployment within the euro area was officially reported at 11.8 percent in March, 2014 with Greece and Spain at 26.7 and 25.3.[43] Unemployment is far lower in Germany thanks to its success in luxury exports, but the country has the highest percentage of low-wage workers in Europe, a full 23.1 percent of its work force.[44] German real wages have been flat since 1990 and the labor share of its national income has fallen below 65 percent, the lowest since at least 1970.[45] Welfare benefits, job security, and pensions throughout the EU are being attacked every day in the name of fiscal rectitude, while the great social gains achieved in the decades after World War II are dissolving into thin air.

Let's now summarize the key points of this chapter. I've argued that the poverty standards used by the official agencies are inadequate because they

---

www.npr.org/2011/10/13/141311902/foreign-policy-americas-pacific-century, accessed May 15, 2014

[42] Eurostat. Accessed May 15, 2014.
www.epp.eurostat.ec.europa.eu/tgm/refreshTableAction.do?tab=table&plugin=1&pcode=t2020_50&language=en

[43] Eurostat news release 70/2014, May 2, 2014.
www.epp.eurostat.ec.europa.eu/cache/ITY_PUBLIC/3-02052014-AP/EN/3-02052014-AP-EN.PDF

[44] *Low Wages in Germany and the European Imbalance Problem*, NachDenkSeiten website. Data is for 2010.
www.nachdenkseiten.de/wp-print.php?p=18499, Accessed May 15, 2014

[45] ILO (2013: 46 & 43)

fail to consider our immense productive capacity. I claim that the only proper standard is this capacity as applied to what's important for a quality life. Measured this way, poverty is the near universal condition of mankind. At the lower end, billions of people live in the direst of circumstances and are condemned to hunger, short lives, filthy slums, stinking pollution, contaminated water, and open fields of waste. Ideology has it that this is the limit of the meaning of poverty and that it's a problem unique to the 'developing' world. But even in richer regions, large majorities live with needless insecurity and struggle to obtain even such basic necessities as a decent home, quality food, healthcare, education for themselves and their children, and a safe neighborhood. Given our massive productive capacity, this way of living as well demands to be branded for what it is—poverty.

Mid-level managers and so-called 'professionals' represent perhaps 20 percent of the workforce and they tend to view things through a middle-class lens that exaggerates their strength within the structure. While the exterior comforts of their lifestyle puts them above official poverty measures, it's largely a façade built on the insecure foundation of the mortgage and the whim of the employer. Life is centered on coping with the ever present stresses of gaining and holding a job. If it's found, then most waking hours are spent either on it or in the commute to it; if it isn't found or it's lost, then only a few months or less separate the unlucky person from seeking destabilizing and often humiliating shelter with family, incurring debilitating debt, or landing in the homeless shelter or street. The big screen television and other accoutrements of middle-class life will offer little condolence. For all the advances in technological prowess since the nineteenth century, we've not progressed very far in what's important. Consider this description of middle-class New England written in 1873; it could be applied word for word today, over 140 years later.

> Very few among them are saving money. Many of them are in debt; and all they can earn for years, is, in many cases, mortgaged to pay such debt. . . . In the faces of thousands of well-dressed, intelligent, and well-appearing people, may be seen the unmistakable signs of their incessant anxiety and struggles to get on in life, and to obtain in addition to a mere subsistence, a standing in society. . . . The poverty of the great middle classes consists in the fact that they have only barely enough to cover up their poverty, and that they are within a very few days of want, if through

sickness, or other misfortunes, employment suddenly stops. No one can describe the secret feeling of insecurity that constantly prevails among them concerning their living, and how it will be with them in the future; and while actual hunger and want may never be known, their poverty is felt, mentally and socially, through their sense of dependence and pride. They must work constantly, and with an angry sense of the limited opportunities for a career at their command.[46]

This two chapter section on wealth and poverty has concentrated on presenting quantitative data and has generally refrained from interpretation. The facts themselves aren't controversial. All agree that wealth is enormously concentrated, great poverty exists in our world, so-called economic life is difficult for a great number, and we have an immense productive capacity. Profound disagreements arise only with interpretation. Mainstream ideology presents the facts as nuanced and complex aspects of the natural condition of a free society whereas I'll argue that poverty and insecurity flow directly from the logic of wealth. It comes down to a clouded ideological justification of power versus a simple acceptance of obvious facts. We'll turn now to an examination of the ancient logic of wealth and the ways it must always position itself as a hostile force against the majority.

---

[46] Ira Steward as quoted in Ewen (1996: 42)

The 5,000 Year System

3

The Tyranny of Inequality

We humans are by nature egalitarian. At least, that is, if we go by the fact we seem to have lived that way for over two million years. While the evidence shows that some inequality existed during this great span along the lines of age, gender, and skill, it wasn't based on class, didn't provide significant material advantage, and wasn't hereditary. Widespread sharing was the rule.[1]

Anatomically modern humans entered the stage about 200,000 year ago and the first "glimmerings" of inequality in some localized areas appear in the archaeological record around 50,000 years ago. They grew more pronounced 20,000 years later and became "especially dramatic" 15,000 years ago.[2] How and why the predominant social organization shifted from egalitarian to unequal hierarchy is unknown but it was a dramatically important event. Archaeologist Gary Feinman has observed that "In the history of the human species, there is no more significant transition than the emergence and institutionalization of inequality."[3]

That inequality didn't exist for virtually the entire span of our species but suddenly became near universal suggests to archaeologist Bruce Trigger that

---

[1] Hayden (2001)

[2] Hayden (2001: 231)

[3] Feinman (1995: 255)

a general acquisitiveness is a part of human nature that's controlled in small societies.[4] Those possessing strong acquisitive drives are called *aggrandizers* by archaeologist Brian Hayden [5] who defines them as "any ambitious enterprising, aggressive, accumulative individual who strives to become dominant in a community, especially by economic means."[6] Research on living hunter-gatherers supports the theory that aggrandizers were well-contained in small societies. David Erdal and Andrew Whiten have observed from their global investigations that "It is characteristic of hunter-gatherers that they bring back to earth, often with a bump, anyone who tries to achieve dominance." They conclude that "The early human mind is likely to have been characterized by psychological dispositions supporting egalitarianism: vigilant food-sharing, informal leadership and counter-dominant behavior."[7] "No alpha domination" is how anthropologist Christopher Boehm sums up the strategy.[8]

Small societies seem to have kept the alpha at bay but as they grew and became capable of producing and storing significant levels of surplus production, the previously successful defense mechanisms were undermined. The dominant long-lived egalitarian social organization of humanity shifted to one of unequal, hierarchical, class based stratification. We don't know how it all transpired but given the brutal hierarchies that were to come, it's clear we're dealing with a catastrophic loss of human freedom.

Warfare appears to have begun around the same time.[9] War, according to anthropologist R. Brian Ferguson, is "organized, purposeful group action, directed against another group that may or may not be organized for similar action, involving the actual or potential application of force."[10] This is a succinct definition not just of war but also of the new relationships of inequality being imposed everywhere by ruling minorities onto 'their' populations. It isn't surprising the two arose at the same time for they're both rooted in the same phenomenon of power.

---

[4] Trigger (2003: 670)

[5] Hayden (1995: 20) Following Clark & Blake (1994: 18).

[6] Hayden (1995: 18)

[7] Erdal & Whiten (1996: 145,148)

[8] Boehm (2000: 40)

[9] Haas (2001: 332)

[10] As quoted in Haas (2001: 331).

At the dawn of recorded civilization, every known society of any significant size was a class based hierarchy. The upper classes were only a few percent and controlled disproportionate wealth, avoided physical labor, and had opulent lifestyles. "A defining feature of all early civilizations was the institutionalized appropriation by a small ruling group of most of the wealth produced by the lower classes." They were based on ideas of social and economic inequality along with strict obedience to authority which was inculcated from early childhood. Legal systems and armed forces were "used to intimidate the lower classes and protect the privileges of the wealthy and powerful." The upper classes universally "agreed about the need to protect their privileges and possessions by keeping the lower classes subservient," relying on at least the passive support of the population which was gained largely because of the pervasiveness and seeming normality of inequality.[11]

Concentrated material power down these lines became the constant unremitting force, the civilization spanning *iron heel*,[12] the most central and unifying theme for the next 5,000 years. It has been outwardly sustained in various ways throughout the ages—taxation on commoners, rent, fees, bribes, corvée, indentured and slave labor, debt accumulation, tribute from weaker societies, and wage labor[13]—but they're all ultimately only details within the larger reality of power, mere instruments within the inequality toolbox. Private property predominates today but this wasn't always the case. What's important isn't the specific tool used in a particular period but rather the structural existence of the vested right to control and appropriate production.[14]

In 1776, 15,000 or so years after our hypothesized transition, John Adams, a prominent lawyer and second president of the US, observed that "Power always follows Property. This I believe to be as infallible a Maxim, in Politicsks, as, that Action and Re-action are equal, is in Mechanicks. Nay I believe We may advance one Step farther and affirm that the Ballance of Power in a Society, accompanies the Ballance of Property in Land."[15] I'll call

---

[11] Information in this paragraph has been taken from Trigger (2003). The quotes are from pages 375, 265 and 667. See also pages 52, 147, 264, 265, and 668.

[12] From the 1908 Jack London novel of that name, referring to capitalism.

[13] Trigger (2003: 376) Corvée is intermittent forced labor.

[14] Trigger (2003: 385-389)

[15] From a May 26, 1776 letter to James Sullivan.
www.britannica.com/presidents/article-9116850, accessed on June 10, 2014.

this the *Adams Maxim* and its relevance lies in its expression of the indelible link between wealth and power. (I take it to apply to all property and not just land.) There has always been a strong correlation between the two in complex societies[16] and it's reasonable to assert that to a very large degree, power *is* wealth and wealth *is* power; they're really just different words expressing the same idea. Societies in which wealth is concentrated will be societies in which power is concentrated and, correspondingly, societies in which power is concentrated will be ones in which wealth is concentrated.[17]

Wealth is minority power over the majority and it's the antithesis of democracy. It's the essence, in fact, of domination and is thereby *tyranny*. According to political philosopher Roger Boesche, this word has been used since the fourth century BC as an "unequivocal insult" for a "harsh and lawless government in which the ruler does not govern for the general good."[18] Aristotle wrote the classical definition that captures some of this but it's far too restrictive. To him, "A tyranny is a monarchy where the good of one man only is the object of government, [whereas] an oligarchy considers only the rich, and a democracy only the poor; but neither of them have a common good in view."[19] The key problem in this is that he limits the age-old insult to monarchies. Didn't Hitler or Stalin rule tyrannically?[20] The real meaning behind tyranny, I suggest, is in its application to any form of rule that's aligned *against* the interests of the majority. Paraphrasing Aristotle, it's a rule where the good of a minority only is the object and the common good isn't in view.

The central fact of recorded history is that all societies have been variations on the theme of tyranny so defined. Throughout every age, a tiny elite has always wielded tyrannical power to subjugate 'its' population into producing goods and services for its aggrandizement. The ever changing historical means by which this has been accomplished are secondary to the unrelenting persistence of a deeply engrained structural power. Wealth is the

---

[16] Trigger (2003: 46)

[17] One may object that there are exceptions and point to the communist systems of the twentieth century. The USSR and communist China represented failed attempts to break from the historic norm and they lasted only decades. They exist again today as oligarchies.

[18] Boesche (1996: 3)

[19] Aristotle (2012: book III, ch VII, 1279b)

[20] Boesche (1996: 82)

root of tyranny and its flip side is servitude. Slavery and serfdom were the icing on the servitude cake; but the cake itself is made of inequality and it's perfectly edible without the icing.

The failure to recognize the pathological nature of inequality is the core barrier to understanding our system today. The problem is that domination and servitude are often imposed in passive ways that disguise the profound antagonism. They hide behind a fog of apparent freedoms while ideology distracts us into believing inequality could somehow be innocent or perhaps just a minor flaw having little relevance. We're fed a series of myths that incorporate the idea the fruits of wealth exist on a separate plane of life. The rich get to own fabulous luxuries, but that's an isolated fact on the luxury plane having no bearing on the wider more important 'economic' one. Wealth in this line of thought can enjoy its toys without affecting the essential freedoms of everyone else; the success of the minority doesn't hurt the majority.

There are two significant errors here. First, wealth diverts production into serving its wealth defense and luxury motives that could otherwise have gone toward improving the living standards of the population. It thereby does hurt the majority. Second, the key fruit of wealth turns out to be the ownership of the economic plane itself. Wealth isn't just luxury; it's above all else power and it ends up with everything. It becomes the owner of the system. The success of the minority thereby becomes the subjugation of the majority. History is clear on this point and it's the essential meaning of the Adams Maxim.

Imagine an agrarian civilization in a remote desert oasis in which all arable land is owned by a tiny minority which has imposed slavery. Most of us today would find this objectionable; but what changes if the population is freed while ownership remains the same? Eliminating slavery is no doubt a significant human rights advance, but the population still owns nothing and must therefore continue working for the owners in a subservient position. The Adams Maxim tells us the balance of power hasn't budged. The individual is no longer tied to a specific owner but he or she can't leave the consolidated class of owners without renouncing his or her existence.[21] [22]

While this seems straightforwardly unjust, there exist a number of arguments that seek to defend such unequal relations. They're ideologies in service to tyranny. Referring to the Critical Theory developed by Jürgen Habermas and others in the so-called Frankfurt School, political philosopher Raymond Geuss speaks of ideology as a "'world-picture' which stabilizes or legitimizes domination or hegemony." He adds that "It is in virtue of the fact that it supports or justifies reprehensible social institutions, unjust social practices, relations of exploitation, hegemony, or domination that a form of consciousness is an ideology."[23]

The most important ones today follow in the tradition of Lockean liberalism. John Locke argued that every man has a natural right to the property arising from his own labor and that government had been instituted to protect it. The state and the majority are seen as subservient to this "law of nature" and have no right to interfere.

> Whatever then he removes out of the state that nature hath provided, and left it in, he hath mixed his labour with, and jointed to it something that is his own, and thereby makes it his property.[24] . . . The supreme power cannot take from any man any part of his property without his own consent: for the preservation of property being the end of government, and that for which men enter into society, it necessarily supposes and requires that the people should have property, without which they must be supposed to lose that, by entering society, which was the end for which they entered into it: too gross an absurdity for any man to own.[25] . . . the natural liberty of man is to be free from any superior power on earth, and

---

[21] Marx (1978c: 205) This is a paraphrase of Marx. In his words, "the worker, whose sole source of livelihood is the sale of his labour power, cannot leave *the whole class of purchasers, that is, the capitalist class*, without renouncing his existence. He belongs not to this or that capitalist, but to the *capitalist class*." Italics in original.

[22] I note that this example could be expanded to a modern industrial and service socioeconomy with little alteration since these sectors end up being just as concentrated as land.

[23] Geuss (1981: 15)

[24] Locke (2011: 12)

[25] Locke (2011: 52)

not to be under the will or legislative authority of man, but to have only the law of nature for his rule.[26]

Locke is arguing for the unbridled prerogatives of wealth as opposed to such other possible "natural" rights as distributional fairness, equality, and democracy. He inserts, however, a significant qualifier—man may accumulate property through his labor, he says, "at least where there is enough, and as good left in common for others."[27] This has been called the "Lockean proviso"[28] and its egalitarian implications are so enormous, it would seem to negate in just fourteen words Locke's entire treatise. It's the "Trojan Horse of right-libertarianism"[29] [30] that can't be taken seriously if one seeks to use Locke as an argument for inequality.

Locke himself doesn't seem to have done so as his paltry effort to get around it consists of the feeble idea that the invention of money somehow solved the problem. Through the existence of gold and silver, he said, "it is plain[!], that men have agreed to a disproportionate and unequal possession of the earth, they having, by tacit and voluntary consent, found a way how a man may fairly possess more land than he himself can use the product of."[31]

Robert Nozick, an influential right-libertarian philosopher, was similarly unsuccessful in his stab at it. He falls back on an unsupported assertion that "the free operation of the market system will not actually run afoul of the Lockean proviso."[32] This is a dubious claim, though, since markets must ultimately reflect the purchasing power and distribution of wealth within

---

[26] Locke (2011: 11)

[27] Locke (2011: 12)

[28] Nozick (1974: 175)

[29] Fried, B. (2004: 69)

[30] Property rights advocates in the US have popularized their association with the term *libertarian* but this dates only back to 1955. Before that and in most of the rest of the world today, the term had been and still is associated with leftist philosophies advocating egalitarian distributions and even the abolition of private property. Anarchist socialists called themselves libertarian as far back as 1858. It's poetically appropriate, notes Karl Widerquist, that property rights advocates have appropriated the libertarian term from people who believe property is theft. There are three distinct groups that refer to themselves as libertarian today—right-libertarian, left-libertarian, and left-socialists. See Widerquist (2009) '

[31] Locke (2011: 19-20)

[32] Nozick (1974: 182)

them. Nozick is making little more than an illogical and factually false proposition that wealth itself, as mirrored by the market, will just happen to leave enough and as good in common for others.

Friedrich von Hayek, another key right-libertarian, argues that private ownership is freedom itself and collectivism the "Road to Serfdom,"[33] but this can't stand up to scrutiny. It perverts normal meaning to associate serfdom to a system in which serfs would be in collective power and therefore not serfs, and freedom to one in which power rests with a tiny few and the majority thereby reduced to effective serfdom.

Liberty in the Lockean liberal paradigm has little to do with democracy and in actuality is aggressively opposed to it. It's an existential clash of principles since inequality (oligarchy) can't be squared with equality (democracy)—they're opposites. The subtle trick in fabricating popularly acceptable arguments for inequality is to paint democracy as tyranny and property as a natural right interwoven into the meaning of liberty. A common strategy is to offer an everyday story having nothing to do with the realities of domination, bring in a group that democratically violates accepted norms, and then derive from it an anti-democratic principle of liberty.

A good example is found in a recent work by right-libertarian philosopher Michael Huemer in which he offers the following story.

Imagine the following scenario, which I shall call the Bar Tab example. You have gone out for drinks with a few of your colleagues and graduate students. You are all busy talking about philosophy, when someone raises the question of who is going to pay the bill. A number of options are discussed. A colleague suggests dividing the bill evenly among everyone at the table. You suggest that everyone pay for his own drinks. A graduate student then suggests that *you* pay for everybody's drinks. Reluctant to spend so much money, you decline. But the student persists: 'Let's take a vote.' To your consternation, they proceed to take a vote, which reveals that everyone at the table except you wants you to pay for everybody's drinks. 'Well, that settles it,' declares the student. 'Pay up.'[34]

---

[33] Hayek (1944)
[34] Huemer (2013: 59) Italics in original.

From this humorously absurd tale, Huemer jumps to the desired conclusion: "Majority will alone does not generate an entitlement to coerce the minority, nor does it generate an obligation of compliance on the part of the minority. More precisely, majority will alone does not provide sufficient backing for a proposal to override an individual's private property rights (your right to your money in this example) or right not to be subjected to harmful coercion."[35]

The trickery here is that his example has nothing initially to do with unequal power. His group is presented as relative equals and the majority action serves to create an inequality against a particular individual. It starts with equality and ends with inequality and we should thus object to it *from an egalitarian perspective*. Let's revise his story just slightly.

> You own all the productive land in your agrarian civilization and, while traveling, end up in a tavern where you sit at the bar with a group of desperately poor strangers. They have no land and are forced into working for you on one of your many plantations where they're paid the market wage which, due to the concentrated ownership and resulting oversupply of dependent workers, is very low. Your wealth is measured at $72 billion whereas the average annual pay of your companions is $4,500.[36] You engage in idle non-philosophic conversation with them and, after a few beers, the question of who will pay the bill arises. You suggest that everyone pay for his own drinks. A laborer then suggests that *you* pay for everybody's drinks. Reluctant to spend so much money, you decline. But the poor man persists: "It's unjust that you have so much while there isn't enough and as good left in common for others." Everyone in the bar agrees. Horrified at this coercion, you rise, pay for your drinks, and fire the men for their gross insubordination.

Here we start with inequality and the question is whether the majority has the right to reduce it. To say it doesn't is to condemn it to unending tyranny, a patently unjust outcome. Contra Huemer, the issue isn't one of minority rights but is rather that of inequality and whether either the majority *or* the minority has a moral basis to impose it on the other. He argues the former

---

[35] Huemer (2013: 59-60)

[36] I refer to the comparison made in chapter one between Carlos Slim Helú's reported net worth and the median annual income in Mexico.

doesn't, to which I agree, but then seeks to use that as a justification for the claim the latter somehow has that right. He attempts to link property with the common nondiscrimination discourse on minority rights but the two aren't just different, they're opposite. The first speaks of the right to possess power over a majority while the second seeks to assure equality for all.

The 'American Dream' ideology is a version of Lockean liberalism that emphasizes *merit*. Equality of outcome isn't important, proponents say, as long as each person has the opportunity to climb the structural ladder to success. A meritocracy, in this view, is the proper goal of a just society. The problem is that there's not sufficient opportunity to go around. We're offered a game of musical chairs having perhaps a hundred contestants but maybe only twenty seats. [37] No matter how widely opportunity is shared, the structure of the game is such that it always produces inequality and ends up violating the Lockean proviso. A tiny few will enjoy power and the majority will be rendered subservient.

The term itself, *meritocracy*, was coined in a satirical sense in the 1950s by sociologist Michael Young with this exact point in mind. In his fictional work, *The Rise of the Meritocracy*,[38] Young presented a future British society in which all positions were determined by "merit" based on the equation *Intelligence + Effort = Merit*. The foreseeable outcome was a tyranny as cruel as any aristocracy of the past. Domination on the basis of intelligence, good looks, charisma, cleverness, brawn, "merit," or anything else has no greater moral claim than noble birth.[39] The problem is the structure, not the selection method.[40]

The only viable argument for inequality, it seems, is down the line that the best and the brightest wouldn't be motivated to achieve great things without great material reward and that without such reward, the inferior majority

---

[37] The number of seats will vary based on assumptions. We found in chapter one that the bottom 80 percent in the US possesses just 7 percent of financial wealth and it's only the top 20 which owns at least the average.

[38] Young (1996)

[39] Some readers still may argue that effort and risk are appropriate bases for inequality. But how can effort be adequately quantified? Who works harder, the janitor or the stock broker? And what of age or physical constitution? Risk is problematic as well given that it's closely related to the logic of inequality itself. Is starting a restaurant by nature risky or is it only so for those without other means?

[40] Poulantzas (1975: 284)

would be worse off. This elitist argument is the gist of Rawls's Difference Principle[41] which justifies inequality as long as it makes the least advantaged better off. It's a leaky bucket. First of all, we're more equal in talents than is often assumed and many of the differences that do exist derive from the advantages bestowed by inequality itself. Second, it's based on a theory of human motivation completely at odds with a great deal of psychological research. The lust for great wealth isn't a key motivator for most people. It's not credible to posit that a person having the capabilities of a general, for example, would choose being a private if the pay were the same. Or that scientific discoveries and artistic creations depend on greed as their guiding light. Introspection tells us that happiness is achieved not through great material reward but through personal relationships and the development of our talents. And third and most important, it ignores the historical and logical truth that once wealth is achieved it consolidates into a force of self-aggrandizement that, by definition, operates *against* the interests of the population. It's difficult to visualize how it could ever be the case that the 'inferiors' would be better off in such a system.

But all this aside, the facts of today make this entire argument beside the point—our knowledge base is so large, we need not worry about the finer points of incentives. New discoveries, while they'd surely keep coming, aren't critical to a society in which productive capacity is already so high; and they're not worth the cost of living in servitude. The state of the industrial arts, as Veblen observed, "is a fact of group life, not of individual or private initiative or innovation ... New elements of insight and proficiency are continually being added and worked into this common stock by the experience and initiative of the current generation, but such novel elements are always and everywhere slight and inconsequential in comparison with the body of technology that has been carried over from the past."[42]

The Adams Maxim captures the fact that power rests with property and so all the arguments in this chapter that spoke in terms of the rights of property are ultimately ones of the rights of power. They fail for the simple reason there's no sound moral basis that can justify the control of power by a minority. It's by definition anti-democratic and thus tyrannical.

---

[41] Rawls (1999: 65)
[42] Veblen (2003: 38)

Systemic inequality overtook humanity perhaps 10,000 years before the onset of recorded civilization and we've been in the clutch of aggrandizers and their philosophic henchmen ever since. Lockean liberalism has been the dominant ideology over the past few centuries and it seeks to present this ancient power as the embodiment of liberty. While it's accepted by many as ideology, it can't reasonably be accepted as a morally viable argument. Putting as it does a natural right to wealth above the democratic will, it's "an assertion of ruling class powers against the people."[43] Liberalism wants to have its cake and eat it too—the cake of moral righteousness embodied in the Lockean proviso and the sumptuous pleasures of its eating made possible only by ignoring it. When all is said and done, the minority's claim of a natural right to own the planet is a laughable proposition. What it possesses isn't a natural right but an actuality of power. Our goal is to understand this power and in the next chapter we'll review its most basic logic.

---

[43] Wood (1995: 230)

4

Motives, Risks, & Dynamics

The word oligarchy derives from the Greek ὀλιγαρχία (oligarkhía) and means *rule by the few*. Aristotle altered it in two key ways so that the classical definition became in effect the *governmental* rule by the *rich*.

> It seems therefore evident to reason, that whether the supreme power is vested in the hands of many or few may be a matter of accident; but that it is clear enough, that when it is in the hands of the few, it will be a government of the rich; when in the hands of the many, it will be a government of the poor; since in all countries there are many poor and few rich: it is not therefore the cause that has been already assigned (namely, the number of people in power) that makes the difference between the two governments; but an oligarchy and democracy differ in this from each other, in the poverty of those who govern in the one, and the riches of those who govern in the other; for when the government is in the hands of the rich, be they few or be they more, it is an oligarchy; when it is in the hands of the poor, it is a democracy.[1]

---

[1] Aristotle (2012: book III, ch. VIII, 1279b-1280a)

By substituting *the rich* for *the few*, Aristotle aligns *oligarchy* with wealth inequality but in emphasizing governmental rule, he misses the essence of its power. The central argument of this book is that inequality, in and of itself, is rule and it's therefore immaterial which class occupies the government at any point in time. The important question, deriving from the Adams Maxim, isn't whether the rich are in government but whether they *exist*; for if they exist, they rule.

Jeffrey Winters, in his work *Oligarchy*,[2] provides a definition that accounts for this distinction and it's the one I'll adopt. Oligarchy isn't the rule by the few nor a government headed by the rich, but the mere existence of wealth inequality. "We enter the realm of oligarchs and oligarchy when the inequalities in question position a small number of rich actors against the masses that are much poorer."[3] The governmental form or mode of production is irrelevant.

Our task in this chapter is to understand the basic logic of this kind of rule. It will turn out to be a remarkably simple job on account of the fact that the subject is something with which we're innately familiar. Inequality is simple and there's no need to make it complicated. With this in mind, I propose that the logic of oligarchy can be reduced to just a few core elements that have remained constant throughout the entire history of civilization. I present them in terms of motives, risks, and dynamics.

Turning first to motives, I'll begin by following Winters and positing that the primary motive of an oligarch is survival. "The relevant and defining political motivations of oligarchs are defensive and existential. Once constituted, an oligarch's paramount objective is to secure, maintain, and retain his or her position of extreme wealth and power against all manner of threats."[4]

One could object here that the history of civilization isn't well characterized by just defense as aggression has been a far more common theme. We can resolve this, though, if we blur the distinction between offense and defense. Regarding defense, the nineteenth century military theorist Carl von Clausewitz has observed that it "follows of itself that we must only make

---

[2] Winters (2011)

[3] Winters (2011,11)

[4] Winters (2011: 39)

use of it so long as our weakness compels us to do so, and that we must give up that form as soon as we feel strong enough to aim at the positive object."[5]

Wealth/power is the positive object and within an oligarchy it's a zero-sum game. One oligarch's gain is another's loss and the best defense against that is often a strong offense. The line between the two is blurred. We can therefore expand Winters' motivational definition to something like: "an oligarch's paramount objective is to secure, maintain, and retain his or her position of extreme wealth and power against all manner of threats, *and to expand it whenever reasonably possible.*" The times when it's reasonably possible and when it's not will vary according to historical circumstances and we witness them as cycles of competition/war and cooperation/peace. I'll use Winters' term *wealth defense*[6] when referring to this motivation but will modify it with a star, *wealth defense**,[7] to remind us it isn't just defense but rather an aggressive often bloody and violent intermingling of offense and defense.

Wealth defense*, though, isn't the only clearly evident oligarchic motive. Wealth holders don't sit on their hoards holed up in dark caves defending themselves against all threats like Wagnerian dragons. They've instead developed a fondness for extraordinary splendor. The psychological drives sparking "conspicuous consumption"[8] entail personal comfort and pleasure and also the display of high social rank. We don't need to quibble between the two; regardless of the underlying cause, we must add luxury consumption.

When all is said and done, I assume two primary oligarchic motives: wealth defense* and luxury consumption. They're intuitive to each of us and they're the foundation upon which to understand our system today.

Let's now turn to the risks against which the survival motive of wealth defense* is directed. We can lean on Winters again here and identify two categorical ones—that from other oligarchs, and that from the population.[9]

---

[5] Clausewitz (1873: Vol 2, 68)

[6] Winters (2011: 6)

[7] Wealth defense* is hypothesized to be the core motivation of oligarchy and will play a central role in what follows. I could think of no word to adequately express the aggressive intermingling of offense and defense, and so fell upon the use of the * which has an interesting astronomical association. The central black hole in our galaxy, estimated to have a mass of four million suns, is named Sagittarius A* (pronounced Sagittarius A star) with the star used to highlight its core significance.

[8] Veblen (2012: 46)

[9] I refer to them as *risks* rather than Winters' term *threats* as this seems better suited to the financial terminology that dominates modern oligarchy.

(He adds the state as well but I choose not to for reasons discussed later in the chapter.)

The inter-oligarchic risk plays out on the micro scale in such forms as business competition, financial dealings, speculation, and fraud, and on the macro between political units, most prominently in war and imperialism. On both scales, geographic expansion and consolidation are ever present tendencies in the development of oligarchic power. Power begets power in a way analogous to the gravitational force in physics and this dynamic has been evident throughout history. It seems to be a basic axiom of oligarchy. Upon the initial transition to inequality at the hazy pre-dawn of civilization, the control of productive resources quickly consolidated into the hands of minorities everywhere and has remained there ever since. We've also seen the power and size of business firms consolidate in the aftermath of the chaos of the nineteenth century. On the macro scale, socioeconomic units started small, competed against each other via endless war, and eventually grew into ever larger geographic sizes. Such was the basic process from the beginnings in Mesopotamia and it reached its maximum extent in Western antiquity with the Roman Empire. The collapse of Rome is the central discontinuity in the history of the West and it brought Europe into a second era of fragmentation. Consolidation started anew though, and through unremitting violence has proceeded to where we are today—a world of some 206 formally sovereign nation states[10] within a global socioeconomy centered on the hegemony of the US.

The drive to maintain and expand power is a bedrock motive of oligarchy and violence is therefore endemic. War has been history's constant theme and intervals of peace have always been short. China, Russia, and the Middle East are the major hot spots today and it's unknowable how events will unfold either there or in other regions that may rise and take their place. I won't try to wade into the details of such matters. The goal of this book is to understand oligarchy as a system and while an important manifestation is inter-oligarchic war, it's not the heart of what the system is. Which group of oligarchs happens to be ascendant at any moment is an ephemeral phenomenon that's immaterial to a structure that has spanned all of civilization; what's important is the unchanging essence of inequality, a

---

[10] The sovereignty of sixteen of these states is disputed by some national governments.

relationship not between competing oligarchs but between oligarchs as a class and the population.

Which brings us to the second categorical risk—that of the population. The inter-oligarchic battle decides which particular oligarchs temporarily sit at the top of the structure but the oligarchy–population one determines whether oligarchy exists at all. The structure itself is negated unless substantial portions of the population are forced into a subjugation in which they lack wealth/power. I'll have much more to say on this in a moment.

From the two motives—wealth defense* and luxury consumption—and the two risks to which wealth defense* is directed—inter-oligarchic and the population—we can derive two primary dynamics that drive the system. They are diversion and suppression.

Diversion is the dynamic of power that assures the population serves the oligarchy's motivational desires *without cost*. It's a relationship of command that's foundational to the system and it must be costless because no oligarchy could long survive if the exercise of diversionary power resulted in its diminution. Costless diversion has been a continuous dynamic throughout all of civilization and we'll examine the ways it's manifested today in chapter seven (*The Diversion-Profit Loop*).

The other dynamic is suppression and we'll need to devote more time to it both here and in the rest of the book because it's more ideologically hidden than is diversion and is also the oligarchy's greatest current challenge given our enormous productive capacity.

When thinking of suppression, it's important to keep in mind that oligarchy is a relationship of power and not a standalone idea of "wealth" innocently removed from any contact with "non-wealth." For oligarchs to exist, they must stand atop and control the hierarchy of inequality. The gradient is crucial; the power of the minority requires the majority be dependent and subservient. They're two sides of a coin and the side of power dissolves if its opposite, the majority, is prosperous and secure.

Suppression is the dynamic by which oligarchic power over the population is maintained. It's the ongoing enforcement of sub-optimal living conditions, insecurity, and poverty in service to the vital wealth defense* need of maintaining the social hierarchy. I differentiate it from diversion in that it's a force imposed against populations over and above that needed to compel them to produce diversion goods and services. The importance of this dynamic rises in lockstep with productive capacity and is therefore crucial in today's world. Should our extraordinary capacity ever be utilized on behalf of the population, the entire structure would collapse. Productive potential must be stifled and populations kept forever dependent: this is the meaning of suppression in modern oligarchy.

More than any other aspect of oligarchy, it's suppression which leads us to conclude the system is hostile. Some readers may not feel comfortable with this idea since it runs counter to the notion there can be a mutuality of interest despite inequality. While we'll examine in the next section some of the many ways it's implemented in the modern world, for now I'd like to present a few illustrations of the thinking and general mindset that links power with suppression.

I turn first to science fiction and the common speculation that a friendly alien species could visit the earth and offer a host of benefits to mankind. As just one of many possible examples, Baum, Haqq-Misra, and Domagal-Goldman posit that "An advanced ETI [extra-terrestrial intelligence] may be capable of solving a great many of humanity's problems, such as world hunger, poverty, or disease."[11] Let's suppose such an ETI does visit the earth, is ushered into an executive committee of the oligarchy, and offers the world technologies that would let everyone live full and prosperous lives. How exactly should we expect the oligarchy to react? The owners of the auto industry, say, to free advanced transportation; agricultural owners to free and unlimited food; energy owners to free energy; Wall Street to eliminating speculation and the collapse of its banks; or the oligarchy as a class to losing all power. The answer is obvious. A visit from a friendly ETI would be a disaster as the oligarchy's entire world position would be destroyed. Its power is based on keeping the population dependent and we should therefore expect it to spare no effort in suppressing the dire threat of a friendly ETI.

We find the same logic in Dostoevsky's *The Brothers Karamazov* when the Grand Inquisitor faces Jesus reappearing in Spain during the Inquisition. While subject to varying interpretations, I believe it provides a vivid portrayal of the enormous self-image of the tyrant, his corresponding contempt for mankind, and the profound need of power to enforce dependency. The Grand Inquisitor considers the returning Jesus a threat and throws Him in jail. Here are a few quotes as he speaks privately to Jesus; how easy it is to visualize a similar conversation with the friendly ETI.

---

[11] Baum, et al. (2011: 12)

Why, then art Thou come to hinder us? . . . tomorrow I shall condemn Thee at the stake as the worst of heretics. . . . Thou hast given to us the right to bind and to unbind, and now, of course, Thou canst not think of taking it away. Why, then, hast Thou come to hinder us? . . . for nothing has ever been more insupportable for a man and a human society than freedom. . . . And we alone shall feed them in Thy name, declaring falsely that it is in Thy name. Oh, never, never can they feed themselves without us! No science will give them bread so long as they remain free. In the end they will lay their freedom at our feet, and say to us 'Make us your slaves, but feed us.' They will understand themselves, at last, that freedom and bread enough for all are inconceivable together, for never, never will they be able to share between them! They will be convinced, too, that they can never be free, for they are weak, vicious, worthless and rebellious. . . . They will marvel at us and look on us as gods, because we are ready to endure the freedom which they have found so dreadful and to rule over them—so awful will it seem to them to be free. . . . Too, too well will they know the value of complete submission! . . . We shall show them that they are weak, that they are only pitiful children, but that childlike happiness is the sweetest of all. They will become timid and will look to us and huddle close to us in fear, as chicks to the hen. They will marvel at us and will be awe-stricken before us, and will be proud at our being so powerful and clever, that we have been able to subdue such a turbulent flock of thousands of millions. They will tremble impotently before our wrath, their minds will grow fearful, they will be quick to shed tears like women and children . . . and they will submit to us gladly and cheerfully. . . . Go, and come no more . . . come not at all, never, never![12]

We know that those in power would act against the interests of the population in the way of these illustrations; we know so because they're doing it now. The human species doesn't need the technology of an ETI or divine intervention to solve its problems for solutions are already in hand. We have the ability to produce food for all and to provide proper shelter, sanitation, clothing, health care, transport, and a virtually limitless number of other

---

[12] Dostoevsky (2009: 314-330)

material needs yet it's being structurally withheld because it would destroy oligarchy.

It's as if we're dealing with two species here, one god-like and the other beast. Dostoevsky and the ETI are examples but it isn't hard to find many others. Here's Nietzsche, "the arch adversary of all slave revolts."[13]

> The essential characteristic of a good and healthy aristocracy, however, is that it experiences itself not as a function (whether of the monarchy or the commonwealth) but as their meaning and highest justification—that it therefore accepts with a good conscience the sacrifice of untold human beings who, for its sake, must be reduced and lowered to incomplete human beings, to slaves, to instruments. Their fundamental faith simply has to be that society must not exist for society's sake but only as the foundation and scaffolding on which a choice type of being is able to raise itself to its higher task and to a higher state of being.[14]

Austrian School economist Ludwig von Mises parrots this sentiment in his praise of Ayn Rand's book *Atlas Shrugged*: "You have the courage to tell the masses what no politician told them: you are inferior and all the improvements in your conditions which you simply take for granted you owe to the effort of men who are better than you."[15]

There's a deeply rooted hostility in oligarchy that would be unthinkable in an egalitarian system. It flows directly from the two class logic of inequality that ensures the population is always positioned as the existential risk to power. It's revealed in every corner of Western culture and it's worthwhile to offer a few more illustrations.

Here's the founder of scientific management in the twentieth century, Frederick Taylor: "Now one of the very first requirements for a man who is fit to handle pig iron as a regular occupation is that he shall be so stupid and so phlegmatic that he more nearly resembles in his mental make-up the ox than any other type."[16] And Dean Acheson, US Secretary of State between 1949 and 1953 and central architect of US foreign policy during the Cold

---

[13] Landa (2010: 133)

[14] Beyond Good and Evil, Part 9 "What is Noble," 258

[15] As quoted in Robin (2011: 91).

[16] As quoted in Meszaros (1989: 61).

War: "I don't think [democracy] is worth a damn . . . I say the Congress is too damn representative. It's just as stupid as the people are; just as uneducated, just as dumb, just as selfish."[17] The US Founding Fathers are idolized by many but they wrote their Constitution out of fear of the people and the desire to contain the democratic threat to property. While a number of quotes are presented in appendix five, here's New York delegate and future Treasury Secretary Alexander Hamilton.

> All communities divide themselves into the few and the many. The first are the rich and well born, the other the mass of the people. The voice of the people has been said to be the voice of God; and however generally this maxim has been quoted and believed, it is not true in fact. The people are turbulent and changing; they seldom judge or determine right. Give therefore to the first class a distinct, permanent share in the government. . . . Can a democratic assembly who annually revolve in the mass of the people, be supposed steadily to pursue the public good? Nothing but a permanent body can check the imprudence of democracy. . . . It is admitted that you cannot have a good executive upon a democratic plan.[18]

Modern conservatism was born as a reaction to the French Revolution and its central core, observes political scientist Corey Robin, is an argument "as to why the lower orders should not be allowed to exercise their independent will, why they should not be allowed to govern themselves or the polity. Submission is their first duty, agency, the prerogative of the elite."[19] Here is its leading historical voice, Edmund Burke.

> The occupation of a hair-dresser, or of a working tallow-chandler, cannot be a matter of honor to any person,—to say nothing of a number of other more servile employments. Such descriptions of men ought not to suffer oppression from the state; but the state suffers oppression, if such as they, either individually or collectively, are permitted to rule. [20] . . . The

---

[17] As quoted in Anderson (2013: 31).
[18] Farrand (1911: 1, 299)
[19] Robin (2011: 7)
[20] Burke (2012: 160)

characteristic essence of property, formed out of the combined principles of its acquisition and conservation, is to be unequal.[21] ... A perfect democracy is therefore the most shameless thing in the world.[22] ... Never, never more, shall we behold that generous loyalty to rank and sex, that proud submission, that dignified obedience, that subordination of the heart, which kept alive, even in servitude itself, the spirit of an exalted freedom![23]

Conservatism, says Robin, has adopted "the language of democratic reform to the cause of hierarchy,"[24] always with the "permanent project" of making "privilege palatable to the masses."[25] Political philosopher Sheldon Wolin notes that conservative theorists have consistently sought to identify mass culture with the traditional one of the lower classes where the pace of change has been slow and literacy limited; the goal being to use the "unthinking or uncritical acceptance of social norms" as a counter-revolutionary force.[26] Like oligarchy, conservatism transcends the era of any individual and links them all. At the same conservative dining table, dinner host Robin seats "Hobbes next to Hayek, Burke across from Palin, Nietzsche in between Ayn Rand and Antonin Scalia, with Adams, Calhoun, Oakeshott, Ronald Reagan, Tocqueville, Theodore Roosevelt, Margaret Thatcher, Ernst Jünger, Carl Schmitt, Winston Churchill, Phyllis Schlafly, Richard Nixon, Irving Kristol, Francis Fukuyama, and George W. Bush interspersed throughout."[27]

"Give him an inch and he'll take an ell"[28] is a sixteenth century saying that well captures a key driving assumption behind suppression. Prosperity is a dangerous 'slippery slope' that must at all costs be avoided. In what reads like a tract from a management tutorial, here are the words of escaped slave Frederick Douglass.

---

[21] Burke (2012: 161)

[22] Burke (2012: 187)

[23] Burke (2012: 176)

[24] Robin (2011: 52)

[25] Robin (2011: 100)

[26] Wolin (2004: 454)

[27] Robin (2011: 34)

[28] An ell is the length of an arm between the elbow and the tip of the middle finger.

Beat and cuff your slave, keep him hungry and spiritless, and he will follow the chain of his master like a dog; but feed and clothe him well, work him moderately, surround him with physical comfort, and dreams of freedom intrude. Give him a bad master, and he aspires to a good master; give him a good master and he wishes to become his own master. Such is human nature.[29]

Douglass seems to have studied Aristotle who, writing about slave management, observed that "if you are remiss in your discipline they grow insolent, and think themselves upon an equality with their masters; and if they are hardly used they are continually plotting against you and hate you."[30] Or it could have been Cicero: "You may distribute, indeed, some show of power to the people, as Lycurgus and Romulus did, but you inflame them, with the thirst of liberty by allowing them even the slightest taste of its sweetness."[31] Or popular eighteenth century British writer Arthur Young: "Everyone but an idiot knows that the lower classes must be kept poor, or they will never be industrious."[32]

The same theme was taken up in the turbulent 1970s in a report written for the Trilateral Commission (TC), an organization formed by billionaire David Rockefeller and others associated with the elite Council on Foreign Relations in order to bring together conservative thinkers in the US, Western Europe, and Japan. The report, entitled *The Crisis of Democracy: report on the governability of democracies to the Trilateral Commission*, decried the growing "excess of democracy" that was arising in conjunction with economic growth. Almost exactly paraphrasing Douglass, it noted that "Instead of appeasing tensions, material progress seems to have exacerbated them," and that "The incorporation of substantial elements of the population into the middle classes has escalated their expectations and aspirations, thereby causing a more intense reaction if these are not met in reality."[33]

The control of populations is the most important challenge of wealth defense* and we gain added insight into its urgency when we observe it has

---

[29] Douglass (2012: 118)

[30] Aristotle (2012: book II, ch IX, 1269b)

[31] Cicero (2010: 37-38)

[32] As quoted in Thompson (1966: 358)

[33] Crozier, Huntington, Watanuki (1975). The quotes are, in order of presentation, from pages 113, 22, and 158.

been an especially difficult undertaking over the past couple centuries. Let's scan the history of this period with a view toward noting a certain regularity to waves of turbulence that fits into a roughly sixty year cycle.

I begin with the French Revolution in 1789 which opened a twenty-five year period of extended war in Europe lasting until 1814. The revolution, with its *liberté, égalité, fraternité*, is widely seen to this day as the key inspiration for populist revolt against undemocratic power. It didn't occur in a vacuum as it was near simultaneous with the farmer rebellions in the US and the growing elite fears of democracy, both of which were subdued with the passing of the 1787 Constitution.[34]

Fifty-nine years after 1789, we find the cataclysmic explosion of 1848, the first revolution in modern European history and the widest. No revolution spread more rapidly, "running like a brushfire across frontiers, countries and even oceans." Within weeks, no government was left standing in all or part of today's France, Germany, Austria, Italy, the Czech Republic, Hungary, Poland, the former Yugoslavian nations, Rumania and parts of Latin America. All were "in fact, or immediate anticipation, social revolutions of the labouring poor." The revolution quickly failed as the original governments retook power within a few months but the events revealed a dangerous "romantic-utopian" passion, a "springtime of the peoples."[35]

Just 66 years later in 1914, we have World War I followed by the Russian Revolution and 30 years of war, chaos, and depression. Communist regimes came to rule over substantial percentages of the global population and presented a considerable threat to oligarchy.

Finally, 54 years after 1914, we run into the outbreak and instability of the sixties and seventies, using 1968 as the specific date. In the sixties we find the height of the protest movements in the US, France, Germany, and elsewhere. The May 1968 uprising in Paris appeared close to overthrowing the conservative de Gaulle government and drew inspiration from the French Revolution. The decade was marked by dramatic attacks on the status-quo, including the Civil Rights movement, Woodstock, the countercultural movement and so on. It also saw top popular leaders in the US—John Kennedy, Robert Kennedy and Martin Luther King—assassinated. The Cultural Revolution in China began in 1966. The Trilateral Commission

---

[34] See appendix five.
[35] Hobsbawm (1962: 10-13)

report mentioned earlier, published in 1975, wrote of the budding "excess of democracy"[36] of this period, harking back to the same phrase used by Alexander Hamilton and many of the US Founding Fathers in 1787.

There are admittedly only a limited number of data points in this historical summary but there can be little doubt that if we experienced the same regularity with comet strikes, there would be substantial scientific concern. If the cycle holds, we should begin looking for the next comet arrival sometime in the 2020s.[37]

Each of these outbreaks brought forth strong oligarchic reactions with the most recent two being the Cold War and the 'economic' agenda of so-called neoliberalism. The Cold War, an "egregious term" for a period of "conflict, war, repression, and ever mounting violence,"[38] was at bottom a war against populations. The threat was never a Soviet or Chinese outright attack, but of an ideology that was attracting many in the 'Third World,' Europe, and elsewhere.[39] While taking the name of communism, the fear in actuality was the age-old one of democracy.[40]

---

[36] Crozier, Huntington, & Watanuki (1975: 113)

[37] 54 to 66 years after 1968 would be between 2022 and 2034. 60 years exactly would be 2028.

[38] Kolko (1972: 6)

[39] See Williams (1972: 105, 222, & 227). As Williams notes (p. 227), "the popular idea that Soviet leaders emerged from war ready to battle the US is not supported by evidence."

[40] The war against the ideology of communism began before the onset of the Cold War. The US sent 13,000 troops into Russia in 1918 in a failed effort to overthrow the new Bolshevik government. In the years prior to the outbreak of World War II, Clement Leibovitz and Alvin Finkel (1998: 17) report that conservative British Prime Minister Neville Chamberlain and his followers "were not trying to avoid a war; their whole intention was to turn Nazi militarism loose in a bloody confrontation with the Soviet Union to end Bolshevism in its heartland. Hitler was to be given a free hand in Eastern Europe so that this common end could be achieved. 'Appeasement' was no more than a public front constructed to appease public disgust with the Nazis." The tacit pact between Hitler and Chamberlain collapsed, according to these writers, because of Hitler's fears that Chamberlain couldn't deliver. This kind of active collaboration with Nazis continued after the war. The FBI and CIA began aggressively recruiting Nazis of all ranks in the 1950s to be used as spies and informants against communists and sympathizers, offering them protection against prosecution for war crimes ("In Cold War, US Spy Agencies Used 1,000 Nazis", *New York Times*, October 26, 2014).

The oligarchy won this ideological battle but it was substantially aided by the fact the USSR and China were poor totalitarian states having no historic culture of democracy. It became possible to link collectivism with these two backward countries and the Cold War itself as one between freedom and totalitarianism. A significant problem would have arisen, though, if the opponent were democratic as the battle line then would have been drawn where it actually lies—between the claimed natural right to wealth, a/k/a Lockean liberalism, and true democracy where the people choose what the natural laws are. The rise of any "democratic hyper-functionality"[41] is the existential threat to oligarchy and substantial resources are assuredly being devoted within the intelligence services to minimizing the odds of that horror ever happening. While the formal Cold War ended with the demise of the Soviet Union, the 'economic' front of neoliberalism continues to this day.[42] In a real sense, the greater Cold War continues.

Much of the world is formally democratic today but we need to keep the relationship between oligarchy and democracy in proper perspective. We've defined the former as concentrated wealth following the Adams Maxim doctrine that if it exists it rules. Democracy, on the other hand, is the rule of the people. The two can't coexist since the people and wealth can't simultaneously rule. Democracy has therefore never existed in the 5,000 year history of civilization. When we speak of those of ancient Greece or of today, we're referring to a particular political form of oligarchy, a formal rather than a real democracy.

Formal democracies have appeared in at least some geographic region for less than 9 percent of recorded history. Except for the couple hundred year experiment in classical Greece, it's brand new. It has been around for less than 250 years in the US although for much of this time only for white males. Blacks formally gained the right to vote in 1870 but then faced such discriminatory hurdles as Jim Crow laws enforcing racial segregation, poll taxes, literacy tests, and residency and record-keeping requirements. Women obtained the right to vote in 1920. Prior to 1867, only one in seven British males had the vote and near universal male suffrage wasn't finally won until

---

[41] Winters (2011: 134)

[42] See for example Gindin & Panitch (2012: 15) "neoliberalism was essentially a political response to the democratic gains that had been previously achieved by working classes and which had become, from capital's perspective, barriers to accumulation."

1918. Universal women suffrage was gained in 1928. Quasi-stable formal democracies have existed in Germany and Italy only since the end of World War II, and in Spain and Portugal since the 1970s. The EU of today is a deeply anti-democratic project. Latin America has a long history of coups against popular governments and formal democracy has been almost a complete stranger to most of Asia and Africa.

That true democracy has never existed and even formal democracy rarely so isn't at all surprising given its gross incompatibility with oligarchy. Democracy "runs against the grain of the most powerful institutions of society. It stands for the attempt to nurture the value of a common good in a society whose main institutions are structured to produce differentials of income, status, and power as a matter of course."[43] The oligarchy has always feared it and has devoted substantial portions of its wealth defense* effort toward its suppression. When popular pressure had become so great that democracy couldn't be denied, the universal response was to bar it from interfering with ownership rights. This has been accomplished through the maintenance of a hegemonic ideology in favor of property, the construction of a great wall between 'politics' and 'economics,' sophisticated techniques of mass propaganda, constitutional barriers of various sorts, institutional and procedural impediments, and assorted extra-legal means like bribes, assassinations, coups, death squads, military action, and so forth. This strange mix of democracy and oligarchy, democratic oligarchy, is a "hopelessly anti-democratic structure" that, when all is said and done, is little more than "a de-facto dictatorship."[44] Democracy has been accepted by the oligarchy, we can conclude, "precisely to the extent that it is *not democratic*."[45]

Here is perhaps a good place to touch on the nature of the state. Since the dawn of civilization, it has always ultimately represented the interests of inequality. According to anthropologist Morton Fried, the state "is a collection of specialized institutions and agencies, some formal and others informal, that maintain an order of stratification."[46] In the same vein, Braudel notes that "The state was there to preserve inequality, the cornerstone of the

---

[43] Wolin (2004: 604)

[44] Boron (2006: 32-33) The author uses the term "democratic capitalism."

[45] Landa (2010: 334) Italics in original.

[46] Fried, M. (1967: 235)

social order."[47] "When the state intervened *against* someone, it was inevitably the masses who had to be contained and returned to the path of duty—that is work." [48] And when it intervened *for* someone, it was inevitably the oligarchy. A good recent example is a reported conversation between Wall Street bankers and President Obama during the height of the banking crisis. "My administration," said Obama, "is the only thing between you and the pitchforks. You guys have an acute public relations problem that's turning into a political problem. And I want to help. I'm not going after you. I'm protecting you."[49] The point isn't Obama as an individual but the structural imperative that the state support the vital interests of oligarchy.

Political sociologist Nicos Poulantzas provides us with a fruitful simplification that conceives the state not as an agent having unique powers of its own, but rather as the condensation of the balance of forces within society. It's not an entity or agent but a relation. This seems persuasive given that it's difficult to conceive how a state could ever be in opposition to the socioeconomic power structure. Any attempt by those holding state office to do so would assuredly result in them being booted from office and replaced by proper managers. Since the dominant force in oligarchy is by definition class based, the state can be reduced to the "materialization and condensation of class relations" with its key responsibility being "to maintain the unity and cohesion of a social formation by concentrating and sanctioning class domination."[50]

The structure of the liberal democratic state reflects the oligarchically weighted balance of forces in many ways but primarily through the separation of the 'political' from the 'economic.' Democracy applies to the former but there are strict limits to the extent it can legitimately interfere in the realm of the latter. Bob Jessop has noted that this form of state is seen by many on both the right and the left as the ideal collective capitalist—the efficient enforcer of law and order, contracts, and property rights, all while claiming electoral legitimacy.[51] The political class struggle is confined to formalized parliamentarism and the economic one to market relations. It's ideal, though,

---

[47] Braudel (1982: 493)
[48] Braudel (1982: 516) Italics in original.
[49] Suskind (2011: 234-235)
[50] Poulantzas (1975: 24-25)
[51] Jessop (1978: 15-17)

only to the extent oligarchy is politically and ideologically dominant and otherwise becomes a serious threat.[52] Democracy and oligarchy, in other words, are compatible only so long as the balance of forces rests with oligarchy and democracy thereby kept neutered.

The concepts brought out in this chapter will form the nucleus of our analysis as we proceed. To summarize, oligarchy has been defined as the existence of wealth inequality, a form of rule that has subjugated mankind throughout all of civilization. Its underlying logic has been broken down into three components—that of motives, risks, and dynamics. The motives girding the system are posited to be wealth defense* and luxury consumption. The two risks against which wealth defense* is directed are from other oligarchs and the population, the latter being existential. And the prime dynamics are diversion, the power to costlessly obtain goods and services, and suppression, the wealth defense* need to keep the population down. The system is always on guard against the democratic threat and wherever democracy has existed, it has always been of a neutered variety. The state is an institution defending the primary forces in society and has thereby consistently aligned itself against the population in service to the oligarchy.

If asked to express the most important theme of this book in just four words, I would answer *the system is hostile.* That this is so is evidenced by the actuality of our brutal history, the widespread existence of poverty amidst plenty, the basic logic of inequality outlined in this and the previous chapter, the aggressively anti-democratic views expressed by authoritative figures throughout all of civilization, and the way the system operates today, the subject of the third section. The hostility, though, is disguised behind ideology of which one of its most important aspects is the proposition the system isn't oligarchy but 'capitalism.' While some argue about the latter's fairness, all seem to agree it's new, complex, and highly confusing. We turn to it in the next chapter.

---

[52] Jessop (1978: 39)

5

Capitalism

The constant throughout all of civilization has been a structure of rule whereby the great majority has lived poorly while facing a tiny minority possessing virtually all wealth/power. We live today in such a system but it isn't named nor understood as such. We instead find ourselves in a Kafkaesque labyrinth called 'capitalism' in which the antagonistic logic of inequality is shrouded and in which the system is presented as one of almost unfathomable complexity far removed from anything that has ever existed.

Many aspects of today are indeed complex and do seem different. Production is no longer centered on agriculture and the level of technology is much higher. The financial sector appears dominant. Workers are free to choose their employer, we have elections, frivolous commodities and advertising bombard us in every direction, and things feel fast, competitive, and chaotic. These are undeniable features of our world but they're ultimately just superficial details having no real bearing on the structural core of power. They're the actions which, as Richard Feynman observed, are often very complicated; but they shouldn't be mistaken for the underlying pattern which is always simple.[1]

---

[1] Feynman (1985: 32-33) See quote on page 6.

An excessive focus on complexity interweaves itself into almost every narrative we have on capitalism. The resulting haze is an effective ideological cloak that has disoriented even some of the sharpest observers. For thousands of years the ruling class of every era has dominated its population in leisured simplicity but now it becomes 'capitalist' and we're told it's doomed unless it succeeds in "constantly revolutionizing the instruments of production" while providing for itself a "constantly expanding market for its products."[2] With the most due regard to Marx and Engels, this is surely untrue. The system is inequality—oligarchy—and the instruments of production and size of the market are mere details. Its strength has nothing to do with whether the instruments of production are the hand shovel or advanced robotics or whether they're constantly revolutionized, and it makes not a whit of difference if the market expands forever or eternally stagnates; it only appeared so during a particular historical convergence of circumstances.

The tendency of the left to view capitalism as something new and complex has caused tremendous harm for it has driven many into an intellectual dead-end from which true understanding can't easily be had. A good example can be found in the words of Ellen Meiksins Wood, a respected scholar in the Marxian tradition.

In modern capitalism, the class relation between capital and labour is rather more difficult to decipher. Here, there is no direct transfer of surplus labour. The workers pay no rent, no tax or tribute, to their employers. There is no obvious way of distinguishing between what workers keep for themselves and what they forfeit to capital. . . . It is not so easy to unravel how . . . capital derives more benefit, in the form of profit, from the workers' labour than the workers receive in exchange in the form of a wage. The Marxist theory of surplus value is a persuasive account of how [the transfer of surplus labour from workers to capitalists] takes place, but the fact that such a complex theory is required to explain what ought to be a fairly straightforward transaction testifies to the opacity of the relation between capital and labour.

The point here is simply that, whether or not we acknowledge that what passes between the worker and the capitalist is indeed exploitation,

---

[2] Marx & Engels (1964: 62-63)

their relationship is not at all transparent, and the means by which, rightly or wrongly, the capitalist appropriates what the labourer produces is by its very nature obscure.[3]

While I may oppose capitalism, it's obscure why I do so! This isn't at all helpful. The exploitation that occurs in 'capitalism' and has dominated the entire history of civilization isn't obscure. What is are the unnecessarily complex theories attempting to explain it. Our vision is clouded and we need to simplify. Newness and complexity, in short, are myths that are among capitalism's most effective pillars of defense against its devastating exposure as nothing other than the sordid perpetuation of ancient domination.

My argument is aligned with that of Andre Gunder Frank but in a reverse sense. He emphasized, as do I, the fundamental unity of the 5,000 year "world system" and the inappropriateness of focusing on modes of production. "The world system-wide reality is the competitive dog-eat-dog war of all against all (a la Hobbes), in which only the few can win and the many must lose. And so it has been for millennia."[4] We differ, though, in that he argued that the system has always been "capitalism" with the prime goal being "ceaseless accumulation."[5] We both see a 5,000 year system but where I'm seeking to bring the simplicity of the past forward to today, Frank is projecting the confusion of capitalism backward into history.

So what exactly is capitalism anyway? Its meaning has always been vague. Although his best known work is *Capital*, Marx never referred to *capitalism*, and the word only became common at the beginning of the twentieth century.[6] Capitalism is the *ism* of *capital*—its defining doctrine, system, or theory; but that doesn't get us too far given that the meaning of capital varies widely depending on where one looks.

The dictionary tells us it's derived from the Latin *caput* or "head." If we open an accounting textbook, we find that *capital accounts* are categories in the net worth section of the balance sheet, *working capital* is readily accessible operating liquidity, and a *capital asset* is an expenditure having a multi-year useful life. Economists insist *capital* is a "factor of production," but to Veblen

---

[3] Wood (2003: 2-3)

[4] Frank (1991: 94)

[5] Frank (1992: 158) as an example.

[6] Braudel (1982: 237)

it's the *capitalized value* of the "presumptive future earning capacity" of a firm, a nebulous quantity depending on "imagined future events."[7] *Capital* can also be living, as we find with both *human capital* and *cattle*, the latter being an exploited animal species which traces its lineage to the same Latin root.

The term arose in twelfth or thirteenth century Italy and had a sense of "funds, stock of merchandise, sum of money, or money carrying interest" and gradually came to mean the *money capital* of a firm.[8] A *capitalist* dates to the mid-seventeenth century and, by the late eighteenth, came to refer to "people who already own money and are prepared to use it in order to obtain even more."[9] *Capitalism* began to appear, but rarely, in the mid-nineteenth century. According to philosopher Pierre-Joseph Proudhon, it's the "economic and social regime in which capital, the source of income, does not generally belong to those who make it work through their labor."[10] The word was essentially banned by economists in the beginning of the twentieth century and became loaded with subversionary meaning after the 1917 Russian Revolution. It didn't merit an article in the Encyclopedia Britannica until the 1926 edition.[11]

Capitalism, it would seem, is a very confused concept. To help gain some clarity, let's turn to a comprehensive, highly sympathetic definition offered by Austrian economist George Reisman.

> Capitalism is a social system based on private ownership of the means of production. It is characterized by the pursuit of material self-interest under freedom and it rests on a foundation of the cultural influence of reason. Based on its foundations and essential nature, capitalism is further characterized by saving and capital accumulation, exchange and money, financial self-interest and the profit motive, the freedoms of economic competition and economic inequality, the price system, economic progress, and a harmony of the material self-interests of all the individuals who participate in it.[12] . . . [It] depends on the institution of economic

---

[7] Veblen (1999: 49)

[8] Braudel (1982: 232-233)

[9] Braudel (1982: 236)

[10] As quoted in Braudel (1982: 237).

[11] Braudel (1982: 238)

[12] Reisman (1998: 19)

inequality, insofar as the latter results from the process of economic competition or, more broadly, from individuals freely engaging in production and exchange, whether they are in competition with one another or not. Economic inequality inexorably emerges from the freedom of the individual to pursue his own prosperity and to keep as his own whatever he achieves. It emerges simply because not everyone is equally intelligent, talented, ambitious, or hardworking, or saves as great a proportion of his income.[13]

There are many points here and it will be useful to categorize them according to whether they apply to the system's structural core, to its details, or to ideology. I'll ignore ideological elements as they're unrelated to our present concerns.

Structural Core
 Private ownership of the means of production
 Pursuit of material self-interest
 Economic inequality

Details
 Monetary
  Saving and capital accumulation
  Exchange and money
  Financial self-interest
  Profit motive
  Price system
 Selection Method
  Freedom of economic competition
  Meritocracy (intelligence, talent, ambition, hardworking, savings)

Ideological
 Cultural influence of reason
 Economic progress
 Harmony of material self-interests
 Freedom

---

[13] Reisman (1998: 145)

I assign to the structural core the elements that define the most basic pattern of the system. Ownership is 'private' which I take to mean non-egalitarian. The prime motive is material self-interest which is expandable to wealth defense* and luxury consumption. And wealth/power is held unequally. Capitalism, we thus find, is oligarchy. If we limited our goal to a very general understanding, we could stop right here for everything else is in the realm of detail or ideology.

The next grouping identifies the details. Money plays a prominent role in capitalism but as we'll discover in the next section, it's a mere token of power and can't therefore be a core element. We commonly miscategorize this token as being part of the core, however, and it causes enormous confusion. Consider the monetary elements listed—savings and capital accumulation, exchange and money, financial self-interest, profit motive, and the price system; what possible meaning can any of these have beyond mere detail? To treat them as core leaves us with nothing beyond money for money's sake, a self-referential "patently absurd" loop in which "one accumulates capital in order to accumulate more capital."[14] It's a view encapsulated in the name itself—*capital*-ism. We may just as well call it *token*-ism or *money*-ism and define it as a coreless structure characterized by the mindless chase of tokens.

The selection method is also a detail as was discussed in chapter three. This is often miscategorized in the same way as money and the result is that surface freedoms end up being mistaken for core ones. The core is structural inequality and it's irrelevant which individuals are selected to fill the various slots within it.

It's not wrong to come up with a word to describe a system having the characteristics outlined above or that it would happen to be "capitalism"; the problem is that we too easily focus on surface details and thereby lose sight of the structural core of ancient and tyrannical power.

Much of the confusion is related to the extraordinary events of the nineteenth century that are often treated as if they were permanent features of the landscape. The century was unique, however, in that it encompassed the greatest material expansion in human history, both geographically and in industry and commerce. Europeans discovered the New World in the late fifteenth century but it was only by the eighteenth and especially the

---

14 Wallerstein (1995: 40)

nineteenth that emigration reached high proportions. The opening of whole continents offered opportunities for many to improve their lives[15] and the term *New World* captures its massive importance. The window was bound to close, though, and it did by century's end as the new resources became consolidated into ever fewer hands. The New World became Old.

If there were no Industrial Revolution but only the introduction of virgin land into the equation, there would be little reason to think the basic dynamics would change. After a competitive struggle, we'd expect the land to become monopolized by a small minority just as before. The age-old force of gravity-like consolidation would lead to a foreseeable end state. The Industrial Revolution did occur, though, and it brought with it a great expansion of the non-agricultural 'dimension' of property—ownership not tied to land but to the control of industrial, commercial, and service sector niches. This dimension, however, turned out to be just as monopolizable as land, a fact well foretold by its history prior to the nineteenth century. Medieval Florence, Venice, Genoa, and seventeenth century Amsterdam are all prominent examples and each were tightly consolidated socioeconomic systems having massive wealth inequalities. There was a great competitive struggle in the nineteenth century to capture control of this expanded property but the forces of consolidation have worked their unceasing magic; the dust has cleared and we find we have traveled a grand circle. Our technology is better now, we dress differently, and oligarchy, as strong as ever, has become fully two-dimensional.

While the expanded second dimension of property added complexity to the picture, it didn't herald the beginnings of a new system. Its competitive aspect was temporary and what differences that do exist between agriculture and the industrial, commercial, and service sectors are in the end minute compared to their ultimate unity as monopolizable property. "The necessary result of competition," observed a prescient Marx while viewing things during its mid-nineteenth century height, "is the accumulation of capital in a few hands and thus the restoration of monopoly in a more terrible form. . . . Finally the distinction between capitalist and land rentier, like that between tiller of the soil and the factory worker, disappears and that the whole society must fall apart into the two classes—the property-*owners* and the propertyless

---

[15] Although of course a great many didn't, especially indigenous Americans and blacks.

workers."[16] This is an apt summation of the core of modern oligarchy and the remainder of the book is devoted to it.

---

[16] Marx (1978a: 70) Italics in original.

Modern Oligarchy

6

The Global Game

As a phase of historical oligarchy, today's system is grounded in the exact same motives, risks, and dynamics that have existed throughout the entirety of civilization. Ideology discourages this claim from gaining mainstream acceptance, however, and so also does the immense complexity surrounding us. How can it be, one might ask, that things could be so simple when they appear so complicated? I believe the best way to overcome the twin barriers of ideology and complexity is through a process of abstraction and simplification so we can come to better see the basic pattern. This is the approach I'll follow in this section and while much will be left out by doing so, we'll gain in return a far clearer view of our situation.

I'll begin by sketching the abstract picture I'm proposing. At its core, modern oligarchy can be thought of in terms of a game, one that's global in scale and derives from the logic of inequality. It has just two idealized classes—the oligarchy which owns all material wealth and *the population* which owns none. Oligarchs compete with each other in accordance with the motives of wealth defense* and luxury consumption but also form a collective unity as a class. The prime concern at the class level is the perpetuation of the game and the enforcement of its rules. The rules seem mostly about money but that's only a surface appearance. Money is a mere token and we'll need to look through it to discover the real dynamics. When we do, we'll find they're nothing other than age-old diversion and suppression.

The heart of the game is the dynamic of costless diversion which is unsurprising given that oligarchy, wealth, and material inequality have no meaning absent this power. It's sustained through the ownership of a portfolio of claims on monetary flows that returns to the holder a sum equal to or greater than what he expended on diversion. For competing oligarchs, it's a zero-sum intra-class battle centered on such strategies as portfolio diversification, calculated risk, and speculation; but at the class level it's a routine structurally guaranteed consequence of the diversion-profit loop, a fundamental flow that will be introduced in the next chapter. Costless diversion, in other words, is provided automatically to the class as a result of the rules; individual oligarchs then compete with each other to capture a sufficient share for themselves.

The game requires pawns to do the work and the most important rules assure the population is perpetually cast in that role. Suppression is a definitional aspect of the whole contrivance and it's strictly enforced by the oligarchy as a class. It takes a number of forms and we'll review some of the most important ones throughout this section.

To recapitulate, modern oligarchy is a game centered on the diversion-profit loop, its rules are written by the oligarchy, oligarchs contend for relative power on a global board in accordance with them, and national populations are the pawns. I'm making many simplifications here and I'll highlight now three of special significance—that there are just two fundamental classes, that the game is global rather than national, and that the oligarchy forms a collective unity. I'll discuss each in turn.

The two class assumption is an idealization. In the real world, large gradations of wealth exist within what we'd call the oligarchy as do similar disparities of relative poverty within the population. There's also an ill-defined intermediate 'middle class' that seems to separate the two. These are complications, though, that distract us from seeing the broader pattern.

As we recall from the first chapter, Credit Suisse estimates that the top 1 and 5 percent of the global population possess 50 and 77 percent of global wealth while the bottom 90 is left with just 12 percent and the bottom majority less than 1 percent. To better appreciate what this means, let's express these numbers in terms of individuals. The average oligarch in the top 1 and 5 percent possesses 376 and 116 times the wealth of the average person in the bottom 90 percent and 2,500 and 770 times that in the bottom majority. [1] If average individual wealth in the bottom 90 percent were represented as a modest single story home, then the portfolio size of the typical oligarch within the top 1 percent would soar to over three and a half times the height of the Empire State Building.[2] I'll use a different analogy for comparing the top 1 percent with the bottom majority. If the wealth of an individual in the latter group were represented as a one mile (1.6 kilometer) stroll to town, then the former would constitute the distance between Madrid and Moscow or, in the US, between Atlanta and San Francisco. Similarly gigantic differentials exist within national populations. Based on Wolff's data in chapter one, the representative member of the top 1 and 5 percent in the US possesses 488 and 165 times the wealth of a person in the bottom 80 percent.[3] I believe the sheer magnitudes of these differentials make it self-evident that a two class model is a reasonable abstraction. Making it more complicated adds shades of grey but at the great cost of rendering the fundamental situation much harder to see.

The second simplification is that the scale of analysis is taken to be global. This fits best with that of the diversion-profit loop which we know to be global given the extensive volume of international trade, transnational supply chains, cross-country ownership links, multi-country subsidiaries, transnational strategic alliances, and so on. Most oligarchic portfolios are globally diversified as well, through either active portfolio positioning or through the diversification existing within most large corporations

---

[1] I calculate these multiples by taking the share of wealth and dividing it by the fraction of the population. In the case of the top 1 percent possessing 50 percent of wealth, I take the wealth share of 50 and divide it by 1 to get 50 (50/1=50). The bottom 90 percent owns 12 percent of wealth and the representative share is calculated as .133 (12/90). The wealth differential is then calculated as 375.9 (50/.133). The top 5 percent possesses 77 percent of wealth or an average of 15.5 (77/5). The bottom 90 percent was calculated above at .133. The differential is 115.8 (15.4/.133). The bottom majority has less than 1 percent (1/50=.02) and the differential with the top 1 and 5 percent is therefore 2500 (50/(1/50) and 770 (15.4/.02)

[2] The Empire State Building in New York is 102 floors.

[3] Taken from Wolff as presented in chapter one. Wealth shares for the top 1, 5, and bottom 80 percent are: 42.7, 72, and 7 percent respectively. Differential calculations: top 1 percent (42.7/1)/(7/80)=488. Top 5 percent (72/5)/(7/80)=164.6.

themselves. The latter is well-demonstrated by national stock exchange data. Corporations within the S&P 500 in the US are reported to receive 46 percent of their revenue from outside the country,[4] the 30 large German corporations in the DAX grouping 60 percent from outside Europe,[5] those in the FTSE 100 75 percent outside the UK,[6] and the NIKKEI 225 corporations 35 percent outside Japan.[7]

There's nothing new about thinking of the system in a transnational way as geographic expansion has always been one of the prime manifestations of inequality. Since being unleashed at the hazy dawn of civilization, its dynamics have guaranteed that those pursuing the goal of power would incessantly seek to expand to the limits of the possible. As early as the twenty-third century BC, for instance, Naram-Sin of Akkad saw himself as "King of the World" and "God" and the expansionist "will–to–power"[8] he embodied has haunted mankind right down to the present day; it's part and parcel of the DNA of oligarchy. British colonialism in the nineteenth century, the German and Japanese attempted conquests of the first half of the twentieth, and the informal American managed oligarchic empire of today are modern examples.

Expansion shouldn't be thought of solely in terms of ever-larger formal empires, though, as they've in fact been rare.[9] The norm throughout history has instead been an integrated system comprised of a multitude of states within and between which the drive for unequal power has sought

---

[4] *S&P 500 2013: Global Sales Year in Review*, Research bulletin issued by S&P Dow Jones Indices, McGraw Hill Financial, August 2014

[5] *DAX Beating S&P 500 by Most Since '06 on Economy Optimism*; article on Bloomberg Business, April 3, 2012, accessed May 22, 2015
   www.bloomberg.com/news/articles/2012-04-02/dax-beating-s-p-500-by-most-since-06-on-economy-optimism

[6] *How British is the FTSE 100—and should you care?*, online article: *Barclays Market Review*, accessed May 22, 2015
   https://wealth.barclays.com/en_gb/smartinvestor/market-review/how-british-is-the-ftse-100.html

[7] *Japan's Global Champions: reinvigorating the nation*, Price Waterhouse Cooper online article accessed May 22, 2015.
   https://www.pwc.com/jp/ja/japan-knowledge/archive/assets/pdf/japanglobalchampions-en.pdf

[8] Wilkinson (2006: 66)

[9] Wilkinson (2004)

gratification not just through war but through the control of monopolizable trade, markets, and resources.[10] Modern oligarchy is such a system and today it spans the world.

The final simplification is that the oligarchy is viewed as a consolidated collective unity. This is a crucial element for understanding modern oligarchy because it places front and center the class-based anti-population hostility that forms the essence of the system. It's in this rule-setting and rule-enforcing class as a whole that we can best recognize the system's pattern and logic and it will be on it where we'll direct our prime focus. We will, on the other hand, be far less interested in the detailed actions of individual competing oligarchs for they're merely the ever changing players in the game.

Let's look closer at the collective nature of the oligarchic class by considering the major form wealth takes today, that being stock shares in large corporations. In the US and other Anglo-Saxon countries, ownership of these companies is widely disbursed throughout the class. Harking back to the classic 1932 work of Berle and Means,[11] Monks and Minow observe that "with rare exceptions like Bill Gates of Microsoft and the late Sam Walton of Wal-Mart, large companies are led by men whose stakes in the company are dwarfed by the holdings of institutional investors."[12] Almost 75 percent of the shares of large US firms, in fact, are reported held by institutions like banks and mutual funds.[13] The actual individual 'owner' has a limited or non-existent role in management, has no right to specific corporate assets, assumes only a limited liability, holds the shares as part of a broader portfolio, and can quickly exit his position through the liquidity of the financial markets. "There are so many owners of the largest American corporations, that it makes little sense to consider any one of them an 'owner'

---

[10] We can point to US President Woodrow Wilson as an illustrative example of the basic mindset—"Since trade ignores national boundaries and the manufacturer insists on having the world as a market, the flag of this nation must follow him, and the doors of the nations which are closed must be battered down ... even if sovereignty of unwilling nations is outraged. ... Colonies must be obtained in order that no useful corner of the world is overlooked or left unused." As quoted in Williams (1972: 72)

[11] Berle and Means (1932)

[12] Monks & Minow (2011: 120)

[13] Glattfelder (2010). As of 2005.

in the sense of an individual with an economic interest in being informed about and involved in corporate affairs."[14]

This vast dispersion lends strong credence to the idea that what's really owned isn't so much percentages of specific corporations but rather a highly liquid slice of the entirety. It's the interconnected web, the market as a whole, that's most relevant. No oligarch really owns the individual large corporations, yet at the same time, every oligarch owns a customized piece of the greater collectivity.

But ownership takes a somewhat different character outside the English-speaking world where it's characterized by *business groups*. These are tightly controlled pyramids of formally independent corporations that are interconnected through hard to decipher cross-ownership ties[15] and in which ultimate control normally rests in the hands of a single family.[16] A distinction is drawn here between ownership and control with the latter requiring anywhere from less than a 10 percent ownership stake for companies with widely dispersed shares up to a bare majority.

The world of business groups is extraordinarily concentrated. Finance professor Randall Morck observes that just "handfuls of wealthy families dominate the economies of India, Korea, Spain, Turkey, other major European countries, and elsewhere."[17] Through pyramidal cross ownership structures, in the late nineties five families in the Philippines controlled 42.8 percent of market capitalization in the country,[18] ten families in Indonesia and Thailand 50 percent of total corporate assets, and 10 families in Hong Kong and South Korea one-third of the corporate sector.[19] Five business groups in Chile controlled almost 50 percent of total assets in the stock exchange in 2002,[20] and in Belgium, Germany, and Canada, ten families controlled 30, more than 20, and 40 percent of market capitalization,

---

[14] Monks & Minow (2011: 125)

[15] Lefort (2010: 398) notes that owners commonly use fantasy names at all levels of the pyramid making it difficult to ascertain ultimate control.

[16] They take various names in different countries. In South Korea they're known as the *chaebol*, in Latin America, the *grupos economicos*, and in Japan, the *keiretsu*.

[17] Morck (2010: 604)

[18] Claessens, Djankov, & Lang (2000: 28)

[19] Claessens, Djankov, & Lang (2000: 3)

[20] Lefort (2010: 397)

respectively. In Sweden, the Wallenberg family alone controls more than 50 percent of the total value of the stock market.[21]

The business groups tend to be widely diversified across both industries and nations and have strong links with large transnational corporations and foreign owners. The largest group in South Korea, for example, is Samsung Electronics and in 2003 it had 85 subsidiaries in 33 countries.[22] As of 2006, 54 percent of its ownership was foreign.[23] The trend in Korea and elsewhere seems to be toward the American style of ownership as a full 42 percent of market capitalization in Korea is foreign owned.[24] Japan is becoming more Anglo-Saxon as well and its keiretsu is "fading away."[25] The largest group in Mexico, controlled by the Slim family, is widely diversified[26] and is even the largest shareholder of the New York Times. Coca Cola holds a 30 percent share in FEMSA, the third largest business group in Mexico and GE a 40 percent share of MABE, the fifteenth largest.[27]

There's every reason to think the transnational collectivization process will deepen further. US and UK investment funds own significant numbers of shares of firms throughout the world and are also lenders through the widespread use of debt securities. State led development has been a prime historical force in the expansion of business groups but it has succeeded mostly by limiting both imports and foreign direct investment. The strategy isn't likely to be viable in an open global system, notes sociologist Paul Windolf, and will need to be reorganized on a transnational level.[28]

Even as they exist today, the controllers of business groups aren't lords of isolated realms; they're widely diversified, their firms are increasingly co-owned transnationally, and global alliances are extensive. Like all oligarchs, their diversion spending is transnational and they're free to place their portfolio bets on the global board as they see fit. They're active players within the transnational game, are members in good standing of the oligarchy, and

---

[21] Morck (2010: 604-605). These numbers are for the late nineties and early 2000s.

[22] Kim (2010: 170)

[23] Kim (2010: 173)

[24] Kim (2010: 173)

[25] Lincoln & Shimotani (2010: 151)

[26] Hoshino (2010: 425)

[27] Hoshino (2010: 444)

[28] Windolf (2002: 225)

play by its rules. I'll therefore not differentiate between the dispersed "shareholder capitalism" of the English speaking world and the business groups. It's one giant inter-connected system.

I conclude that modern oligarchy is best thought of in terms of a global web of collective ownership. The more powerful the oligarch, the greater his proportionate share of it will be. It's a simplification, but like the others discussed, it captures the essential truth. We gain from it the vital perspective that the real owner of our world is the collectivity, the oligarchy as a class, and what it owns isn't so much individual corporations but the system as a whole.

Viewing ownership as ultimately in the hands of a single entity enables us to better distinguish what's going on between the two classes. This becomes especially clear if we filter from view the legal fiction of corporations. What then stands out is no longer the corporate shells but the collective power to command production. We end up with just the oligarchy and workers and nothing in between. We drop the fictions called "Starbucks," "Samsung," and "General Electric," and gain in their place the stark vision of a single power in command and multitudes of workers who every day follow their orders to serve coffee, produce electronic products, manage power plants, generate financial statements, and what have you.

The oligarchy as a class has a definable set of interests and these have been institutionalized for quite some time into a series of practices, rules, organizations, and structures that I'll refer to as *finance*. This is a vague word having a wide variety of meanings but it's always linked in some way to money and wealth. I'll use it as a shorthand term for the collective interest of the class. It's the core of power in modern oligarchy, what one observer has called the "infrastructure of the infrastructure."[29]

Rudolph Hilferding used the term in this way in 1910, arguing that consolidation had created the single unified entity of *finance capital.*

Thus the specific character of capital is obliterated in finance capital. Capital now appears as a unitary power which exercises sovereign sway over the life process of society; a power which arises directly from ownership of the means of production, of natural resources, and of the whole accumulated labour of the past, and from command over living

---

[29] Cerny (1994: 224)

labour as a direct consequence of property relations. At the same time property, concentrated and centralized in the hands of a few giant capitalist groups, manifests itself in direct opposition to the mass of those who possess no capital. The problem of property relations thus attains its clearest, most unequivocal and sharpest expression at the same time as the development of finance capital itself is resolving more successfully the problem of the organization of the social economy.[30]

This is an excellent summary of our condition today although it can be argued that the subsequent outbreak of the World Wars showed Hilferding to be premature in its global application.[31] While it took the extraordinary violence of the first half of the twentieth century to bring that about, the fact of the matter is that given only modest variations in terms, Hilferding's insight applies to all eras of oligarchy. Concentrated power, after all, is old, eruptions of ruinous competition always transitory, and power by its nature timelessly hostile to the population. What's unique in modern oligarchy is the degree ownership has become both collectivized and centralized within the monetary rules of finance.

Finance in the way it's being defined here isn't an industry or sector of the economy but is rather the "unitary power" of oligarchy, the crystallization of its rules and interests. It's diffuse with tentacles branching to every industry, sector, and productive activity. Its myths and world-picture belong to oligarchy and 'sound finance' is behavior in accordance with them. In the words of anthropologist Karen Ho, finance is "cloaked in its abstractions and universality" and "part of the discursive power of the financial market is precisely its representation as abstract, its seeking to be everywhere and claiming to be nowhere coupled with its particular mission and claims to freedom, democracy, property, and prosperity."[32] Financial institutions enforce collective oligarchic rules on the management of corporations, states, and entire populations. They're "the voice of the financial markets" and "thus occupy a unique social position representing both 'the market' and the corporate entities that are subject to the market."[33]

---

[30] Hilferding (1981: 235)
[31] Panitch & Gindin (2004: 4)
[32] Ho (2009: 37)
[33] Ho (2009: 5-6)

Like capitalism, finance wraps itself in a mystique of complexity and sophistication and proudly revels in a meticulously dressed "culture of smartness."[34] We shouldn't be fooled, though, for there's nothing inherently difficult about collective ownership or the logic of inequality. As Veblen noted a century ago, finance is

> largely a matter of artless routine, in which the greatest ingenuity and initiative in the premises are commonly exercised by the legal counsel working for a fee. A dispassionate student of the current business traffic, who is not overawed by round numbers, will be more impressed by the ease and simplicity of the maneuvers that lead to large pecuniary results in the higher business finance than by any evidence of pre-eminent sagacity and initiative among the pecuniary magnates.[35]

There exists a well-funded academic discipline devoted to the subject of ownership and it appropriately calls itself *finance*. Its prime focus is on the management of wealth and a great deal of ink has been spilled on the issues of gain, risk, and especially diversification. Academic finance's emphasis on the latter is pertinent as it presses home from a different angle the essential importance of collective ownership and the unitary nature of the oligarchic class.

An awareness of diversification became prominent with the work of economist Harry Markowitz in the 1950s and was extended in the sixties by finance professor William Sharpe and economists Jack Treynor, John Lintner, and Jan Mossin who each developed separately what came to be known as the Capital Asset Pricing Model (CAPM). Markowitz and Sharpe won the economics version of the Nobel Prize in 1990 for these efforts.[36] While aspects of CAPM have been criticized, it continues to be an influential theory. Of particular note is its conception that the ideal and most efficient portfolio is the weighted average of everything; of every stock, bond, and financial asset that exists. It represents complete and absolute diversification and it's called the *market portfolio*. This, academic finance tells us, should be the portfolio goal of every oligarch.

---

[34] Ho (2009: 40)

[35] Veblen (1908: 126)

[36] Along with economist Merton Miller for work in a separate area.

The oligarchy by definition possesses the fully diversified market portfolio. To the class there can be no valuation risk in holding it for it's simply the ownership of everything. There's only one risk that's pertinent and it's existential—it's the risk of losing it, of having the game overturned. Finance theory calls this a *systematic risk*, one that can't be diversified away. Academic finance offers oligarchs a montage of intricate mathematical methods to both assess individual risk and value portfolios but these tools are useless at the class level. Systematic risk stands outside its realm of expertise and the thought of applying a market valuation to planet Earth, i.e. to the market portfolio, is an absurdity; unless, that is, there were an alien species to which it could be sold. (God help us if there were!)

Both finance and the market portfolio are embodiments of the collective oligarchy which, as a diversified unity, isn't in competition with itself. The notion of competition, in fact, fades into an obscure haze as it isn't so clear how it can be the case that diversified oligarchs compete at all. Shouldn't an oligarch be indifferent to the contest between Coke and Pepsi if he owned both equally? And should he not similarly be apathetic to inter-sectorial battles as long as his portfolio were diversified? Of course he should—that's what diversification means. Management competes for market share and is harshly disciplined if it dare deviate from the principles of sound finance, and workers always and everywhere are in a desperate struggle. But in the god-like heavens above the market portfolio, we find serene tranquility with life taking something of the air of a Roman senatorial luxury box in a Coliseum contest in which each senator owns a stake in all the gladiators.

That, at least, is the ideal of diversification. In the real world, individual oligarchs do place bets and deviate from the portfolio suggestions of academic finance. But as we proceed, it's the perspective of the oligarchic class as a whole, embodied in both finance and the market portfolio, which will be the main means of gaining a better understanding of our socioeconomic system.

To recap the main points of this chapter, modern oligarchy is visualized as a global game having two fundamental classes—the oligarchy which hovers above the board as owner and the population which is subjugated into the role of pawn. Its heart is the diversion-profit loop which sustains the oligarchy by guaranteeing to it the unending power to costlessly divert production in service to its motives. Individual oligarchs position their ownership portfolios to capture their share of the systemic monetary flows arising within it. The class as a collectivity owns the entire means of production as conceptualized by the market portfolio and has, through the institution of finance, established the basic rules and practices. The two key concerns of finance follow from the dynamics of age-old oligarchy—to assure the efficient operation of the diversion-profit loop and to keep the global population firmly in its place. We'll take a much closer look at this game in coming chapters and will begin now with an examination of the diversion-profit loop.

7

The Diversion-Profit Loop

Diversion is the dynamic by which the oligarchy forces the population to produce goods and services in fulfilment of its motivational desires of wealth defense* and luxury consumption. It's one of the two fundamental dynamics of oligarchy and the goal of this chapter is to explain the way it operates today.

Let's begin by looking at the essential flow as it has existed throughout all of civilization.

Diversion Command Issued ➜ Diversion Produced

We get from it two important pieces of information. The first is that diversion is ludicrously simple. The second is that it isn't an equal exchange like we'd expect to find in 'capitalism.' It's a command in the full military sense of the word. Generals don't purchase compliance from privates, they command it; and what that means is that no units of power are lost in the process. If they were, if issuing orders entailed a cost, then power would flow downward and the two ranks would eventually meet somewhere in the middle. It's the same with the oligarchic class; if it were to lose units of power in the process of commanding diversion, then power would flow downward to the population and oligarchy would quickly collapse. The power of diversion must be structural for oligarchy to exist and it can't therefore encompass a 'thing' that's spent or exchanged. At the macro level, diversion has to be costless— it can't be paid for.

This simple power relation, though, is obscured in our modern world by an outer veil of money. We'll find throughout this section that money is a key source of confusion and the problem here is that it creates an illusion of exchange.

A general's command is clearly not an exchange but it seems different for transactions involving money. When an oligarch pays money to workers for his diversion, it appears to be a proper exchange completely unlike the general's orders. To see it's not requires we look at the entire transaction. Here's an example using a historically typical flow.

Diversion Purchased via Money ➔ Diversion Produced ➔ Money Returned via Taxation

The oligarchy in this case purchases diversion goods via a monetary payment to workers, the diversion is produced, and the monetary sums advanced are returned via taxation of the workers. If we focus only on the purchase, the transaction seems like one of exchange, but when we widen our view we can see it's just an illusion. Money flows in a giant oligarchic loop that's integrally tied to diversion. It starts with a command that's issued via money and closes with its return via taxation. The key point is that money must parallel the power it represents. For oligarchy to exist, diversion must be monetarily costless.

The idea is the same when we turn to modern oligarchy with the exception being that profit takes the place of taxation. (I'm using profit here and throughout the rest of the book as a generic term for all monetary income associated with ownership. It includes corporate profit, interest, rent, and also high wages and bonuses tied to an owner-like position.) Diversion and profit are linked in modern oligarchy in what represents the most fundamental flow of the system, the *diversion-profit loop*.

Let's begin exploring it by asking a most elementary question—where does profit come from? It can't be from workers since they can spend no more than the wage received. (I ignore rising worker debt as it's self-limiting.) Wages are a source of revenue through sales, but they're also a cost. For the system as a whole, they must net to zero—workers are simply not profitable.

A firm can't make a profit selling only to its own workers; the consumer sector can't make a profit selling only to consumer sector workers; US business can't make a profit selling only to US workers;[1] and the greater system can't make a profit selling to workers period. This quandary isn't solvable by charging a higher profit margin as that's not the issue; profit can't be generated no matter how owners manipulate pricing, the cash inflow from sales can't be greater than the cash outlay in wages.

This is a great paradox for those whose baseline is capitalism but it makes perfect sense from the perspective of 5,000 year oligarchy. The ever pragmatic Roman senator wouldn't consider it a profitable venture to add more slaves to his latifundium simply to grow more food for the enhanced enjoyment of his very same slaves. Slaves aren't a source of profit, they're merely workers. The medieval lord would likewise roar with laughter at the proposition his serfs producing strictly for themselves could be of any benefit to him. Oligarchy has never operated in the interest of laborers, be they slaves, serfs, or modern workers; they're only "a necessary evil" whose cost is best minimized. "If wages are cut heavily," observed philosopher Rosa Luxemburg, "capital does not worry about having to produce fewer means of subsistence for the workers, in fact it delights in this practice at every opportunity."[2]

Luxemburg was puzzled by the mystery of profit and considered it a "blatant tautology, a dazzling circle."[3] She recognized that profit couldn't come from the worker and concluded it could only arise from interactions outside the system, particularly colonialism. Once the entire world was brought within it, however, the source of profit would dry up and capitalism would thereby collapse. Her insight that profit had to come from a source beyond the worker was correct but she erred in accepting the conventional monetary wisdom that capitalism's "aim and goal in life is profit in the form of money and accumulation of capital."[4]

A significant advance in this area was made by Polish economist Michal Kalecki. His profit equation, described by economist Hyman Minsky as a

---

[1] This applies of course to all countries.

[2] Luxemburg (2003: 441)

[3] Luxemburg (1972: 51)

[4] Luxemburg (1972: 54)

"profound insight into how a capitalist economy works,"[5] plainly shows how profit is generated in a static economy. In a closed system with no state spending,[6] it's:

Profit = Capitalist Consumption + Investment[7]

While supporting Luxemburg's view that profit can only arise from an 'other' outside the wage process, the equation shows there's no need for colonialism or any other type of expansion. Profit is automatic whenever capitalists spend on personal consumption or investment.

This is a fantastic simplicity! Capitalists themselves are the source of the profit they crave. They crave their own spending. This isn't a dazzling circle, though, it's circular nonsense. Whatever it is, we have a zero-sum loop. If capitalists spend a quadrillion trillion on consumption or investment, they 'earn' a quadrillion trillion in profit, a net cash flow of zero. If they spend nothing, they 'earn' nothing, again a net cash flow of zero. We can resolve this apparent absurdity if we drop traditional notions of profit and recognize the system as oligarchy. We then get from the equation a mathematical expression of the 5,000 year historical truth that the power of the oligarchy to spend is always self-sustaining and costless.

Let's apply this insight to the taxation example previously discussed. What, one might ask, is the source of the taxation money that perpetually finds its way into the bank accounts of the oligarchy? The answer is self-evident—it arises not from workers but from diversion spending. It's the same with profit. Profit is the return loop of oligarchic spending and it's a structurally guaranteed sum for the oligarchy as a class. (I'm emphasizing the core idea here and am excluding for now other sources of profit that will be discussed in this and following chapters.)

The Kalecki equation is a significant achievement but to many it will be confusing. The problem is with motivation; while the place of capitalist consumption within the equation makes perfect sense, the role of investment is obscure. Luxury consumption is a core motivation of oligarchy, but are we

---

[5] Minsky (1986: 151)

[6] We'll address state spending and international trade in upcoming chapters.

[7] Kalecki (1969: 45). This is the short version of his equation applicable to the assumptions mentioned. Its derivation is presented in appendix one as is the expanded version of the equation.

to believe that regardless of purpose or beneficiary so also is the mere act of investment? The answer is most definitively not, but it's best for now to defer this question and emphasize instead the fundamental insight that oligarchic spending is self-funding. We'll return to investment later.

To understand some of the key implications of the diversion-profit loop, we'll need to adopt the perspective of the oligarchic class. As we found in the last chapter, the class as a unity is the owner of the market portfolio, the sum total of every corporation on the planet. That's an extremely complex aggregation which will have to be simplified in a way that helps our analysis. A common simplifying method practiced by financial analysts is to categorize all output into business sectors according to what's produced. Dow Jones,[8] for example, publishes over a hundred such sectors with names like oil and gas producers, iron and steel, coal, aerospace, automobiles, clothing and accessories, health care providers, pharmaceuticals, hotels, water, and so on and so forth.

While this is a helpful step, we're still left with a great deal of complexity that isn't organized in a way that suits our purpose. The goal is to understand the diversion-profit loop and that's a two class phenomenon. Our interest isn't in *what* is produced for that's just detail; it's rather *for whom* it's produced. We're interested in whether it's produced for the oligarchy or for the population and we therefore need just two fundamental sectors.

All output is ultimately for the benefit of one of the two classes and that will be the basis for the sectors. It's immaterial what exactly is produced in each but we can speculate it would include things like luxury jets, yachts, mansions, fine food and wine, servants, guards, financial advisers, and exquisite clubs for the oligarchy and modest housing, basic food, mass entertainment, and cheap beer for the population. It's also of no relevance whether output is for immediate consumption or investment; our only concern is the final beneficiary. I'll call these sectors the *diversion sector* and the *population sector*; the first providing luxury consumption and wealth defense*

---

[8] The online market data page of the Wall Street Journal provides comprehensive listings of industries and sectors.
www.online.wsj.com/public/npage/all_industries.html?mod=mdc_uss_p glnk, accessed on August 3, 2014.

goods and services for the oligarchy and the second whatever living standards the general population may require.[9]

This sectorial division is realistic given the existence of the two fundamental classes. We don't notice them in the real world because most corporations aren't segregated in ways that make them obvious. The divide usually exists internally within corporations and isn't therefore easily measured. Its lack of visibility, however, has no bearing on the essential point that it flows from the structural necessities of oligarchy.

Let's proceed, then, by conceiving of the market portfolio as composed of these two sectors along with all banks, a cohort of managing executives, entrepreneurs, exploitable natural resources, and an unlimited number of workers. Hovering above it as owner is the oligarchy. The diversion-profit loop begins with the oligarchy sending money into the market portfolio to acquire diversion and ends with the return to it of monetary profit. The timing of when diversion goods are produced isn't important; they could be generated in response to specific orders or in advance in anticipation of them. The basic idea is illustrated in Figure 1.

---

[9] Some goods and services are used by both classes. I'll assume there are legions of capable cost accountants at our disposal who are able to come up with reasonable methods of allocating such output into the proper sectors.

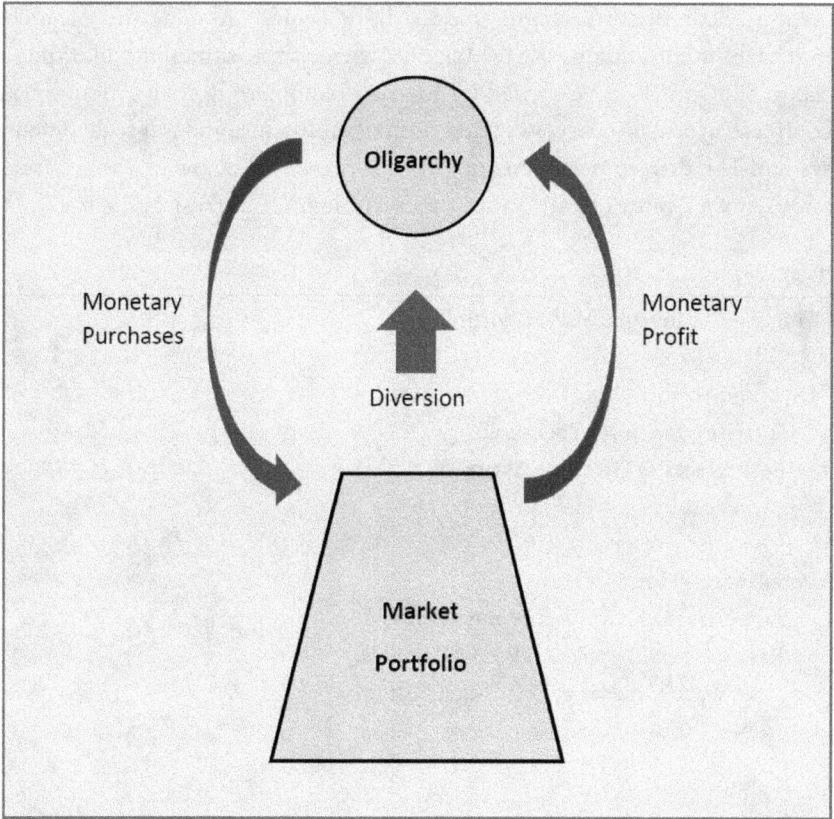

Figure 1: The Diversion-Profit Loop

We gain from this perspective the important insight that the market portfolio isn't a profit producing entity for it has no magical power to create 'profit' out of thin air. What it creates is diversion goods and services and these are costless because worker wages are both an expense and a revenue netting to zero. "Workers spend what they earn, capitalists earn what they spend" is a quip that succinctly sums it up.[10] Oligarchy has no need for its workers to be profitable, the idea actually doesn't make sense; what it has an existential need of is that they be costless.

Let's now delve deeper into this most central flow in order to bring out some key points. We'll do so by first working through a simple example based

---

[10] This is commonly attributed to economists Joan Robinson or Nicholas Kaldor.

on the "department" scheme utilized by Kalecki.[11] Assume the oligarchy purchases a glittering new $1.5 billion luxury yacht, something like the 24 cabin, 536 foot Eclipse owned by Russian billionaire Roman Abramovich, complete with two helicopter pads, a mini-submarine, and a missile defense system. The flow of diversion and profit is presented below in Table 2 using a format we'll return to at various times throughout the rest of the book.

Table 2: Diversion-Profit Loop—Yacht Example

$1.5 billion enters the Market Portfolio	
Diversion Sector:	
Total Revenue from Yacht Sale	1.50
Less: Wages in Diversion Sector (W)	(1.00)
Net Profit—Diversion Sector	.50
Population Sector:	
Revenue from Diversion Sector Wages (W)	1.00
Revenue from Population Sector Wages (w)	.75
Less: Wage Expense in Population Sector (w)	(.75)
Net Profit—Population Sector	1.00
Total Profit	1.50
$1.5 billion exits the Market Portfolio	
In Billions	

Starting from the top, the $1.5 billion yacht order enters the market portfolio in the form of payment to a yacht manufacturing firm in the diversion sector and is reflected as revenue. The firm pays wages (W) to its workers of $1.0 billion and thereby nets a profit of $.50 billion. These workers use their $1.0 billion in wages (W) to buy goods in the population sector where it's reflected

---

[11] The two sector model I'll be using throughout the remainder of the book is inspired by Kalecki's three "department" "scheme of reproduction" that was also used by Marx (Kalecki (1969: 80). His three departments are *investment goods, capitalist consumption,* and *worker consumption.* I eliminate the investment goods department and assign its output to the ultimate beneficiary—the oligarchy or the population. The basic logic otherwise follows Kalecki.

as revenue. The population sector staffs up to meet this demand and hires its own workers who are paid wages (w) of $.75 billion. These workers don't represent a net cost to the population sector, however, as they'll also spend their wages within the sector. Net profit in the population sector therefore ends up being equal to the wages paid in the diversion sector (W). The combined profit of the two sectors ($.50 and $1.0 billion) equals the yacht purchase price and the diversion-profit loop is thereby closed.

Two important points are illustrated here. The first is that whatever is spent on diversion is returned as profit. The second is that population sector workers are never in themselves profitable. Wages are paid out, -w, and then return, +w, and the net is zero: -w + w = 0. The population sector by itself isn't a profit center; it's simply costless. Its profit can only come from without, in this case the wages paid in the diversion sector. As long as there's outside demand, a population sector profit is inescapable because productivity is such that workers can produce more than they consume. To summarize,

$$\text{Population Sector Profit} = W + (-w + w) = W$$
$$\$1.0b + (-\$.75b + \$.75b) = \$1.0b$$

Total profit is the sum of the profits in the two sectors.

Profit = Diversion Sector Profit + Population Sector Profit
Profit = (Price of Diversion Good - W) + (W - w + w)
Profit = ($1.5b - $1.0b) + ($1.0b - $.75b + $.75b)
Profit = $.5b + $1.0b = $1.5b

That profit is equal to the purchase price rests on the fact workers are costless as can be seen in the second row above. Wages (W and w) net to zero and the only thing left is the purchase price. The end result is that the diversion good, the yacht, is produced and delivered by the market portfolio and the monetary price paid is returned via profit. The oligarchy will thusly enjoy the fine noble splendor of sailing the world's seas in princely style and without cost. Those who built it will live for another day but will never set foot on its deck. This is the nature of oligarchy; it's a structure of costless diversion.

Many claim that 'capitalism' is driven by profit but this exercise shows such views to be incomplete. 'Profit' is actually a problematic term given that it isn't really 'profitable'; there's no mysterious increment being added to the equation, only the banal return of what was spent. A yacht was produced in this case, though, and in that sense it was a 'profitable' expenditure. But it's not necessary for a diversion good to be produced for profit to be issued. Any monetary order sent into the market portfolio from outside will exit as profit.

Even a charitable contribution to the population would produce profit as the population would then spend more than it was paid in wages. While a diversion good wouldn't have been produced, the population would end up living better at no cost to the oligarchy. This brings home in a different way how the Kalecki equation should be interpreted. Suppose the oligarchy consisted solely of do-gooder saints who spent only on charity. Charitable expenditures would enter the market portfolio and profit would thereby be output. Kalecki would have had to re-write his equation to this:

Profit = Charity

The only reasonable meaning is that charity is self-funding for the owners and thereby costless. (And also, therefore, not really charity.) We can see from this that the elements one chooses to place on the right side of the equation are completely open as long as they sum to the entirety of oligarchic spending.

While the oligarchy as a whole has a virtually unlimited capacity to command production, individual oligarchs are constrained in two basic ways. The first is by the total volume of monetary orders entering the market portfolio from the entire class as this determines the extent of system wide profit. The second is the share of this collectively generated pool their particular portfolios are able to capture. An individual oligarch's lifestyle is thereby a collective phenomenon tied to both class-wide spending and the way his portfolio relates to it.

The subsidiary role of the population sector is a central aspect of the game of modern oligarchy and it will be helpful to expand a bit more on this. I'll do so by noting an important corollary to the principle that whatever monetary sum enters the market portfolio will exit as profit. It's that no transaction completely confined within the market portfolio will be able to generate a profit over its relevant life. For there to be profit, there must be a monetary order from outside. Assuming no such infusion, the population sector is incapable of being profitable except to the extent some other inside entity like a bank or the diversion sector incurs an offsetting loss. As it can't on its own generate a monetary profit and by definition doesn't produce diversion, it's of no worth to the oligarchy beyond its role in sustaining the lives of diversion sector workers. This is a key piece of the game's logic and it does much to explain the population's poor living conditions.

All things being equal, population prosperity is determined by the number of workers hired in the population sector. The greater are the resources devoted there, the greater is the output available for workers in both sectors and the more their wages will buy.[12] But there's no profit to be had from this prosperity since the population sector on its own is always a breakeven. No matter how high the output, the net must be zero because wages are both an income and an expense. If the population sector were 50 percent larger in the yacht example, for instance, the profit emitted by the market portfolio would remain completely unchanged. As Kalecki's equation requires, profit is locked at the amount spent by the oligarchy—"capitalists earn what they spend." The wage level, as reflected in population sector output, is irrelevant. It applies both ways as well; reduced output in the population sector won't create profit. Workers are neither a net revenue nor a net cost because they "spend what they earn."

There are two crucial points to be taken from our discussion so far; first, the purpose of the market portfolio is costless diversion and profit is nothing other than an 'unprofitable' return of what was spent, and second, workers in themselves can't generate profit.

We're now ready to return to investment and inquire how it can be profitable according to Kalecki's equation. We've already seen that everything the oligarchy spends returns to it as profit and we're thereby free to put any categories we wish on the right side of the equation as long as they sum to total spending. Kalecki chose *investment* as one of his categories and it's thusly 'profitable.' But we also learned the population is never profitable given it can only spend up to its wage. How can it be, then, that investment in the population sector could ever be profitable?

This confusion is resolved when we realize we're dealing with differing perspectives. To owners sitting on the outside, the purpose of the market portfolio is diversion and the meaning of profit is that it renders it costless.

---

[12] The assumption is that given our productive capacity, each worker is capable of producing more than he or she consumes.

But to the managers of corporations within the market portfolio, the goal isn't diversion but rather the capture of the largest possible share of oligarchic spending.[13] The motive from within, in other words, is monetary profit.

The question a corporate CEO, a banker, an entrepreneur, or a finance executive must ask before any investment outlay, therefore, is whether it's likely to be 'profitable' from this perspective—will it capture profit? As we're concerned with the system as a whole, the question reduces to whether an investment will be profitable for the market portfolio. We'll find that the profitability of investment is determined strictly by class beneficiary and that only investment in goods and services that will be bought by the oligarchy can be profitable.

Let's consider an example in which we contrast two investments that differ only in whether the beneficiary is the oligarchy or the population. The assumption in both is that financing starts from inside the market portfolio; should an oligarch seek to play the role of entrepreneur or bank, he would need to travel inside to do so. We look first at a diversion sector investment.

Table 3: Profitability of Diversion Sector Investment

	Stage 1	Stage 2	Total
Bank financing of $10 billion			
Diversion Sector:			
Sale of New Investment		20	20
Bank Loan to Pay Wages	10	(10)	0
Investment Wages Paid	(10)	0	(10)
Net Profit: Diversion Sector	0	10	10
Population Sector:			
Revenue: Diversion Sector	10	0	10
Net Wages Pop Sector	0	0	0
Net Profit: Pop Sector	10	0	10
Net Profit from Investment	10	10	20

In Billions

---

[13] This is an idealization since many of the CEO's themselves are oligarchs. For purposes here, I separate the role of manager from the class position.

Table 3 shows the outcome of a $10 billion bank financed investment in the diversion sector which will lead to a product consumed by the oligarchy. The financing covers the wage expense to produce the investment and the final product is sold for $20 billion. I break the transaction into two stages—the first being the period during which the investment is produced and the second when the loan is repaid and the resulting output sold. We find that the investment yields a total market portfolio profit equal to the sales price of $20 billion and that it's divided equally between the two stages. Stage 1 yields a profit of $10 billion because diversion sector wages are paid from the bank loan and those wages are spent in the population sector. Whatever additional wages are paid in the population sector to service these workers net to zero. Stage 2 produces a profit of $10 billion as well which is the net between the $20 billion sales price coming from outside the market portfolio less the repayment of the bank loan.

Using the exact same assumptions, let's now consider in Table 4 below an investment in the population sector.

Table 4: Unprofitability of Population Sector Investment

	Stage 1	Stage 2	Total
Bank financing of $10 billion			
Diversion Sector:			
Net Profit: Diversion Sector	0	0	0
Population Sector:			
Sale of Investment	0	20	20
Bank Loan to Pay Wages	10	(10)	0
Investment Wages Paid	(10)	0	(10)
Investment Wages Revenue	10	0	10
Net Wages: Population Sector	0	(20)	(20)
Net Profit: Pop Sector	10	(10)	0
Net Profit from Investment	10	(10)	0

In Billions

Just as in the diversion case, the population sector reports a profit in stage 1 since the bank loan is used to pay wages to the investment workers which are then spent within the population sector. The final product is similarly sold for $20 billion in stage 2 but the proceeds come not from outside the market portfolio but from wages paid by population sector firms. The rechanneling of $20 billion in wages so that workers can buy the new product means that population sector firms experience a $20 billion reduction in revenue from their base business and their wage expense therefore exceeds income by this amount. Since the sales proceeds come at the expense of the population sector itself, i.e. it's an intra-sector transfer, total revenue nets to zero and stage two therefore reports a $10 billion loss as the bank loan, the source of stage 1 profit, is repaid. The profit over the life of the transaction is zero.

What we find here is a vital fact that applies to all population sector investment and to consumer loans as well—they can't create profit in the market portfolio. They can only offer illusionary timing difference stage 1 profits that must always be reversed in stage 2. We can reduce this to the following equation.

Profit on Investment = [Stage 1: Financing] + [Stage 2: (Sales Price - Financing) - Offset]

Stage 1 will always yield a profit in the population sector as the investment wages are spent. Stage 2 will yield a profit only to the extent the sales price isn't offset by a reduction in revenue elsewhere. There's no offset for diversion sector investment since the sales price comes from the oligarchy sitting outside the market portfolio, but there's always one when dealing with the population sector and it serves to eliminate the stage one profit. Illusionary Stage 1 timing difference profits are routine aspects of loans and investments in the population sector and their contribution to bubbles and crashes will be explored in chapter eleven (*The Grand Casino*).

Since population sector investment is never profitable over its applicable life, we can rewrite the profit equation in the following manner:

Profit = *Capitalist* Consumption + *Capitalist* Investment

Or, in oligarchic terms,

Profit = Luxury Consumption + Wealth Defense* = Diversion[14]

We're now able to state this chapter's central conclusion on diversion and profit in modern oligarchy. Profit is a fixed quantity arising from diversion.[15] Corporations capture their share of it by either producing output in the diversion sector for sale to the oligarchy or by producing output in the population sector *for sale to the workers who produce diversion for the oligarchy.* Both profit and the corporate motivation to generate output trace directly to diversion. There's no incentive to invest in the population as a stand-alone activity except as a zero-sum effort to gain market share at the expense of competing firms. Workers are never profitable in and of themselves. We should expect, therefore, that investment in them will either be minimal or the result of uncoordinated action.

But what then of the Kalecki equation and the prominent spot it gives generic investment? Its purpose is to explain the determinants of profit in specific accounting periods and it's not wrong. In the Table 4 population sector example, it would correctly report a $10 billion profit in the stage 1 accounting period based on the $10 billion investment, and it would then correctly report the $10 billion loss in the stage 2 accounting period based on the $10 billion "disinvestment." What I seek to show, and what the Kalecki equation doesn't clearly capture, is that the overall profitability of investment is determined by class beneficiary. This is made plain when we categorize investment by class and consider profitability over its relevant life.

Our political and economic discourse has generified investment into a classless 'good.' Undifferentiated investment is considered by many to be the most important aspect of capitalism, even its crux. To economist Hyman Minsky, it's the "essential determinant" of the economy with all else being "secondary" [16] and to Max Weber, private investment is capitalism's "governing principal."[17] Investment has a formidable ideological appeal as well given its association with productivity, profitable gain, and a puritan-like abstention from consumption. Hardly a day passes in which a politician or

---

[14] This can be derived in the same manner as Kalecki derived his and I compare the two in appendix one.

[15] This is a simplification and we'll bring in the complexities of the state, international trade, and speculation in upcoming chapters.

[16] Minsky (1986: 171)

[17] Weber (2011: 91)

learned economist doesn't rise in great profundity and propose tax breaks or some other scheme to promote it.

But investment in what? Investment, like 'jobs,' is an empty signifier standing for nothing. It's a mystification that raises all investment to the same level and thereby steers us away from thinking of the specifics of what needs to be produced. The solution for improving the lives of slum dwellers can then become not one of investment in sanitation, housing, food supply, clean air, and the like but rather the construction of a new five star casino hotel. The hidden reality behind it all is that it's never about generic investment; it's about profitable investment.

The reification of undifferentiated investment is a huge distraction from the insight that the system is driven by antagonistic power and not by some existential urge to 'invest.' Diversion and suppression are the key dynamics and the oligarchy can be expected to invest only when it furthers them. There's no gain to be had from investing in population benefiting output; it yields nothing to the oligarchy while increasing the power of the population. One of the prime drives, in fact, is to disinvest in the population and we can see the success of that effort in every corner of the world.

Investment is often linked to that supposedly ultimate goal of capitalism, *accumulation*. But we can't allow ourselves to get misled here either. The prime motives are luxury consumption and wealth defense*, not 'accumulation' whatever this vague word may even mean. If we have oligarchy, then by definition the means of production have already been accumulated; the market portfolio is already owned. For the class as a whole, what matters is the accumulation of power and this is reflected not in terms of accumulated investment but in the oligarchy–population relationship. If a thousand oligarchs owned everything ten years ago and today also own everything, they accumulated nothing of real import. But if the population is poorer today via effective suppression, then the oligarchy did accumulate relative power and is thereby in a stronger position. As Jonathan Nitzan reminds us, *"Power is the very essence of accumulation."*[18] And for the oligarchy as a whole, what this means is the size of its "differential power"[19] over the population.

---

[18] Nitzan (1998: 205). Italics in original.

[19] Nitzan (1998: 193). Nitzan is referring here and in many other places to differential power between capitalists. The same concept, though, applies to the two fundamental classes.

One thing that does tend to accumulate is knowledge[20] and it's the basis for our high level of productivity. The motives of oligarchy, however, aren't conducive to maximizing the application of knowledge; quite the contrary, they're focused on limiting its dispersion.

The claim, then, that capitalism is intimately tied to investment doesn't hold water. It, along with all spending,[21] is a determinant of output and employment but the central driving forces are the motives behind oligarchy. I'll have more to say on investment in the next chapter.

We've assumed so far that workers always "spend what they earn," but what if they don't? What if they save? Revenues then wouldn't cover the wage expense and the market portfolio would report a reduced profit. The oligarchy would be effectively transferring ownership rights to workers, a dire malfunction since workers can't be permitted to acquire significant ownership if oligarchy is to exist.

That oligarchy is as old as civilization tells us that formidable safeguards have always been in place. Beyond the sound finance dogma of austerity and low wages, the oligarchy also relies on the psychological onslaught of the global half a trillion dollar a year advertising industry.[22] It's an interesting mix—the dual passions of keeping wages low yet spending high. Consumption must be suppressed while, at the same time, encouraged with all the sophistication of modern psychological theory. The term *consumer capitalism* signifies a great deal more than we often realize. Consumption linked with capitalism tells us that the systemic goal isn't the maximization of worker consumption of goods but is rather the capitalist re-consumption of the wage.

It's easy to conceive of a thermostatic mechanism that would assure the wage is consumed. Should workers begin to save, then population sector companies would suffer reduced profit. The companies would accordingly cut back, the laid off workers would spend their savings to live, and the natural order would thusly return. How it's accomplished, though, is unimportant; the historical record and the logic of the situation are both

---

[20] It's not inevitable of course and may be reversed by war, disease, or natural catastrophe.

[21] Including through the state.

[22] Plunket Research, accessed August 25, 2015.
www.plunkettresearch.com/advertising-branding-market-research/industry-statistics

unequivocal—workers have never been able to save to any significant degree and they can never be permitted to do so. It's a bedrock principle of oligarchy.

This chapter has covered some important points on modern oligarchy. We've found that profit is crucial but the name of the game is luxury consumption and wealth defense*. These are rendered costless through the diversion-profit loop. Profit is a guaranteed sum for the oligarchy as a whole but not for the individual; what makes one a successful oligarch is that he own a portfolio that captures a sufficient percentage of the collective profit pool to render his expenditures costless.

The population's role in the game is limited to that of pawn. Workers aren't a source of profit and their purpose in life is tied to producing diversionary goods and services for the power and enjoyment of the oligarchy. While they're not a cost, the game provides no incentive to expand production for them beyond that required for the sustenance of those in the diversion sector. The real world result is marginal investment in areas that would benefit the population, high levels of poverty as measured against productive capacity, rampant crime, ongoing political tensions due to 'economic' pressures, and environmental degradation arising from the desperation to secure a living. The situation, however, is far worse than even this would indicate. This is so because the people of the world aren't just diversion producing pawns, they're also the sole existential threat. We turn to this aspect of modern oligarchy in the next chapter.

8

Suppression

No aspect of wealth defense* is more important than maintaining the wealth differential over the population for without it, oligarchy ceases to exist. The way it's achieved in any era will vary but a key determinant is the level of productive capacity. When low, the process focuses on maximizing diversion through a zero-sum struggle against the population for limited resources. But things are different when productivity is high. Diversion today has become routine and oligarchic desires are satiated long before capacity has been reached. We're no longer in a zero-sum situation as productivity is more than capable of providing plenty for all. The production problem has been solved and this is good news, but for the oligarchy it's a mixed blessing in that the differential still needs to be maintained.

This is the main challenge in modern oligarchy and it has led to a modification of strategy; from one of applying an active coercive force to assure sufficient diversion to one of defensively sealing off productive potential against the threat of its use by the population. There has been a shift in focus, in other words, from the offensive enforcement of diversion to the no less hostile defensive imposition of suppression.

As discussed in chapter four, suppression is the dynamic by which the oligarchy maintains the power differential over the population. While not widely recognized as such, it's interwoven into the rules of the game and is so widespread it's impossible to hide. It's a tribute to the immense power of ideology that the harshness of an all pervasive suppression blends virtually unnoticed into what's seen as the legitimate order of things.

The basic method of suppression in modern oligarchy is extraordinarily simple and can be thought of in terms of a duality between collective action and competition. The oligarchy maintains power by acting collectively as a class and minimizing competition within its ranks while imposing the exact opposite condition on the population—denying its ability to act collectively and forcing it to compete. In this chapter, we'll concentrate on how this plays out in the realm of the 'private' market; in the next (*Money and the Oligarchic State*), how it operates in the 'public' sphere of the state; and in chapters ten (*The Transnational Oligarchy*) and twelve (*Global Oligarchic Governance*), how it works in the international context.

Before proceeding, though, I believe a few words should be said to support what I take to be the self-evident fact we do indeed have a massively underutilized sustainable productive capacity. The proper scale for determining our capacity is global. Oligarchy has long transcended state boundaries and so also have the sources of labor. Immigration has been a key provider for centuries and production supply chains today are integrated on a transnational basis in service to a global market. Outsourcing has become routine. Within this global system is a gigantic 'reserve army' of desperate people looking for work. The International Labor Organization (ILO) reports that almost 202 million are unemployed, a figure higher than the entire US workforce. A realistic accounting, though, puts the effective number far higher since a very significant percentage who are categorized as employed are cut off from modern productive methods. Of the employed, 48 percent are classified as "vulnerable," 26.7 percent live on $2 per day or less, and "informal employment" is widespread. [1] Workers everywhere intuitively know they're replaceable, an unsurprising fact given that, as economist Joseph Stiglitz has noted, just a small percentage of the global population can produce all the food and manufactured goods that can be bought.[2] The enormous pool of excess labor will likely continue to swell

---

[1] Data in this paragraph is from ILO (2014: 11-12).
[2] Stiglitz (2010: 24)

given the intensifying progression in automation.[3] Finally, there exists a significant leverage potential deriving from the fact that fixed overhead is already accounted for. A relatively small number of additional workers would therefore be capable of substantially increasing output. I think the only reasonable conclusion is that made by economist Stephen Marglin—"In practical terms, labor supply is unlimited, not only in the poor countries, but in the rich countries as well."[4]

Let's now examine the key ways the 'private' market incorporates the suppression dynamic of keeping non-diversion output low. We'll start by observing that suppression in our era of high productivity has nothing to do with the direct needs of diversion. Workers are costless and their employment could thus expand to the limits of the global workforce without affecting the oligarchy's material lifestyle one iota. Despite this, the rules of finance recognize that any such enlargement would indicate a severe systemic illness. Only the 'efficient' market portfolio is a healthy one with efficiency defined as producing diversion at as low a labor input as possible. Its state of health at any point in time can theoretically be assessed through a metric I'll call the *diversion margin*—the ratio of diversion to total output.

A high diversion margin means a healthy and efficient market portfolio. A pure slave society would arguably mark the summit of health as workers would be forced to labor for nothing beyond bare sustenance and nearly all output would thereby go to the oligarchy.[5] The diversion margin would approach 100 percent. At the other extreme, the margin would drop to the low single digits if the population sector expanded to meet unutilized sustainable capacity. It would mean a sick and inefficient market portfolio. The diversion margin, we can see, isn't a measure of diversion but of suppression and of the corresponding health of the oligarchy.

While the data required to calculate this metric isn't provided by governmental statistical agencies, we do have access to an imperfect[6] parallel—the *profit margin*. This is the ratio of profit to total output and, just

---

[3] The likely effects of productivity growth on employment and wages are discussed in appendix two.

[4] Marglin (2010: 3)

[5] I say arguably here because all methods of enforced labor have the potential for extremely high efficiency. Unrestricted 'flexible' wage labor could be even more efficient than slavery in that unproductive fixed costs could be substantially reduced.

[6] For reasons that will be discussed in future chapters.

as with the diversion margin, it's not a measure of profit but of suppression. At any given level of profit, the metric is maintained only by limiting the denominator, total output. And that, the maximization of the profit margin, is the prime monetary drive of modern finance.[7]

A significant historical challenge to achieving it has been intra-class competition in the population sector.[8] The term "price war" is commonly applied to periods when this has been high but it's more accurate to think of them as output expansion wars. The means by which they're controlled is a central element of modern suppression and it will be helpful to examine it through a thought exercise.

Suppose the population lived on beer alone and the population sector therefore consisted solely of breweries. The sector consists of workers with wages totaling 100 units and at that staffing, produces 2,000 bottles of beer. Diversion sector wages also total 100 units although it's immaterial to us what they're producing for the oligarchy. Given these assumptions, we can calculate the price of a bottle to be .1 unit (200 in combined wages/2,000 bottles produced). We assume the oligarchs drink something more refined which is part of their diversion spending. The profit for the population sector is the sum of wages in the diversion sector, 100, and the profit margin is 50 percent as calculated below.

Population Sector Profit = $W + (w - w) = 100 + (100 - 100) = 100$[9]
Profit Margin = Profit / Output = $W / (W + w) = 100 / 200 = 50\%$

For whatever reason, the managers of the breweries become gripped with an urge to capture market share from their competitors and decide to expand production. Beer output rises five-fold to 10,000 bottles and the higher employment needed to produce it brings population sector wages to 500 units. The price per bottle accordingly drops to .06 unit (600 in combined

---

[7] The *Return on Investment* is another common financial ratio and it's a measure of suppression in the same way. Given any profit level, the ratio is maximized only through limiting investment output. We can relate these ratios to the basic oligarchic principle that the population is never profitable.

[8] There's no danger from competition in the diversion sector since the population doesn't benefit.

[9] W and w represent diversion and population sector wages respectively in the same way as was presented in the previous chapter.

wages in both sectors/10,000 bottles). None of this new activity, however, can be profitable since profit is a fixed quantity coming from diversion sector wages. Profit remains stuck at 100 and the profit margin plummets to 16.67 percent.

Population Sector Profit = W + (w - w) = 100 + (500 - 500) = 100
Profit Margin = Profit / Output = W / (W + w) = 100 / 600 = 16.67%

Such is the outcome of a price war in the population sector—total profit remains unchanged while the profit margin declines with increasing population sector output. The oligarchy doesn't benefit, the population becomes more prosperous, and the market portfolio suffers a severe bout of inefficiency. Regardless if one speaks in the language of finance or suppression, the cure is the same—the oligarchy must come together collectively and restrict population output.

Note that each population sector firm increased its wage expense while also lowering prices. That this didn't cause losses illustrates the important point that profits, wages, and prices aren't related to each other in the ways we normally think. Profit is the monetary valuation of what's produced for the oligarchy, wages are the monetary sums paid to workers and have no effect on profit, and monetary price is the relation between output and wages.

Since this is counterintuitive yet goes to the heart of suppression, it may help to extend this example a bit further. Suppose there are four brewing companies in the population sector—firms A, B, C, and D—with each controlling one-fourth of the market. Table 5 below summarizes the entire exercise from the perspective of firm A.

Table 5: Profit, Wage, and Output from the Perspective of Firm A

	Initial	Price War
Revenue from Diversion Sector Wages	25	25
Revenue from Population Sector Wages	25	125
Wage Expense	(25)	(125)
Net Profit	25	25
Profit Margin	50%	16.67%
Total Bottles Produced	500	2,500
Price per Bottle	.1	.06

Firm A increased its wage expense from 25 to 125, expanded production from 500 to 2,500, and reduced its price from .1 to .06. Many will assume this would create losses but they'd be ignoring the fact that one-fourth of the additional wages it paid out are returned to it as they're spent by its workers and that it will also receive as revenue one-fourth of the higher wages received by workers in firms B, C, and D. In this way firm A recovers its entire incremental wage outlay. Wages and output have nothing to do with profitability when we consider the system as a whole. This is because profit is diversion and workers aren't a cost.

But the ideology of capitalism is obsessed with 'cost.' Everything according to the dictates of finance has a cost and this serves as an effective constraint on public understandings of what's possible. "Who will pay for it?" is the ever-repeating refrain. Who, though, paid the cost of the new employees here? No one did because there was none; prices, in fact, dropped 40 percent. Cost is a mythological concept having no real basis in a system with massively underutilized capacity.[10]

---

[10] An economist may argue that there are always "opportunity costs" in the real world. An increase in employment in beer production, for instance, would come at the "expense" of not using that labor to produce something else of value. While this is true in a micro sense, it misses the macro point of this exercise which is that beer production stands for population sector output in its entirety. The population sector in toto can expand virtually without limit and without cost. The specifics of what exactly is produced (including leisure time) will involve "opportunity" trade-offs but these are micro-scale details within the population sector. In the example, it would amount to the choice between IPA's and stouts.

This carries forward in the way we commonly use the analogy of a pie when thinking of income distribution. The world is seen as zero-sum and the two classes get their desserts based on how it's cut, a larger share for one meaning a smaller for the other. The beer example, though, shows this to be nonsense, for in actuality the two portions of the proverbial pie are unrelated. A more appropriate analogy is that of a balloon with a high profit margin corresponding to severe underinflation. Conceiving income distribution in this way derives from the identity between profit and capitalist spending in Kalecki's profit equation. Kalecki observed that changes in the income distribution weren't due to variances in profit (capitalist spending) but rather from the growth or constriction of total output.[11] I'm not arguing we should inflate the balloon to its full extent as we need nothing close to such levels to live well. My point is that the metric of the profit margin and the rhetoric of 'cost' are key ways we're kept poor.

A historical demonstration of what we've been discussing can be found in the price wars of the late nineteenth century. These were fostered by the predominance of small independent firms, an expanding New World, and rising productivity levels and the result was what we'd expect—collapsing prices, higher output, rising real wages, and declining profit margins. Labor militancy also increased.[12] This massive multi-decade price war was a sickness in the oligarchic system and the only possible cure was intra-class cooperation. The large corporation thus emerged and price competition eventually became a museum piece of the nineteenth century. The purpose of the new corporate system, noted Nitzan, was "not to enable large-scale industry, but rather to prevent it from being 'excessively' productive."[13] Veblen branded it for what it was—*sabotage*.[14]

Pricing today is based on the 'going' profit margin as determined by the financial markets; it's a collective phenomenon reflecting the relative power between the two classes. What this means in our daily lives is that despite our productive capacity, we experience not an ever expanding balloon of

---

[11] Kalecki (1971c: 95)

[12] This is a good example supporting the oligarchic fear that rising prosperity leads to a 'slippery slope' of rising expectations, a key point made in chapter four.

[13] Nitzan (1998: 190)

[14] Veblen (2001: 4)

prosperity but an unending struggle in a deflated world of high profit margins characterized by brands, image, and superficiality.

While recognizing the monopoly-like nature of this new corporate system, some observers maintain that companies do compete when it comes to investment. Kalecki himself held that inter-firm competition of this type is significant, saying that "capitalists do many things as a class but they do not invest as a class."[15] Given what we've discussed in this section so far, however, I don't see this as credible. The giant oligopolistic firms are collectively owned by the oligarchy and engage in ongoing cooperative behavior in maintaining profit margins. It makes little sense to posit these same companies aggressively compete when it comes to investment. The logic of finance is an important check given that population benefitting investment can never prove viable on a macro scale. Competitive investment wars can occur but they end just like price wars because they're harmful to the general interest of the oligarchy.

Economist Joseph Schumpeter dismissed the lack of firm level competition as irrelevant compared to the "perennial gale of creative destruction" that forces corporations to adopt to new methods of production, organization, and transportation which, he said, "incessantly revolutionize the economic structure from within, incessantly destroying the old one, incessantly creating the new one."[16]

Products and production methods do continuously change and these have undoubtedly brought benefits to the population. We travel today, after all, via cars, trains, and planes and not the stagecoach and we have computers, the internet, and cell phones to boot. They've brought costs as well— environmental degradation, military weapons capable of destroying humanity, increased surveillance over populations, job replacing automation, offshoring, and so on. But regardless of the extent of these kind of changes, they're always peripheral to the core power relation that underlies them. The structure of oligarchy has shown itself impervious to the gales of creative destruction as whatever is destroyed is quickly rebuilt for the new technological environment. Within the "revolutionized" structure that's created on the ruins of what has been destroyed, we find nothing other than the exact same ancient logic as before. Population benefitting production

---

[15] Kalecki (1971a: 152)
[16] Schumpeter (1947: 83-84)

continues to be unprofitable and the need for suppression grows even further with the expanded capacity. Our technology is remarkably sophisticated and it has given many of us access to some new and improved commodities,[17] but it would be a serious mistake to think we could ever make any fundamental progress in the most important elements of our quality of life as long as oligarchy remains in place.[18]

We need only consider how Schumpeter's gales have played out since the turn of the twentieth century to see this is true. Shortly after the "Banker's Panic" tempest in 1907 and 1908, devastating winds swept the world between 1914 and 1945, blasting in two World Wars and a Great Depression; it was followed by 25 years of relative postwar prosperity between 1950 and 1975, albeit including (and largely caused by) two deadly hurricanes in Korea and Vietnam killing millions and a Cold War that almost destroyed the planet; leading finally to our current 40 year storm of declining wages and living standards that has also brought an unending series of regional crises[19] and a gigantic eruption that has stymied the world since 2007. The weather forecast offers no relief.

It's a horrendous record albeit not one that should surprise us given the forces generating the climate. The odds this kind of unending destruction could ever yield anything creative for the population are miniscule; the best we could ever expect from Schumpeter's interminable gales would be a temporary respite, perhaps an "occasional mild breeze." [20] As historian William Appleman Williams observed, "American capitalism has never since 1861 functioned effectively enough to decrease economic misery over any significant period of time; save as it has been stimulated by war or cold war."[21]

I conclude that the oligarchy through corporate consolidation has successfully protected itself from the dangers of undue intra-class

---

[17] By no means have all of them improved. Our food supply for instance is widely thought to be of inferior quality and freshness than in the past as it's tainted by pesticides and industrial production methods.

[18] Mainstream economists claim that progress depends on ever rising productivity but this is most unlikely. I address this issue in appendix two.

[19] To name just a few, the Latin American debt and savings and loan crises of the eighties; the East Asian and Mexican crises along with the dot.com crash of the nineties; and the real estate bubble and subsequent crash in the 2000's.

[20] Baran & Sweezy (1966: 74)

[21] Williams (1964: 83)

competition. This applies to investment as well and Schumpeter's perennial gales do nothing to alter the situation. The collectivization of the oligarchy, however, isn't by itself sufficient to contain the population. There's an opposite side of the coin that needs addressing as well and it's that workers must be prevented from themselves collectivizing. It's crucial, in other words, that the oligarchy collectivize *and* that workers compete.

Be it through unions or the state, there's no greater threat to modern oligarchy than a collectivized population; it's a dagger aimed at the heart of inequality. Labor historian Jeremy Brecher summed it up this way: "ordinary people—together—have potentially the greatest power of all. It is their activity that makes up society. If they refuse to work, if they withdraw their cooperation, every social institution can be brought to a halt."[22] Collectivist ideas are radically insubordinate and their suppression has therefore always formed the foundation of wealth defense*.

The oligarchy has armed itself with formidable defenses against the eternal popular threat and they begin with the ideology of competitive individualism. If the population accepts it, then the threat is contained without further ado as the vast oversupply of workers enabled by our enormous productive capacity will render the lone individual powerless. This is the rule of the "invisible hand" and it's the best of all worlds since the work of suppression is handled automatically through the impersonal asymmetry of 'market forces.' It's tyranny without the tyrant, the gloss of freedom without its substance.

We call it neoliberalism today and to its proponents it represents the natural order. Within its vision, workers are individualized atoms living alone in the brutal world of perpetual global competition. The rules are those of finance—wages and living standards should be 'flexible' and competitively low; state spending modest and its budget balanced; imports minimized in favor of exports; and a great wall built to protect the 'economy' from the popular will. This is the way of peaceful modern oligarchy and, as Margaret Thatcher famously said, "there is no alternative." She was right in the sense that a collectivized population can't be an alternative if the 5,000 year structure of inequality is to survive.

Individualism, however, will never prove completely satisfying and collectivist pressures will regularly boil from below. Oligarchic defenses are

---

[22] Brecher (1997: 5)

deep and include assorted constitutional barriers to effective democracy; the influence of money to corrupt the political process; the ownership of the public media and its ability to shape opinion; anti-union laws such as the Taft-Hartley Act in the US; the ability of corporations to relocate, outsource, subcontract, and automate; the global power of finance to provoke crises against renegade populations; and ultimately the power of the police, military, and intelligence forces.

The era of modern oligarchy has been one of enormous turmoil but the oligarchy nevertheless seems to have ended up with a remarkable victory. In the face of rising global democracy, unions, communism, anti-colonialism, two World Wars, a Great Depression, the cultural outbreaks of the sixties, and ever growing productive capacity, it today is as outwardly healthy as ever. The class is collectivized on a global scale to a degree that has never previously existed and the population, correspondingly, has been forced into a downward spiral of brutal individualized competition.

The magnitude of success is evidenced by the existence of widespread poverty and insecurity coexisting with our immense productive potential. It can also be seen through the monetary metric of the profit margin. The ILO reports that the labor share of national income for sixteen higher income OECD nations hovers around 65 percent while being lower in the 'developing' countries. In China, it's 47 percent.[23] The profit margin, the inverse of the labor share, is therefore 35 percent in the OECD and 53 percent in China. As noted by the ILO, however, a significant percentage of labor income is paid to top executives[24] and thereby understates the profit margin. If we used Piketty's US data[25] showing that 12 percent of labor income flows to the top one percent and transferred that to the oligarchy side of the ledger, we'd end up with an OECD profit margin of 42.8 percent.[26]

Profit is an imprecise measure of diversion[27] and we need to take the published figures as indicating only a general magnitude. But if we accept a rounded 40 percent as a reasonable ballpark, what does that mean? It means

---

[23] ILO (2013: 43-45) Data is for 2010

[24] ILO (2013: 43-44)

[25] Picketty (2014: table 7.1)

[26] 35% + (12% X 65%)

[27] It can include stage one profits discussed in the preceding chapter, state spending as will be discussed in chapter nine, and speculative bubbles and fraud as will be discussed in chapter eleven.

first that the total output for nearly all of mankind is just 50 percent higher than what's produced for the tiny minority that's the oligarchy.[28] It also gives us a pointer to a solution. If the profit margin were reduced from 40 percent to 5 percent while keeping diversion constant, then population benefitting output would rise by a factor of over twelve.[29] This is the essential suppressionary meaning of the profit margin.

Populations can't easily force the oligarchy to reduce the profit margin. They may at times succeed in gaining higher wages, but corporations control pricing and can thereby sustain the margin regardless of the wage. Without pricing power, the realities of excess labor, immense technological capacity, and ever advancing automation would self-evidently lead to rampant rises in output, sharp declines in prices, huge increments in real wages, and a near disappearance of profit margins. Median wages, though, haven't increased in forty years, indeed they've declined, profit margins have increased, and the basic monetary trend is moderate inflation rather than sharp deflation, all prima facie evidence of the fantastic success of the suppressionary effort.

I've argued in this chapter that the key challenge facing the oligarchy in our era is maintaining the wealth differential over the population in the face of massive productive capacity. This has elevated the importance of suppression and we find it most prominently expressed in the language of finance. Because it seems second nature to many of us, it's easy to overlook the hostility of the force lurking behind it. It's helpful to reflect on the fact it would be impossible for oligarchy to exist were its logic such that it encouraged the full use of our productive capacity. The structure of oligarchy demands that finance be what it is.

Suppression in our era can be thought of in terms of a duality between collective action and competition, the oligarchy reserving the former for itself and the latter for the population. This chapter has emphasized the ways it operates in the 'private' realm but, as we'll now see, the underlying logic is identical when it comes to the 'public' sphere of the state. The crucial rules are again that of finance and the key goal is to deny the ability of the population to act collectively.

---

[28] 60% share for the population / 40% share for the oligarchy.

[29] Population Benefiting Output = Profit / Profit Margin - Profit. The starting case is: $1 / .4 - 1 = 1.5$. If the profit margin were reduced from 40% to 5%, then it would be: $1 / .05 - 1 = 19$. 19. Dividing the latter number by the former, we get an expansion of output of 12.67 times (19.19 / 1.5).

9

Money & the Oligarchic State

We need to put the state in proper context to understand its role in modern oligarchy. The system is a structure of power grounded in the minority control of the means of production. Oligarchs as a class sit at the pinnacle of the hierarchy, drive the system, and rule over a propertyless population. The state isn't an independent actor in this schema but is rather a set of institutions within which the relative power of the two fundamental classes play out.

That the balance of power rests with oligarchy means that it controls the institutions of the state in the areas relating to its vital interests. The vital interests are diversion and suppression and the state performs a wide range of functions in service to them; these include property protection laws, courts, prisons, the military, police, intelligence, covert action, education, propaganda, and so on. The population is the existential risk and the key danger is that it would capture the important state institutions and use them in its collective interest. Wealth defense* demands that this be prevented and the population denied any significant access to the levers of the state, especially its power to spend.

The structure requires that the state be an anti-democratic institution in furtherance of suppression and this poses a management problem in a culture that's democratic. Ideology is the main means by which oligarchy and democracy are reconciled and it has been remarkably successful. Large numbers everywhere seem to accept the most basic doctrines—that we're best off "standing on our own two feet" as individuals and entrusting our prosperity to the market; that taxation is a burden to all and should be kept low; that the state is like a household and should balance its budget and avoid debt; that the state should limit itself to matters of defense (military, intelligence, etc.), law and order (police, prisons, courts, etc.), and basic infrastructure; and that spending on 'entitlements' and 'welfare' is wasteful, inefficient, and financially unsound.

This 'public' agenda is aligned tightly with that of the 'private' one discussed in the last two chapters. We found there that 'private' diversion is the essential purpose of the market portfolio and here we see that 'collective' diversion in the form of military, police, etc. is the essential purpose of the state. 'Private' spending in the interest of the population was found to violate the dictates of sound finance by being unprofitable, inefficient, and by harming profit margins; here we see that 'collective' spending for the population violates the purpose of the state and is likewise inefficient and financially unsound. The agendas are identical, in fact, and this gives us a smoking-gun clue that their motivating force is the same.

The ideologies surrounding state spending are extraordinarily powerful and to see through them requires that we first step back and consider what it is that the state spends. The easy answer is money, but we need to dig further and consider what that means. It turns out that this is a tricky issue for if we go off in search of the thing called "money," it won't be found. This is so because it doesn't have an actual physical existence; in the words of anthropologist David Graeber, it "has no essence; it's not 'really' anything."[1]

Some theorists assert it's best thought of not as a 'thing' but rather as an abstract measuring unit of a thing. It's like an hour or an ounce or a centimeter, and just as we can't see these units, we can't see money.[2] But it's clear that the hour, ounce, and centimeter measure time, weight, and length; what is it that money measures?

It measures credit says economist Alfred-Mitchell Innes, developer of the 1914 *Credit Theory of Money*—"Credit and credit alone is money."[3] The base

---

[1] Graeber (2011: 372)
[2] Innes (1914: 4)
[3] Innes (1914: 12)

requirement is that there exist an institution with strong enough credit that we don't cash its liabilities but instead let them continuously circulate. The banking system is such an institution and what it does is substitute the credit of parties lower in the monetary hierarchy with that of its own. It has a creditor–debtor relationship with its borrowers, but it's a debtor to greater society as its IOU's, its deposit accounts, are accepted and circulate as money.

This gives the banking system the power to create money through the process of lending. When a bank extends a loan, it credits the borrower's deposit account in return for the promise to repay it plus interest. Where did the banking system get the money? From nowhere; bank money isn't a thing, it's rather a mere reflection of the fact its liabilities circulate. The loan was 'funded' by an increase in total circulating liabilities. The only limit to the amount of money banks can create in this way is the creditworthiness of borrowers, their demand for loans, and the continued public acceptance of the banking system's liabilities.

The credit theory provides some important insights but it limits itself by wrongly placing the banking system at the top of the power hierarchy. Banks aren't at the top for they're subordinate to the state. A rival theory, the *State Theory of Money* developed in the early twentieth century by economist George Friedrich Knapp, takes this into account. It sees money not as bank credit but as a creature of the state. Keynes promoted this view, noting that it's the state and not banks which has the power to write and enforce the laws.[4] Economists writing in the so-called Modern Monetary Theory paradigm follow Knapp and Keynes in asserting state monetary primacy and emphasize the importance of the power to tax as the ground for it.[5] But the state theory is problematic as well for it also wrongly places its preferred agent at the top. The state is a mere institutional shell and can't, therefore, be the ultimate backing for money. For that, we must look to the top of the power hierarchy, the oligarchy.

A fruitful angle for seeing the relation between money and the oligarchy is provided by sociologist Heiner Ganssmann. He views money as a kind of shared understanding one finds in a language and turns to Wittgenstein. "The

---

[4] Keynes (1930: 5) In his words, the state has always had "the right not only to enforce the dictionary but also to write the dictionary."

[5] Wray (2014) The MMT School has been an invaluable resource in developing a stronger understanding of money.

pawn in chess neither has meaning in the sense of representing something, of being a sign of something, nor is it just the piece carved out of wood. What the pawn is, is determined by the rules of chess."[6] Following this line of thought, we can understand money as the tokenized expression of the rules of the game of oligarchy. The various national currencies of today mean nothing but what the rulebook says about them; how they're to be created, how they're to be distributed, and what their power to command will be. The state is the institutional manager and the money it or the banking system issues is a social construction defined by these rules. It's not a thing but a token of the power of oligarchy and, just as there's no effective limit to what the oligarchy could spend, there's no real constraint on what the state could spend. It's impossible for it to run out of money.

This is an immense institutional power that poses a significant threat; not that the state would spend per se, but that it would be captured by the democratic spirit and do so in the interest of the population. To protect itself, the oligarchy has developed an elaborate series of restrictive laws, procedures, and mythologies which can be lumped together under the rubric of 'sound public finance.' Since the rules of money are the rules of the game of oligarchy, every nuance of sound public finance must support and further oligarchic goals. They must enforce the power of wealth, suppress the population, and bail out the system when needed. If they didn't do these things, then the game wouldn't be called oligarchy.

The various national central banks and treasuries along with international financial agencies like the International Monetary Fund (IMF) and World Bank are the key monetary institutions today and together they form an elite club operating in the collective interest of the global oligarchy. The IMF has played an important role in assuring strict conformance with the principles of sound public finance. It has been rock solid throughout the decades in its consistent demands for privatizations, reduced state spending, deregulation, austerity, trade liberalization, balanced budgets, balanced trade, high interest rates, and central bank 'independence.' The IMF's "unofficial agenda," according to former World Bank chief economist Joseph Stiglitz, is controlled by finance[7] as was more or less 'officially' confirmed by its Director General between 1987 and 2000, Michael Camdessus, who

---

[6] Ganssmann (2012: 20, 28, & 44)

[7] Stiglitz (2003: 206)

emphasized that the IMF "did not circumvent the discipline of the financial market, but came to reinforce it."[8] The same can be said of the World Bank which has long been a reliable partner of the IMF. We had a taste of the character of that partnership when we looked at its *2014 World Development Report* in chapter two and I examine it further in appendix four.

The US, the European Monetary Union, and many countries have built legal barriers to reinforce the so-called independence of their central banks. These don't bestow real independence, though, for the central banks are agents of oligarchic policy and operate within tight bounds. The question isn't about central bank independence from government—it doesn't exist; but of government independence from the population which, in the places where it counts, most certainly does.

The paradigm of sound public finance is the monetary reflection of the wealth defense* need that the state limit all spending that would benefit the population. One of the main ideological means by which this is accomplished is through the requirement that spending be 'financed' via either taxation or debt. Beyond the fact that both methods are made difficult, the financing principle itself is important for it establishes the point that the state isn't an agent of unlimited resources. The real issue has nothing to do with unfinanced spending, though, as it's concerned only with assuring it doesn't accrue to the benefit of the population. The so-called "quantitative easing" programs of the Federal Reserve and the European Central Bank (ECB) have been 'money printing' operations and have thereby violated the financing requirement but the experts have accepted them, albeit uneasily, because they've been directed at propping up asset prices and haven't been accompanied by any undesirable increment in population spending.

It's not hard to show that common understandings of the financing methods of taxation and debt are mere mythologies in support of suppression. I'll start with taxation and observe there are two key aspects of it that are at odds with the mythological storyline. First, the state has no obvious need to tax at all since it's the authority over the currency and could theoretically produce it at will. The notion it depends on taxpayers for money is patently at odds with the facts. And second, the idea that taxation represents a burden is flawed. Taxes are a cost only to the population and pose no burden to the oligarchy. While keeping the first point in mind, let's

---

[8] Panitch & Gindin (2012: 240)

expand on the second for it will no doubt seem counter-intuitive to many readers.

Taxation is a different kind of phenomenon for the two classes. The population is bound inside the confines of the market portfolio and depends on oligarchic wages for survival. Taxes levied upon it represent true costs. Real benefits like social security and healthcare may be associated with them, but the bottom line must end up a net wash as spending in other areas will be reduced to pay the taxes.

Taxation of the oligarchy, however, is a different affair. It was exempt from taxes throughout a good part of its 5,000 year history given that their main purpose was to force populations into producing diversion. While it seems to be the case today that the oligarchy does pay taxes, this is only an appearance. The truth, deriving from Kalecki's profit equation,[9] is that the oligarchy doesn't incur a tax burden for state spending, only the population does. This is so because the oligarchy owns the market portfolio and whatever the state spends flows directly into its coffers via the diversion-profit loop. Any taxes paid are thereby offset by increased profit. Taxation for the oligarchy is thus a net wash. This is guaranteed by its structural position at the top of the ownership hierarchy and it's almost as nonsensical to think of taxing the oligarchy as it is of taxing the state.

An example will help reinforce the point. Suppose the oligarchy spent 100 monetary units each year on diversion and it was decided the state should increase its military expenditures by ten units to be financed by income taxes on the oligarchy. The new state spending flows into the market portfolio via,

---

[9] The inability to effectively tax the oligarchy by any 'normal' means is reflected in an expanded version of the Kalecki profit equation. See Kalecki (1971b: 39):
Before Tax Profit = Capitalist Consumption + Investment + Income Tax Revenue
The assumption is that the state spends the income tax revenue. We eliminate it on both sides and end up with:
After tax profit = Capitalist Consumption + Investment
Reformatted to the diversion equation, we find:
Before Tax Profit = Diversion + State Spending Financed by Oligarchic Taxation
And, eliminating taxation and state spending from both sides:
After Tax Profit = Diversion
I note that state spending financed by taxes on the population wouldn't yield a profit to the oligarchy since population spending is reduced elsewhere in order to pay the taxes. The state has simply redirected the spending of the wage.

say, military weapon purchases or the direct hiring of soldiers and exits as profit, the total of which now rises to 110 units. Ten units of taxation then return to the state leaving the oligarchy in the same position as before but with increased military output. The tax didn't affect 'private' diversion at all as it was 'paid for' by the profit that flowed from the state spending.

Figure 2 illustrates the basic flow. We find a zero-sum loop beginning with state spending and ending with taxation. I keep the heavy diversion arrow pointing to the oligarchy since we can assume the military spending served a diversionary wealth defense* purpose.

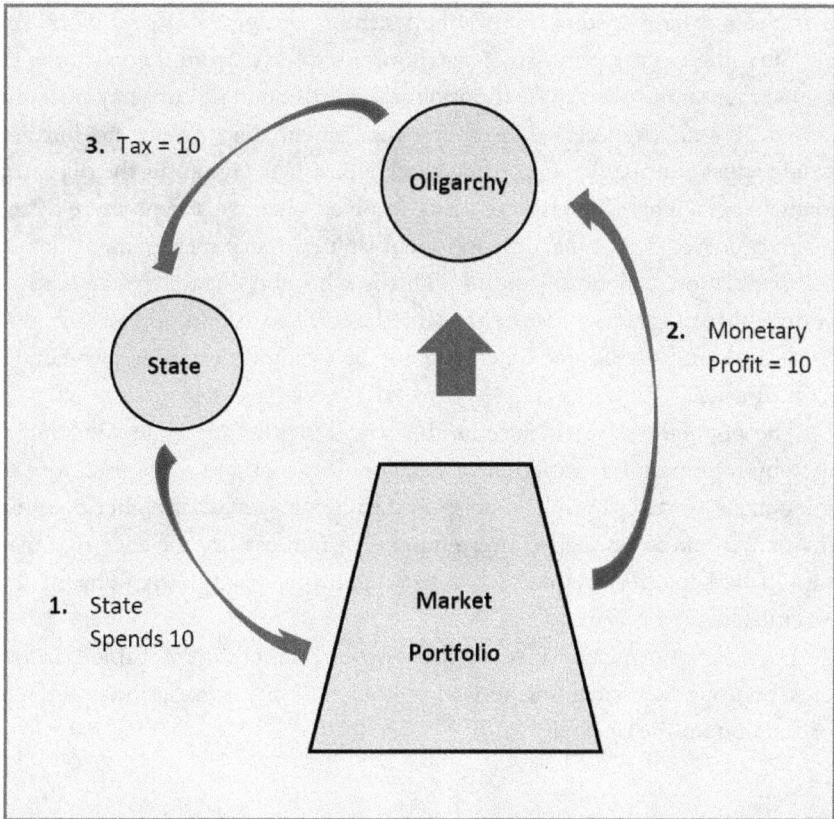

Figure 2: The Market Portfolio and Taxation

The oligarchy didn't incur a cost and if the word is to have any meaning, it wasn't taxed. To claim otherwise would be like saying a worker paid a tax even though he or she received a subsequent refund. Or that the cost of an

$8 six pack of beer was actually $10 because that was the amount initially tendered to the cashier, ignoring the $2 change given back. Taxation is a real cost for the population but it's not for the oligarchy.

Because of its position at the top of the hierarchy, the oligarchy can't be taxed under normal circumstances as long as the state spends the money.[10] The only exception would be if the market portfolio were operating at full capacity before the added spending. The new spending would then be offset by a reduction elsewhere and thereby yield no net profit. Only in such a case would the oligarchy suffer a potential decline in diversion and possibly incur a real cost. This would be a most rare event given our high productivity, one that has only happened in the twentieth century during the World Wars.

What then is the purpose of taxation? As we saw from the example, its primary function seems to be the apolitical one of draining currency from the system. It's an exercise in currency management that, posing no burden, would appear incapable of arousing much interest. Yet we know the oligarchy loathes taxes. This is a paradox that's resolved once we accept we're in the realm of ideology and that the opponent isn't currency management (taxes) but population benefitting output. This is what the oligarchy fears and to control that risk, taxes must be presented as dire costs and opposed on that basis. To admit they weren't a cost would be to admit output had no limit; a clear disaster.

The population largely accepts this world-picture and state spending is thereby suppressed. It experiences taxation as a cost and seeks therefore to minimize it for itself. While it's disposed to favor somewhat higher taxes on the rich, it can be persuaded by arguments of fairness or efficiency that they should be kept 'reasonable.' It's a most harmful misunderstanding of the essential logic of oligarchy.

Let's dig a bit further into this most powerful mythology. Table 6 below presents four state spending scenarios along with the corresponding effects of taxation on the oligarchy.

---

[10] The state could use the proceeds to retire debt and in such a case the oligarchy wouldn't be taxed either—it would simply be swapping state bonds for cash. We'll address state debt later in the chapter.

Table 6: Taxation is not a Cost to the Oligarchy

Diversion	State Spending	Before Tax Profit	Tax	After Tax Profit	Tax on Profit	Tax on Diversion
100	0	100	0	100	0%	0%
100	25	125	(25)	100	20	0
100	100	200	(100)	100	50	0
100	900	1,000	(900)	100	90	0

Assume that basic population needs require state spending of 900 units and the oligarchy's demand for luxury and wealth defense* is satiated at 100. Four scenarios are shown in which diversion is held constant while state spending and taxes increase. The key point is that there's nothing special about any of the tax rates for no matter how high or low, the oligarchy achieves its diversion without cost and suffers no burden. Ideology ignores this and simply asserts that taxation is a burden that, beyond a certain point, is both unfair and inefficient. Perhaps that rate is claimed to be 20 percent of profit. As we can see from the second scenario of the table, such a rate would limit state spending to just 25 units, a level far below what's necessary. The real issue isn't the tax rate but the extent the output balloon should be inflated to support population needs. If they were met as per the fourth scenario, then state spending would account for 90 percent of output and a 90 percent tax rate would be applied. One can imagine the inevitable screams of "soaking the rich" but they would be baseless since the oligarchy would have suffered no burden. For every tax rate that fails to meet its needs, it's the population that's actually being "soaked."

We can imagine a few objections here, the first being down the lines of fairness. Work would be performed in producing the additional goods and services, after all, and surely those doing it should be compensated. Is it fair they should be ordered to work for nothing? The tax, though, wouldn't be assessed on those doing the additional work and who are now enjoying an employment they otherwise wouldn't have had; it would be on the owners of the means of production. It's true they wouldn't earn an after tax profit (nor incur a cost), but this is always the case for population benefiting output regardless of whether it's financed 'publicly' or 'privately.' *It's a structural fact of oligarchy that the population can never be profitable.* The 'fairness' argument turns out to be nothing other than a justification for keeping the output balloon underinflated. It's the exact same one that seeks to keep the profit margin high. Excess capacity exists in the market portfolio and the state in this case is simply ordering it utilized at no cost to anyone. It's a strange moral principle that would see this as unfair.

Another possible objection concerns practicality. Would there not be a lack of incentive for corporations to expand output to meet the new demand? While this is arguably a valid 'economic' point, it only reiterates what has been said—there's never an incentive to expand population sector output. The structural logic of inequality assures that any state effort down these lines won't be profitable at the level of the market portfolio and will be viewed by the oligarchy as a hostile act. The goal of this exercise, though, isn't to claim the state could easily violate the basic rules but to demonstrate that taxation isn't a cost to the oligarchy and that the real issue is suppression.

One could nevertheless reasonably argue that high tax rates wouldn't have any important effects on incentives. The diversion sector would be unaffected since the state would only tax what it had added. As for the population sector, while taxes would be higher, so also would pre-tax incomes. An investor would thereby have a much higher chance of success than in a low tax environment albeit with reduced after tax winnings. The net would be the same in both cases.

Yet another objection could be that the expansion would unfairly benefit oligarchs with portfolios weighted toward the population sector because only those firms would receive the extra income while all oligarchs would pay the higher tax. The simple response is to suggest to those with poorly diversified portfolios that this is just part of the risk of the game and that they should perhaps study up on portfolio theory.

Finally, there's an international objection that warrants closer scrutiny. It's that while taxation isn't a cost to the oligarchy taken as a whole, a higher rate in one nation could adversely affect that country's oligarchs to the benefit of foreigners. The local oligarchs would pay the entire higher tax yet would receive only part of the profit as some of it would leak across the border into the global system. While this is also an issue of diversification, we'll examine it further in the next chapter. It doesn't at all change the important conclusion that the oligarchy as a class doesn't incur a tax burden.

The second financing method is called debt and it also is wrapped in the thick fog of mythology. Populations have been taught to view it through the perspective of their own personal lives and see the state as like them, a lowly household forced by economic imperatives to sit at a barren kitchen table and humbly balance its budget to avoid bankruptcy. That public debt is a great danger is widely incorporated into our political culture and laws and nations everywhere are suppressing spending because of it. The EU has built restrictions into its constitution that require each member country to keep its total debt below 60 percent of GDP and its annual deficit under 3 percent. Greece, Spain, Portugal, Ireland, and Italy have been forced into brutal depression because of debt. The US congress must annually approve a debt ceiling and conservative forces throughout the world are routinely proposing balanced budget amendments.

A state, though, is not at all like a household; the former is the authority over its currency and can create it at will[11] while the latter is powerless. Linking the two gives us an entirely false world-picture.

Let's pause a moment and consider what's "functionally" taking place when the state spends and taxes.[12] It's extraordinarily simple. When it spends, the end result is that deposit accounts of recipients are credited; and when it taxes, deposit accounts of taxpayers are debited. A host of operational details exist in-between but they needn't concern us here as we're interested only in functional outcomes. The state may choose to couple its spending with taxation but it's not necessary it do so; it has the full capacity to credit deposit accounts without simultaneously debiting them.[13] Again, it can create its currency at will and doesn't depend on the debits of taxation to fund the credits of spending.

When the state spends in excess of taxation, it creates money in a way similar to banks. It's called *deficit spending*. The state, though, is higher in the hierarchy and is creating money to which there's no further recourse. It therefore, unlike bank money, can't reasonably be considered debt. A depositor at a bank could walk into its lobby and demand that the bank redeem his or her deposit account in hard cash, i.e. paper units issued by the

---

[11] The well-known problem in Europe is that the member countries have ceded their monetary power to the ECB. For purposes here, the 'state' in Europe is the EU. States which have ceded their power over the currency are neutered entities that can't really be considered full-fledged states. They're more like the individual states in the US—mere parts of the more powerful whole.

[12] This is the approach adopted by economist Abba Lerner that he termed *Functional Finance*. Lerner (1943)

[13] I'm ignoring self-imposed legal prohibitions.

state, and the bank would thereby be forced to redeem its debt. The former depositor would now have state money but the end of the road will have been reached. It would be a silly exercise if he or she then proceeded to walk over to the national treasury and demand the cash be redeemed for a different kind of money. The basic unit of account is state money and it's a non sequitur to claim its issuer could be in debt.

When the state spends via a deficit, monetary orders enter the market portfolio in the standard way and flow to the oligarchy as profit. The key difference with what was shown in Figure 2 is that since there's no taxation, the deficit spending accrues to the oligarchy as after tax profit. This is reflected in the expanded Kalecki profit equation.[14] Figure 3 below illustrates the flow assuming ten units of deficit spending.

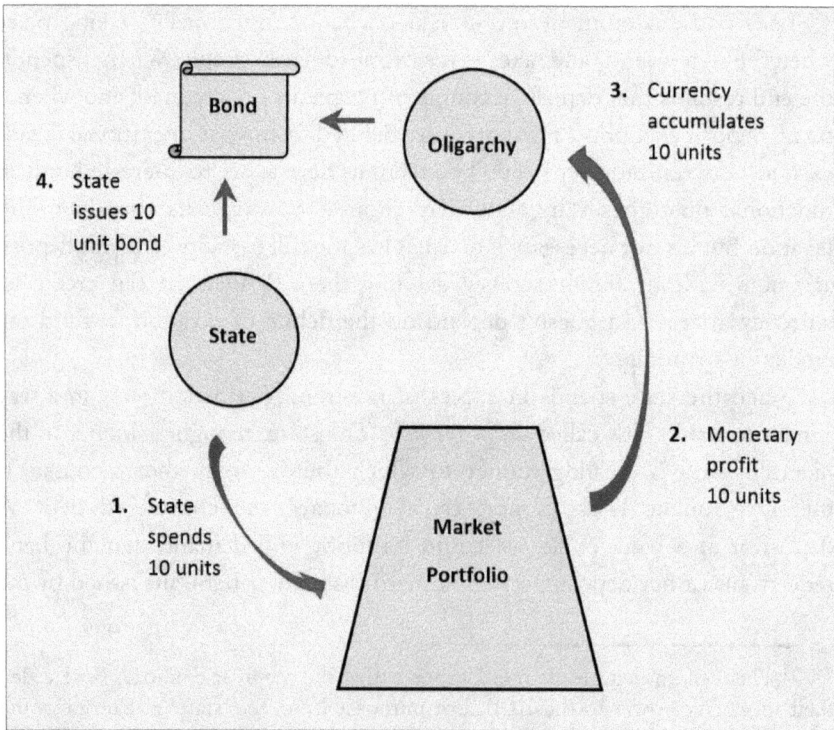

Figure 3: The Market Portfolio and State Debt

---

[14] The full Kalecki equation includes deficit spending as a profit item. Kalecki (1969: 49). See appendix one.

We've discussed a number of monetary circuits so far and each has represented a closed loop in which monetary sums flow out of the oligarchy or its varied institutions and then return to it. Diversion spending enters the market portfolio and returns as profit; corporate wages return as sales; bank loans return with repayment and, if not repaid, return as population sector profit; and taxes paid by the oligarchy return as profit. It's a bit different with deficit spending—the loop begins with the state, the issuer of the currency, and ends with the oligarchy. Regardless of which class benefits from the deficit spending, the end result is an accumulation of currency in the hands of the oligarchy.

Widely accepted orthodoxy has it that the state should pay interest on this currency and there are a number of ways it could do so. It could, for instance, offer savings accounts or certificates of deposit into which the oligarchy could deposit the funds. Or, in what would be the exact same thing, it could issue 'bonds.' Bonds in essence are savings accounts and that's what 'public debt' really is—an interest bearing savings account. As Warren Mosler has put it, "Over the course of time the total number of dollars that have been drained from the banking system ... is called the federal debt. A more appropriate name would be the Interest Rate Maintenance Account (IRMA). The IRMA is simply an accounting of the total amount of securities issued to pay interest on untaxed money spent by the government."[15] Bonds, according to economist Stephanie Bell, "provide the private sector with an interest-earning alternative to non-interest bearing government currency and allow the government to spend in excess of taxation while maintaining positive overnight lending rates."[16] They're part of monetary policy and don't finance deficits.[17]

The functional result of the flow illustrated in Figure 3 is that the state has channeled monetary sums to the oligarchy which has then deposited them into a state provided savings account we call a bond. If the state had not offered the bond or the oligarchy refused to buy it, then the currency would simply accrue in non-earning deposit accounts. Absent purposeful proactive monetary policy action by the state to sustain them, deficits will drive interest rates to zero because of rising levels of non-earning deposit

---

[15] Mosler (2012: 34)
[16] Bell (1998: 20)
[17] Wray (1998: 2)

accounts. (For the Figure 3 illustration, we should visualize the new bond as becoming part of the market portfolio. The diversion arrow is omitted as we make no assumption whether or not any was produced.)

At first glance it would seem that deficits are a fantastic deal for the oligarchy—in exchange for nothing, it receives both a free flow of profit and an interest bearing bond to put it in. Even the population sector is transformed into profitability through deficit magic, a direct contradiction to the logic we've discussed so far. Yet we know deficits are a complete anathema and entire populations are routinely brought to their knees because of them. Why does the oligarchy reject the fountain of free profit? This is a puzzle for those who insist the prime systemic goal is profit but it becomes clear when we think in terms of the motives of diversion and suppression.

To help sort this out, let's first note that the oligarchy is unlikely to object to untaxed spending on such collective wealth defense* purposes as the military, police, bailouts, and so on. These are crucial diversion expenditures and the manner in which they're financed is irrelevant. The trouble arises when the population benefits. While it's true that deficit spending yields profit in the population sector, it comes at the gigantic cost of upending the most basic flow of oligarchy. The population, via the state, rises above its station and gains the immense power to order production. It becomes an agent for itself and the game itself is imperiled. The oligarchy receives in return a flow of currency but what possible value can this have when the diversion-profit loop already gives it an unrestrained power to spend? It has no need for these extra monetary tokens.

We're dealing here with one of the most important fronts of the inter-class war for the entire façade risks collapse if the state's power to spend is seen as unlimited. Deficits must be presented not as savings accounts but as actual hard debt. The state is thereby reduced to the household, the population pushed back to subservient debtor, and the fundamental rules and logic of oligarchy returned. Deficits lose their magic once they become debt and no longer produce profit in the population sector; they're mere advances on future wages, offering nothing of value to the oligarchy. Populations see only the image of debt and fear it, accepting the myth that the upfront benefits must come at the great cost of future austerity. The mythologies of debt are most effective stories.

Interest rates on this 'debt,' as mentioned, are maintained by central banks as part of their monetary policy and they are key tools of suppression. High rates are almost always good in the doctrines of sound public finance and we are certain to hear howls of anguish in the financial media whenever it perceives them as being too low. A few reasons the oligarchy supports high interest rates are:

- They increase the cost of purchases requiring credit and thereby reduce the real wage.
- They reinforce the notion that public debt is dangerous by imposing a high cost.
- They're a key weapon against excessive wage demands and high employment.
- They reduce the threat that budding entrepreneurs could advance into the oligarchy through borrowed money.
- They provide the oligarchy with a larger piece of the pie through high yielding loans to small businesses.
- They channel extra income to the upper middle-class, a key ally for the oligarchy.

Central banks establish what's called the "risk free" interest rate and while they normally focus on short term maturities, their policy decisions determine rates at all points on the yield curve. The applicable rate for ten year maturities in the US in March, 2014 was 2.73 percent. This is low by historical standards because of a policy decision to sustain asset values in the aftermath of the crisis beginning in 2007 and because of public pressure in the face of an especially weak global economy. But it nevertheless represents an annual risk free transfer to the oligarchy of $27,300 per million of wealth. As recently as June, 2006, a more typical, albeit still low, yield of $51,500 was in place, an amount higher than the annual US median household income. The contrast between the riskless return on wealth and the risky return on work is even starker in 'developing' countries. The ten year yield in Mexico in March, 2014, for example, was $63,200 per million and was as high as $86,900 in June, 2006, over 19 times the country's median annual disposable household income.[18]

---

[18] Using the OECD figure of $4,500. OECD (2014: 86). Yields in this paragraph were obtained from the St. Louis Federal Reserve Fred system.

We've found in this chapter that the state is something of a necessary evil for the oligarchy. Inequality requires the institutions of the state but there's the ever-present risk that the population could capture its powers and use them for democratic purposes. A thick ideological fog has accordingly been constructed which seeks in every which way to explain why the spending power of the state must be constricted. The myths center themselves on the idea of cost (taxation or debt) and they've been extraordinarily successful in sowing a deep confusion. The common conception of the state as a real independent entity is a big part of the problem as it distracts us from what's essential. It's not an actor but only an institutional shell and we gain a great deal of clarity by filtering it out. We can then better appreciate how money is in fact the measure of social relations within the language of oligarchy and that it has significance only in the unequal way it's distributed and the power it commands. The discourses on 'state' spending, 'state' taxation, 'state' debt, and 'state' interest rates take on a strangely artificial character that can't so easily hide the hostile logic that's driving it all.

Intermission

We're over halfway through our examination of modern oligarchy and have covered the basics of diversion, suppression, and state spending. Let's take a break here and consider a brief illustrative narrative that highlights some key elements of our oligarchic world.

You are an oligarch and live in the luxury confines of Park Avenue. You own a fully diversified share of the market portfolio which consists of the 500 corporations in the S&P 500 stock grouping. Because of your wise compliance with portfolio theory, your chief financial advisor tells you it's immaterial how any particular company or sector performs. Your only risk, he says, is a "systematic" one which seems as unlikely to occur as a comet strike. You're in the comfortable position of perpetually receiving extraordinary sums of money and thereby living extraordinarily well.

You think yourself superior in your social station and like being part of the upper crust.[1] As a moral person, you don't of course wish to see too much abject poverty, but you wouldn't feel very good if an extra-terrestrial being suddenly offered to convert all apartments everywhere to the same cultured opulence that permeates Park Avenue. You recognize that your most

---

[1] Taken from a quote of an upper class woman in a large mid-western city in Domhoff (2006: 4).

eminent rank demands there be a great number of inferiors and that you have a vested interest in keeping the 'working-class' working-class.

It may appear that the source of your river of gold is the 500 corporations in your portfolio, but it's not. Your glittering lifestyle is rooted in the structure of oligarchy and the place within it in which you sit. The mounds of money that regularly find their way into your bank account are the mere return flow of what the class as a whole had previously expended on diversion plus whatever had been spent by the state. What's important isn't profit per se, but the fact your position is forever self-sustaining. While it's not obvious to you, the real causal order is the reverse of what it seems—you and the other oligarchs live extraordinarily well and therefore receive extraordinary sums of money.

The corporations in your portfolio aren't independent entities, they're legal fictions collectively owned by you and the other oligarchs. They're intertwined in complex partnerships, alliances, joint ventures, and cross-ownership relations; they share many of the same directors, are audited by the same accounting firms, and use the same 'best practices' promulgated by the same management advisory companies; their officers and directors attended the same schools, belong to the same clubs, and strut through the same revolving door between Wall Street and Washington; and they all operate according to the strict dictates of finance. What you own isn't so much the corporations but a slice of the great structural web.

Your servants along with workers throughout the city toil every day to make your life the fine splendor that it is, commuting on the subways and buses from their modest housing and slums outside the gates. The entire system is based on the twin pillars of diversion and suppression and you consider it the natural order of things. The dynamic of costless diversion enables you to put these people to work serving your refined tastes while suppression keeps them in a dependent state of relative poverty.

While the capacity exists for them to live far better, the concept of using it for that purpose is inconceivable to you for it could never be profitable. The idea is frankly absurd. To even hint at it forever brands the speaker as either stupid or a revolutionary. You're neither. You once thought it would be nice if the workers lived better, but your learned friends disabused you of that notion. Not only would it be financially unsound, it would threaten your way of life. Imagine if the doormen, servants, and the great mass of workers were less deferential! The thought is alarming and makes you queasy, even hostile. Nothing is more natural or essential than keeping the worker in his or her proper station. They're not your equal and constantly need discipline; many of them are as stupid as an ox. Let them make it on their own in the competition of the free market.

Agitators on the left unconscionably want the state to do more for these people by infringing on your sacred natural rights. How *dare* they threaten to raise your taxes or sink the nation into debt! Democracy is perhaps fine in theory but there are strict limits that must never be breached. All your friends agree that the proper role of the state is minimal and revolves solely around protecting your fundamental rights to life and ownership. The great philosophers have argued for this limited range of duties for millennia and it's the only possible basis of freedom. Protection from the hoards is the state's sole obligation; how *dare* any state or group of individuals do more. Or less.

10

The Transnational Oligarchy

Modern oligarchy is a system that appears both global and national and this poses a significant analytical challenge. The question is whether we should approach it from the bottom up or the top down. The first focuses on individual nation-states and sees the global system as their simple summation while the second views the system as a single global whole with the states being mere incidental parts. I argued for the latter in chapter six on account of the pervasiveness of transnational ownership and production links and in this chapter we'll consider the issue further. We'll find that matters like trade, production, currencies, taxation, and state debt require a global approach if we're to avoid confused and erroneous conclusions.

I argue specifically against a mainstream ideology that centers itself on the parts and leaves us with the false inference that the system is fundamentally inter-national rather than inter-class. The goal is to untangle these myths and I believe an effective way of doing so is through an extended thought exercise that attempts to present the opposition between the global whole and the national parts in a way that's simple yet still captures the essential idea. I turn to it now.

Assume a global playing board that's divided into two nation-states; one of them is called Leymanville and its currency is the dollar, the other

Kaiserland and its currency is the euro.[1] The currencies trade at parity. There are two oligarchic groups in the game, the Goulds and the Habsburgs,[2] and they collectively own between them the entire global market portfolio which consists of a few large corporations and banks. Both groups are fully diversified per finance theory with the Goulds owning 60 percent of the total and the Habsburgs 40 percent.

They, along with their corporations and assorted subsidiaries, are completely transnational and have no loyalty to either nation. While most of the Goulds live in Leymanville and the Habsburgs in Kaiserland, the location of their residences is of no importance for as owners they float above the board. Cemented on the surface are the populations of both states, the pawns, and we assume they've been successfully suppressed so that unemployment and poverty are endemic.

I argue this is a reasonable abstraction of modern reality for it presents a global system divided into national parts in which oligarchs have the ability to diversify their portfolios across the entire board.[3]

The managers of the corporations decide where production occurs between the two nations and they do so according to sound financial principles. We'll suppose they've organized it so that diversion production is split equally between Leymanville and Kaiserland.

Because diversion encompasses both countries, the Goulds and the Habsburgs will end up using both currencies. There's no home monetary unit for either group as the one required for any purchase will depend on where it was produced. In the present case, an equal mix of dollars and euros are required because that's how the managers have divided the diversion sector. We'll assume that the Goulds end up spending 600 billion and the Habsburgs 400 billion monetary units in diversion split evenly between dollars and euros and they obtain them by borrowing the sums from the banking system. This is summarized in Table 7 below.

---

[1] In honor of the demised Wall Street firm and the German word for emperor.

[2] Named after the 'robber baron' Jay Gould who is claimed to have said "I can hire one-half of the working class to kill the other half," and the Royal House of Habsburg, one of the most powerful royal houses in European history.

[3] Not all oligarchs will fully diversify in accordance with finance theory of course but that's irrelevant for us as those who don't are simply making zero-sum intra-class portfolio bets. One will win and the other lose with no effect on the class as a whole.

Table 7: Gould and Habsburg Debt to Acquire Diversion

	($)	(€)	Total
Gould Debt	$300	€300	600
Habsburg Debt	200	200	400
Total Debt	$600	€400	1000

In Billions

Whereas the diversion sector has been split evenly between the nations, we'll suppose that corporate management has concentrated 60 percent of the population sector in Kaiserland. The income statement and trade balance categorized by nation is summarized in Table 8.

Table 8: Leymanville & Kaiserland Income Statement and Trade Balance

		L-ville ($)	K-land (€)	Total
	Income Statement			
	Diversion Sector			
a	Gould Diversion	$300	€300	600
b	Habsburg Diversion	200	200	400
c	Total Diversion	500	500	1000
d	Less: Diversion Wages	(250)	(250)	(500)
e	Net Profit Diversion Sector	250	250	500
	Population Sector			
f	L-ville Diversion Wage Rev	100	150	250
g	K-land Diversion Wage Rev	100	150	250
h	Net Population Sector Rev	0	0	0
i	Net Profit Population Sector	200	300	500
j	Net Profit	$450	€550	1000
k	Gould Split (60%)	270	330	600
l	Habsburg Split (40%)	180	220	400
	Trade Balance			
m	Gould Diversion in K-land	$(300)	€300	0
n	Habsburg Diversion in L-ville	200	(200)	0
o	Diversion Sector Trade Bal	(100)	100	0
p	L-ville wages spent in K-land	(150)	150	0
q	K-land wages spent in L-ville	100	(100)	0
r	Population Sector Trade Bal	(50)	50	0
s	Net Trade Balance	$(150)	€150	0

In Billions

As shown in row *e* above, diversion sector profits are the same in both nations. Kaiserland's population sector, though, receives 60 percent of total diversion wages (rows *f* and *g*) and is therefore more profitable (row *i*). We assume that staffing of population sector workers in both nations is such that they are a break-even (row *h*).

Because of the way the managers have divided total production, Leymanville has a trade deficit of $150 billion and Kaiserland a corresponding surplus of €150 billion (row *s*). The cross-border transactions involving the population sector—Leymanville workers using their dollar wages to buy goods in Kaiserland denominated in euros (row *p*) and Kaiserland workers using their euro wages to buy goods in Leymanville denominated in dollars (row *q*)—were handled via currency swaps, a routine service offered by the banking system. The net was a 50 billion swap from dollars into euros which represents the population sector trade deficit of Leymanville (row *r*).

Regardless of the trade balance between the nations, though, it's the oligarchic groups that are the actors and, as shown on rows *k* and *l*, each ends up with its ownership share of total profit in a currency mix determined by where production occurred.

The diversion-profit loop ends with the oligarchic groups repaying their debt to the banks as summarized in Table 9. Both execute currency swaps from euros to dollars summing to $50 billion, the exact reverse of that done to handle the population sector trade deficit.

Table 9: Gould & Habsburg Debt Repayment

	($)	(€)	Total
Gould:			
Debt	$(300)	€(300)	(600)
Repay from Profit	270	300	570
Repay from Swap	30	0	30
Net Position	0	0	0
Habsburg:			
Debt	$(200)	€(200)	(400)
Repay from Profit	180	200	380
Repay from Swap	20	0	20
Net Position	0	0	0
Oligarchy Position	$0	€0	0

In Billions

This is a basic exercise that ignores a host of real world complications but it shows the simplicity that underlies the basic pattern of the transnational system. Diversion is stable and it's irrelevant where production takes place or how the currencies are mixed. Regardless, both oligarchic groups receive their percentage interest in the whole and will have acquired their diversion at no cost. The currencies take on a transnational character that parallel the realities of ownership and production. The globally diversified oligarchy is indifferent to where production occurs because the system transcends the state and is inter-national only in a trivial sense. Inter-national statistics like the trade balance therefore have no important meaning.

This, though, flies in the face of the ideology of sound finance which insists that national trade balances are crucial numbers. It also seems at odds with Kalecki's profit equation which places the trade balance as an element of profit, net exports being an addition and net imports a subtraction.[4] It's not that Kalecki was wrong, however, it's that this part of his equation is based on a nation-state paradigm that's irrelevant given the wider scale of analysis.

In a transnational system, nation level trade deficits become meaningless because no matter where production takes place, profit will be divided amongst the oligarchs per their global ownership stake. This was demonstrated in Table 8 where we can see that while the location of production affected the profit allocated to the nations (row *j*), it had nothing to do with the final profit distribution going to the oligarchs (rows *k* and *l*) nor did it affect their ability to retire their debt (Table 9). It's possible that the Goulds or Habsburgs could incur something that resembled a trade deficit but it would only mean that its diversion spending exceeded what it recovered in profit and that it therefore either spent beyond its ownership power or wasn't properly diversified across the proper scale of the system. While bad news for the oligarchs involved, it isn't something that should trouble the rest of us.

Despite its lack of meaning, the inter-national trade balance plays a significant ideological role in the furtherance of suppression. In the example, we can imagine financial experts in both Leymanville and Kaiserland condemning the former's deficit and the failure of its workers to "live within their means." It's an effective storyline and it will be helpful to take a closer look at it.

According to orthodox economic theory, a trade deficit should be impossible over any intermediate term. The basic idea, taken from a supposed equilibrium mechanism conceived by David Hume in the eighteenth

---

[4] See appendix one for the full equation.

century,[5] is that market forces would drive the deficit country's currency value or wage rate down versus the surplus one and thereby bring trade into balance.

We lack a mechanism in our example, though, that would adjust currency values given that everything so tidily netted to zero (Table 9). The argument for a wage adjustment is on stronger ground and runs down the line that unemployment is higher in Leymanville because of the trade deficit and this will force its workers, out of sheer desperation, to accept less for their work. On the other hand, wages would rise in Kaiserland because of the trade surplus and the supposed extra demand for workers there. All this is a bit dubious, however, as we assumed high pre-existing unemployment in both nations and we could also expect at least some immigration into Kaiserland. But there's nevertheless a reasonable basis to think the threat of starvation could force workers into adjusting their wage demands.

Let's assume, then, that the equilibrium argument of the economists is correct and trade will eventually balance by reducing the wages of deficit country workers versus that of the surplus. Workers in the former will import less because they're poorer and export more to the latter who are now richer and everything will neatly sum to zero. Does this lead to a more optimal and efficient world? The economists say it does. It brings to all the splendid benefits of free trade which is both efficient and *Pareto optimal*,[6] a state of

---

[5] See Hume's *Of the Balance of Trade*. His equilibrium mechanism is known as the "price-specie flow."

[6] *Pareto optimality* or *Pareto efficiency* is a widely cited economic concept that's tightly aligned with the status-quo. It ignores the question of whether the pre-existing distribution of power is itself optimal and implicitly brands as sub-optimal any effort to change it. It's reasonable to believe this was Vilfredo Pareto's intent. He detested democracy and is often linked with fascism. "When Mussolini marched on Rome, the old Pareto is said to have risen from a sick-bed and utter a triumphant 'I told you so!'" (Landa 2010: 48). He favored a harsh Darwinian laissez-faire capitalism, one in which the weak would be brutally weeded out.

"All species of living beings would degenerate without the operation of selection. The human race cannot escape this law. Humanitarians may be able to close their eyes to this truth, deliberately ignoring it, but this can in no way alter the facts. In every race reject-elements are produced which must be eliminated by selection. The grief and suffering caused by this are the price which has to be paid for the improvement of the race. This is one of the many cases in which the good of the individual is in opposition to the good of the species." (As quoted in Landa 2010: 46)

affairs by which nobody could be made better off without making someone else worse off.

But this is efficient and optimal in a very strange kind of way. Stripped to its essentials, the equilibrium argument boils down to the proposition that unemployment is best cured through reductions in wages and/or increases in worker inequality. Wages in Leymanville are deemed either too high or those in Kaiserland too low or some combination of the two. As is always the case with orthodox economic advice, the pain falls on workers to the benefit of the oligarchy. That the population of Leymanville suffers by it is obvious but so also would that of Kaiserland.

Consider the inevitable chain of logic that flows from the medicine of the economists: 1) wages decline in Leymanville and employment is thereby increased at the expense of workers in Kaiserland; 2) workers in Kaiserland are thereby forced to reduce their pay to keep or regain their jobs and this results once again in losses of employment in Leymanville; 3) wages thereby further decline in Leymanville and employment is restored at the expense of workers in Kaiserland; 4) workers in Kaiserland are then forced again to reduce their pay to keep or regain their jobs . . . and so the spiral goes forever downward.

The nature of this poison is clear; it's the same price war logic that was rejected by the oligarchy at the turn of the twentieth century—it's a rat race to the bottom that benefits only the oligarchy in its collective goal of suppression. It's an example of the basic suppressionary method of forcing competition upon populations. The end result isn't only lower global wages, but reduced employment as well since the population sector will have been decimated because of the lower pay.

I conclude that both the equilibrium argument and the ideology of inter-national trade have no basis in a world of transnational ownership and massive productive capacity. The real issue isn't that production needs to be balanced between artificially drawn borders but that it be organized in a way that brings prosperity to everyone.

I note that in the example, populations of both nations are being suppressed and the socioeconomy is therefore in a state of gross Pareto sub-optimality. Their lot could be improved without making the oligarchs worse off in any direct material sense. The original transition to inequality some 15,000 years ago, we might add, was also most assuredly not Pareto optimal.

Suppression operates on a global scale and the defensive options available to populations at the nation-state level are limited. The most common means by which they try to ease their condition is through pressuring their state to increase spending. It's a routine dynamic worldwide and it's instructive to examine the ways by which the oligarchy overcomes it.

Suppose the population in Leymanville demanded that its state increase spending to alleviate high unemployment and poverty. The first hurdle within the logic of the global system would be that higher taxes on its resident oligarchy would be a complete non-starter. This isn't only because the Goulds would threaten to move themselves and their wealth out of the country, but also because any tax so levied would represent a straightforward transfer to the Habsburgs.[7] While the oligarchy as a class is the owner of the market portfolio and therefore doesn't pay taxes, tax rates within a nation that are above the global norm impose direct costs on local oligarchs. If Leymanville instituted such a tax and it continued to any significant degree, the Goulds would eventually be wiped out and Leymanville would become owned by the Habsburgs. There would end up not being a domestic oligarchy to tax at all, a euthanasia no oligarchic state could permit.

To illustrate, suppose the Leymanville state levied a $100 billion tax on the Goulds and spent it on poverty relief. The sum would enter the global market portfolio and would be output as profit, with 40 percent going to the Habsburgs and 60 percent to the Goulds. The functional result would be that the Habsburgs received $40 billion at the direct expense of the Goulds.

Unequal taxation of this kind is radically unsustainable and we must conclude it doesn't occur in the real world. Be it in the fine print of the tax laws or the willingness of state authorities to accept tax havens and fraud, oligarchic taxation must converge to the global norm.

Absent an unlikely global tax hike, the people of Leymanville will have no choice but to finance their $100 billion spending via a deficit. This too, though, faces near insurmountable hurdles as we shouldn't expect the global oligarchy to long accept any significant violation of the tenets of sound public finance.

---

[7] I assume here that the Leymanville population is operating within the rules of the game of oligarchy and isn't intending to confiscate oligarchic property in order to institute some form of socialism.

We've seen in Tables 7 through 9 that the basic diversion flow is stable and what makes it so is it comprises a closed loop of oligarchic spending. What is spent on diversion is returned as profit, the bank loans are repaid, and currencies net to zero. Leymanville's deficit, however, introduces instability into this tranquil picture by inserting 'excess' currency, i.e. currency over and above that used in the basic diversion flow.

The deficit enters the market portfolio, outputs as profit, and is shared by the two oligarchic groups in proportion to their ownership interest. At the end of the process, the Goulds and the Habsburgs will hold Leymanville state bonds of $60 billion and $40 billion respectively. (We can assume they acquired the bonds since their only other choice would be to let the currency sit in their non-earning deposit accounts.) The bonds serve no tangible purpose for either group, though, since the entire market portfolio was already owned before their issuance. They add nothing to the equation and aren't even real assets in the normal sense of the word since any ultimate repayment could only come at the expense of the oligarchs themselves. We're dealing with currency and there's no means by which it could be 'paid off' without taking it from somewhere else.[8]

The only real question for the combined oligarchy is how long to hold the excess before generating a crisis and thereby ending the poverty assistance. We need not hypothesize an actual closed door meeting here; all that's needed is the realization that the Leymanville deficits violate the most basic rules of the game and therefore must be put to an end. The issue will be ideologically presented as an inter-national problem but it's so only in a trivial sense; at root it's inter-class. Both oligarchic groups fear the rising prosperity of Leymanville and worry about the example it poses for Kaiserland. A currency or 'debt' crisis will eventually ensue and the populations of both nations will be taught a valuable lesson on the dangers of unsound public finance.[9]

A likely way it would happen is via a currency crash, a sharp rise in interest rates, a decline in the value of Leymanville debt, and much higher

---

[8] If the population were forced to pay, the oligarchy would reap lower profits in the population sector.

[9] Prior to the onset of the crisis we'd expect the most knowledgeable 'insiders' to dump the bonds onto the more gullible.

unemployment as a result of a collapse in 'business confidence.' [10] Mainstream economists will hail these occurrences as the outcome of their prized equilibrium mechanism and their predictable 'solution' will be to eliminate state aid, slash wages, and impose a balanced budget, all with strict international supervision.

Many accept this dynamic as the normal, efficient, and fair workings of the financial markets but the underlying reality is extraordinarily brutal. The poverty assistance imposed no cost to the oligarchic groups. They incurred no reduction in diversion and, while the bonds never had real value, they were obtained without a monetary expenditure. The rejection of the bonds, in short, is a rejection of poverty relief and it takes us to the heart of oligarchy—population output not only is unprofitable and lacks value, it's an existential risk. The experts will blame the crisis on excessive wages and unsound budget and trade deficits but this is nonsense. It was an action *provoked* by the oligarchy in service to its vital wealth defense* need that the population always and everywhere be suppressed.

There's only one acceptable means of helping the poorest in a nation and that's through the taxation of workers. In this way the overall prosperity of the population doesn't advance, oligarchic power is protected, the cost dynamic of taxation is reinforced, deficit spending doesn't occur, and various factions of the population are helpfully set against each other. Such taxes predominate throughout the world and take forms like the value added tax on consumption in Europe and sales, social security, and real estate taxes in the US.[11]

---

[10] It could also happen in a more bureaucratic manner as we've witnessed in the EU suppression of the European 'periphery.' In that case, the crisis would take all of the forms mentioned except that of a currency crash.

[11] The real estate tax can appear progressive since it's based on the value of the home but it's actually highly regressive to the extent it applies to non-existent wealth. Compare two families who put their life holdings into the purchase of their home, one $5,000 down for a $100,000 unit with the remainder financed and the other $500,000 down on a $1,000,000 home. If the tax rate is 1.5 percent of home value, then the effective wealth tax rate for the first family is 30 percent (tax of $1,500 / $5,000 wealth) while for the second, it's only 3 percent ($15,000 / $500,000). A far more equitable tax would be on wealth rather than real estate value with an equitable allowance for basic housing. As an example, a wealth tax rate of 3.27 percent would yield the same total tax revenue (total tax revenue of $16,500 / total wealth of $505,000 = 3.27%) and the poorer family's tax bill would drop from $1,500 to $163

The key issue in all this isn't global oligarchic taxation or deficit spending or 'unsustainable debt' or relative wage rates or trade deficits for none of these involve identifiable costs; it's rather that of denying the ability of populations to live better than the most optimal and efficient flow of diversion would otherwise require.

We gain a deeper sense as well that the value of any national currency within the global system is grounded in its observance of the suppressionary rules of sound public finance. The global acceptance of the British pound in the nineteenth century, for instance, integrally depended on its conservative monetary policies centered on a constricted democratic franchise. Likewise, the two major currencies of today, the dollar and the euro, are each backed by pro-oligarchic controls on population welfare and wouldn't long retain their global credence without them. In this way we can think of global currencies as transcending the state in the same way as does ownership. They must speak the language of oligarchy and that language has long been transnational.[12]

We've found in this chapter that the global market portfolio is stable as long as it sticks to its essential task of generating diversion output. The global population is a mere commodity locked inside it and the rules of the game continuously force it into submission. The ideological stories supporting this state of affairs revolve around the supposed dangers of trade deficits, budget deficits, excessive taxation, unsustainable debt, uncompetitively high wages, and the unquestioned need for workers to compete. Underlying them all is the myth of the parts and we've seen that it's untrue because the system is a global whole.

(3.27% x $5,000). It would drop even further if the tax rate were progressive and had a basic housing allowance.

[12] We may wonder about the dollar and the sustainability of the US budget and trade deficits. As we've discussed, though, the issue isn't trade or budget deficits for in themselves they're meaningless. The US state maintains the central position within the global oligarchy. It's playing a crucial role in trying to bring China and other nations of Asia into the Western dominated oligarchic system, is maintaining one of the stingiest welfare regimes in the world, is the global military power, and is leading the global movement to reduce oligarchic taxation and expand oligarchic principles. Of course its deficits and currency are widely accepted. We'd expect the value of the dollar to decline sharply though should a rogue populist government ever rise to office and attempt to increase social spending at a pace above that of the rest of the world.

It's laughable, in fact, to speak of populations as ever being in deficit for it's in reality always the opposite. They've instead, everywhere and for the entire span of civilization, been locked perpetually into a massive systemic surplus: forever being forced to export outside the market portfolio to that most ancient of systemic importers, the oligarchy.

The market portfolio is a gargantuan transnational diversion machine encompassing the world; the oligarchy owns it and requires it be used only to further its existential interests. Woe to national populations that dare interfere. Into it go orders from the globalized oligarchy in the form of any acceptable transnationalized currency, and from it come diversion and monetary profit in the form of those same currencies. It's simplicity itself and it can ultimately be reduced to something as basic as this:

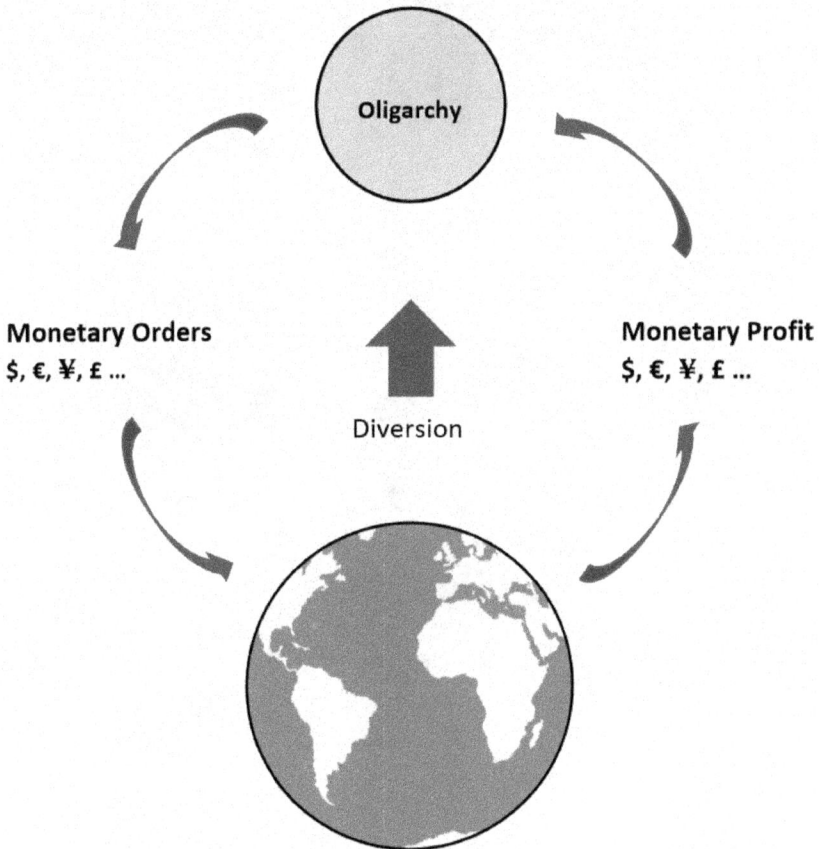

Oligarchy

Monetary Orders
$, €, ¥, £ ...

Diversion

Monetary Profit
$, €, ¥, £ ...

Figure 4: The Global Diversion-Profit Loop

11

The Grand Casino

The preceding chapters have presented a picture of an oligarchy that's the diversified owner of the market portfolio and thereby united in the collective business of rule. It's an important perspective as it eliminates the messy noise of inter-oligarchic strife and puts into vivid relief the fundamental class relation that's the heart of the system. The real world, of course, isn't so serene and this is because of the insatiable oligarchic thirst for relative power. Oligarchs are united as a class against populations but at the same time they're engaged in a Hobbesian contest of each against all that's the inescapable outcome of the primal motive of wealth defense*. Excluding war and imperialism, the central battlefield is in the grand casino of the financial markets.

Power in modern oligarchy is measured in terms of monetary wealth, a valuation assigned by the financial market on all claims to the profit streams that flow within the market portfolio. The values depend entirely on the perceived future earning capacity of the claim and oligarchs therefore devote enormous wealth defense* resources to trying to predict the future. It's a futile effort, though, for the future is unknowable to all except the insiders who have the power to manipulate it. "The outstanding fact," noted Keynes, "is the extreme precariousness of the basis of knowledge on which our estimates of prospective yield have to be made."[1] Valuations aren't based on knowledge of the future for that doesn't exist but rather on an ever-changing consensus formed by the mass psychology of the class. This consensus moves in a herd-like fashion with optimism breading further optimism and pessimism further pessimism in a feedback loop that billionaire oligarch George Soros has called "reflexivity."[2]

The fundamentals of the future can't be known and, as Soros notes, "lone investors who hitch their fortune to the fundamentals are liable to get trampled by the herd."[3] Many therefore give up on prediction and simply follow the existing trend with hopes of exiting before it reverses. *The trend is your friend* is their rallying cry and it's common wisdom on the casino floor. Patterns in historical prices are also studied in what's called "technical analysis" to help identify profitable entry and exit points. Both trend following and technical analysis are widespread wealth defense* strategies that Soros sees as reasonable. "Just as certain animals have good reasons to move in herds, so do investors."[4]

The herd dynamic of a mass psychology seeking to foresee what's unforeseeable leads to repeating cycles of bubbles and crashes. Bubbles are dynamical price progressions in which assets are purchased not for their rate of return but in the hopes they can be later resold at higher prices to someone else, "the greater fool."[5] Or, as Keynes put it, in hopes "to outwit the crowd, and to pass the bad, or depreciating, half-crown to the 'other fellow.'"[6] Ride the bubble, profit from it, and exit before collapse—that's the name of the game and it's the heart of Wall Street and of trading rooms everywhere. Any asset can serve as the casino chip: commodity exports, commodity imports,

---

[1] Keynes (1964, 149) He goes on to say "Our knowledge of the factors which will govern the yield of an investment some years hence is usually very slight and often negligible. If we speak frankly, we have to admit that our basis of knowledge for estimating the yield ten years hence of a railway, a copper mine, a textile factory, the goodwill of a patent medicine, an Atlantic liner, a building in the City of London amounts to little and sometimes nothing; or even five years hence. In fact, those who seriously attempt to make any such estimate are often so much in the minority that their behavior does not govern the market." (pp 149-150)

[2] Soros (2000, 58)

[3] Soros (2000, 64)

[4] Soros (2000, 64)

[5] Kindleberger & Aliber (2005: 13)

[6] Keynes (1964, 155)

agricultural land at home or abroad, urban building sites, railroads, new banks, discount houses, stocks, bonds, glamor stocks, conglomerates, condos, shopping centers, and office buildings.[7] To which we can add the food supply, insurance, and even tulips, one of the biggest bubbles of all going back to 1636. The wagers can be played in many ways and they almost always involve leverage[8]—put and call options, futures contracts, swaps, collateralized debt obligations (CDO's), credit default swaps (CDS's), arbitrage between financial instruments, and so on almost ad infinitum, all of which can be positioned from the long or short side.[9]

Bubbles and the crises resulting from them are endemic to oligarchy. They occurred at regular ten year intervals throughout a good part of the nineteenth century—1816, 1826, 1837, 1847, 1857, 1866, and 1873—and in the early twentieth in 1907, 1921, and 1929.[10] After a brief respite in the couple decades after World War II, the seventies saw a bubble in bank loans to Latin American countries leading to a massive debt and foreign exchange crisis in the early eighties. In the latter eighties, we saw the gigantic bubble in Japanese real estate and stocks and the failure of thousands of US savings and loans. The early nineties brought us the collapse of the junk bond market with losses (and gains to some) of over $100 billion along with the British exchange rate crisis of 1992 involving speculative attacks against the pound. Speculation in real estate and stock prices in Thailand, Indonesia, and other Asian countries led to the Asian Crisis of 1997 and the related currency crashes in Russia and Brazil. The Mexican peso crashed by more than half versus the dollar in 1994-95 leading to the collapse of almost all its banks. The close of the twentieth century brought the crash of the US stock bubble concentrated in the information technology and dot.com sectors and we're still dealing with the aftermath of the mortgage and debt collapse beginning in 2007.

One of the main challenges in this form of the wealth defense* game arises from the fact that a great deal of the profit streams within the market portfolio are illusory and therefore bound to reverse at some unknown point.

---

[7] Kindleberger & Aliber (2005: 17)

[8] Financing the bet through borrowed money.

[9] Buy or sell.

[10] Kindleberger & Aliber (2005: 24)

I present in Figure 5 below a schematic that attempts to shed some light on the situation using the two sector model.

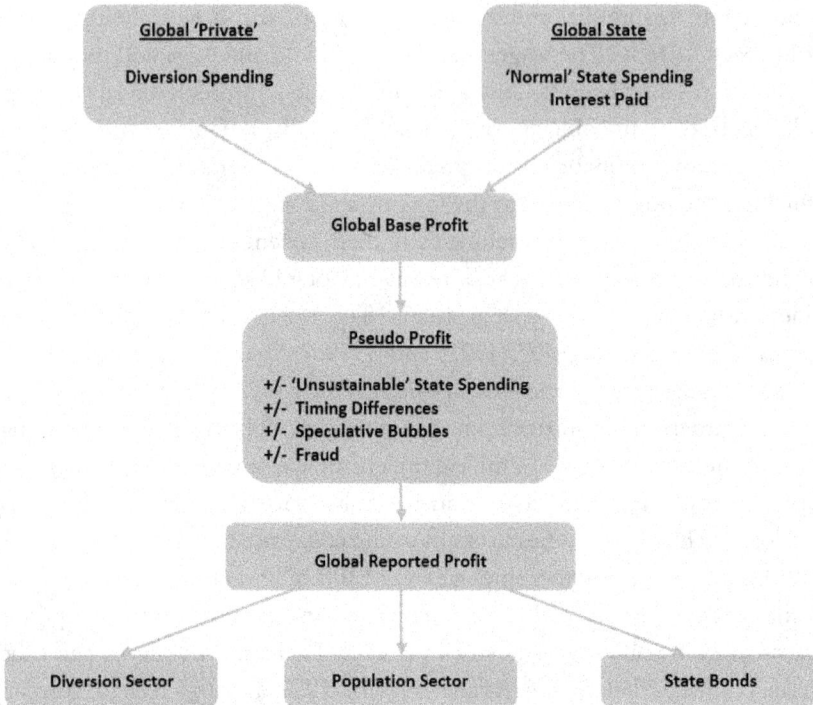

Figure 5: Real and Pseudo Profit

At the top of Figure 5 are the drivers of 'real' profit which I'll call *Global Base Profit*. It consists of 'private' diversion and 'normal' state spending along with whatever interest the state decides to pay. State spending is considered normal if it's more or less accepted by the oligarchy as being in line with sound public finance. Global Base Profit is for all intents and purposes a guaranteed sum and so there's minimal risk associated with it—it's simply the structurally determined return of what enters the market portfolio.

The profit that's reported, though, can differ substantially from the base as it includes such pseudo items as 'unsustainable' state spending, timing differences, speculative bubbles, and fraud. Unsustainable state spending is that which wouldn't be characterized as normal per above and would likely lead to future austerity. Timing differences, as discussed in chapter seven, are concentrated in the population sector and represent first stage profit that's destined for reversal in the second. We'll return to this along with speculative bubbles and fraud below. The sum of these items is added to Global Base Profit to yield *Global Reported Profit* which is output mainly as corporate profit or interest in either the diversion or population sector, or as interest on state bonds.

Almost all speculative bubbles can be traced to the dichotomy between real and pseudo profit illustrated in Figure 5. For an activity to be stable within the structure of oligarchy, it must lead to or support a consumption purchase by either the oligarchy or the state, the latter being so only to the extent it's 'financially sound.' Bubbles usually involve in one way or another a speculative rise in activities which directly or indirectly depend on the population for ultimate payment. This would include bubbles on real estate, stocks of firms selling to the population, loans to workers, and loans to states. As it's a fundamental principle of oligarchy that the population sector in and of itself can never be profitable, any profits that accrue outside the normal diversion flow are just timing differences that must reverse.[11]

Bubbles are driven by ever mounting credit and economist Hyman Minsky's *Financial Instability Hypothesis*[12] provides some added insight. Minsky categorized credit into three types: "hedge finance" where repayment can be made through normal cash flow; "speculative finance" where interest but not principal can be made out of regular cash flow; and "Ponzi finance" where regular cash flow is insufficient to meet either interest or principal and repayment depends on price appreciation. Credit advanced in the standard flow of diversion would always be sustainable and therefore classifiable as hedge finance. To the extent it's directed to speculative activities beyond normal diversion, though, and especially when it depends on the population for repayment, it will on the whole fail and should be classified as Ponzi finance.[13] A bubble in population housing, for example, would generate profit as new homes were constructed and loans extended that increased consumption spending. So also would expanding consumer debt. But these are examples of Ponzi finance since the loans and investments are just

---

[11] The state, however, always stands ready to bail out the system when needed.

[12] Minsky (1992)

[13] I emphasize "on the whole" as individual investments may succeed at the expense of others. Also, we should be clear that normal population sector activity in service to diversion is sustainable.

advances on future wages. Profits can be sustained only so long as new lending and investment continue at the elevated pace. When that ends, so does the bubble. Population consumption then falls as the loans are repaid and the investments will prove unprofitable to the population sector as a whole.

The key to success is to ride the game and exit at the last moment before the music stops. When it does, the Ponzi valuations collapse into thin air and all that remains is the fundamental value derivable from stable sources. For the winners, almost always the insiders, it's a glorious victory; only for the losers—the foolish oligarchs who didn't exit in time and the population—is it a crisis. As far as the population goes, though, we shouldn't overplay the idea of crisis for it carries the implication that the 'good-times' of the bubble were normal. If there were no speculative excess, the 'normal times' for the population would be far worse.

Bubble collapses are a means by which the size of the oligarchy is culled. As 'robber baron' Andrew Mellon allegedly said, "In a depression, assets return to their rightful owners." Recessions and depressions are not only functional for the insiders but also for the oligarchy as a whole in its relationship with the population. The hard times are viewed by business leaders, noted Domhoff, as a "saving grace" to "keep the expectations of workers in check."[14]

The world of the casino has become naturalized to an extraordinary degree; so much so that even notable authorities like economic historian Charles Kindleberger and economist Robert Aliber tell us we should think of its worst excesses as normal. We shouldn't be surprised by them, they say, because "Swindles, fraudulent behavior, defalcations, and elaborate hustles are part of life in market economies."[15]

The regularity of such events attests to the normality of casino logic but these observers surely err in identifying the culprit as market economies. There's little basis to think markets in and of themselves, absent the passion for unequal power, would be corrupt. This was one of Braudel's central points in his trilogy on capitalism. He argued that *the market* is very different from *capitalism*, the former being a place not of fraud and hustles but of openness and transparency in the sense of traditional town markets with the

[14] Domhoff (2006: 193-194). This is a quote from a CEO.
[15] Kindleberger & Aliber (2005: 166)

latter being a malevolent force that hovers above and controls and corrupts it. "It is the shadowy zone, hovering above the sunlit world of the market economy."[16] It sits on the "top floor" of the system and it seemed "diabolical to common mortals" even in the fifteenth century.[17] Capitalism to Braudel isn't the market, it's the "anti-market, where the great predators roam and the law of the jungle operates."[18] It's the realm of "gambling, risk-taking, cheating" where the "rule of the game was to invent a counter-game, to oppose the regular mechanisms and instruments of the market, in order to make it work *differently*—if not in the opposite direction."[19] Just a few wealthy merchants in sixteenth century Genoa or eighteenth century Amsterdam, he notes, "could throw whole sectors of the European or even world economy into confusion"[20] and the same power concentration exists today. The corruption that's part of life to Kindleberger and Aliber doesn't belong to "market economies" but to all economies within the structure of oligarchy. Only there do we enter the shadowy zone of swindles, fraud, defalcations and hustles.

"The inference from the historical record is that swindles are a response to the greedy appetite for wealth stimulated by the boom,"[21] they say; but we can take it a step further—the greedy appetites themselves are where the booms were born. They note that fraud is endemic and "many-faceted": "the directors swindle the stockholders, the senior management swindle the directors, the security underwriters swindle both the owners of the firms that they are bringing to the public and the stockholders, borrowers swindle the bank lenders, and one group of employees may swindle another."[22]

Fraud is indeed rampant in this great orgy, but we shouldn't use the word uncritically. The dictionary tells us it's "a deception deliberately practiced in order to secure unfair or unlawful gain."[23] We're quibbling with nuance here, though, when we consider that our long history has been rooted in systemic

---

[16] Braudel (1992: 24)

[17] Braudel (1992: 562)

[18] Braudel (1982: 230)

[19] Braudel (1982: 578) Italics in original.

[20] Braudel (1992: 24)

[21] Kindleberger & Aliber (2005: 20)

[22] Kindleberger & Aliber (2005: 187)

[23] The Free Dictionary. Online at http://www.thefreedictionary.com/fraud, accessed July 13, 2014

unfairness and that the laws themselves have been written, interpreted, and enforced by the winners. Fraud at bottom is just another technique of wealth defense* that, like all the rest, has its own particular risks and rewards.

We need not look far to find ample evidence of the immense popularity of this technique. Numerous accounting frauds were exposed at the beginning of the twenty-first century including such giants as Enron, Global Crossing, WorldCom, Tyco, Alephia, and Waste Management. Enron provides an excellent example of how fraud systemically extends beyond the corporate boundary. It wasn't just a case of Enron which filed for bankruptcy in late 2001, but of its accounting firm, Arthur Anderson, which certified its financial statements and was paid $52 million for mostly non-audit work in 2000; investment and commercial banks who were paid several million dollars in fees and had knowledge of questionable practices; the security analysts of these firms, the majority of whom rated Enron a "strong buy" or "buy" shortly before it collapsed; and the law firms and credit agencies which were paid substantial fees. The latter rated Enron's debt "investment grade" even after most of the negative news was out and the stock was trading at just $3 per share.[24] The mortgage and debt bubble that led to the global crisis beginning in 2007 was replete with similar kinds of fraud.

Bernie Madoff, former Chairman of the National Association of Securities Dealers (NASD), prominently swindled investors in his fraudulent hedge fund out of billions. Volkswagen is another good example. The world's second largest car manufacturer was caught red-handed programming its diesel engines to conceal the fact its emissions exceeded US standards by up to forty times.

Fraud amongst politicians is also rampant. Perry Anderson provides a "fresco" of recent political corruption in the EU; from sixteen year ruler of Germany Helmut Kohl, who accumulated two million deutsche marks in slush funds from illegal donors, to French president Jacques Chirac who was convicted of embezzling public funds, abuse of office, and conflicts of interest, to Germany's Gerhard Schröder whose government guaranteed a billion euro loan to a company weeks before he stepped down and joined the company, to a French minister for the budget who was discovered to have between €600,000 and €15 million in hidden accounts in Switzerland and Singapore, to French president Nicolas Sarkozy who is accused of receiving

---

[24] Albrecht (2005)

some $20 million from Muammar Gaddafi for the electoral campaign that took him to the presidency, and finally to Spanish Prime Minister Mariano Rajoy who is said to have received kickbacks totaling a quarter of a million euros over a decade, passed to him by his party's treasurer for twenty years who is now in prison for accumulating €48 million in undeclared Swiss accounts.[25] Similar paintings hang in the art galleries of every country on earth.

These kinds of frauds, though, are but the tip of the great iceberg of systemic moral fraud. Informal price collusion, misleading advertising, the power of money in corrupting democracy, and tax avoidance through legal tax havens are obvious examples. So also are the friendly ways corrupt governments throughout the world are treated. As Pogge observes, the core rich countries self-interestedly treat corrupt leaders as entitled to speak for their people. They're given the right to borrow in the people's name, buy weapons systems to keep themselves in power, sell national resources, and either put their hoards in rich country banks or hide them in legally sanctioned tax havens.[26] Such treatment is a central aspect of the global system and is as fraudulent as the leaders themselves.

This chapter has taken a cursory look at the inter-oligarchic wealth defense* struggle within the financial markets. These markets value wealth via an ever-changing class consensus on unknowable future events and this leads to repeating cycles of booms and busts. The booms are self-reinforcing and even oligarchs who believe they're witnessing a bubble are incented to hop on board to prevent their wealth from declining versus the rest of the class. The mass psychology of the financial market herd, like all of oligarchy, is a collective affair and can be opposed only at great risk.

An enormous level of resources are diverted to the casino game and it represents a horrific waste to the population. Its influence is so all-embracing that some have even defined the system itself as a casino. This is a significant overstatement, though, for it mistakes what's mere detail for the core. Speculation, bubbles, and fraud don't exist independently in and of themselves but derive from the motive of wealth defense* within the structural logic of inequality.

---

[25] Anderson (2014)
[26] Pogge (2008: 29)

12

Global Oligarchic Governance

Power in our world is defined by inequality. It, and not national governments, is what ultimately confines us, what circumscribes the range of the possible, and what imposes poverty and insecurity. What governs us are the rules of the global game of oligarchy and in this chapter we'll briefly examine how they play out in the modern system.

Inequality is a fractal-like phenomenon that shows itself at every scale. The unequal power that reigns over the planet's population is itself unequally distributed and is disproportionately weighted toward oligarchs from the US, other English speaking nations, and Western Europe. As we can see in Table 10 below, the US alone comprises just 4.5 percent of the global population but accounts for a full 31 percent of its billionaires, is home to 29.5 percent of its large corporations, possesses the dominant world currency, and overshadows all in military spending. If there's a global capital today, it's located in the US and the 'homeland' is the core West.

Table 10: Geographic Inequality of Oligarchic Power

	US	Other English	West European	Total Core	Remainder
Population	4.5%	1.8%	5.0%	11.3%	88.7%
Billionaires	31.0	6.4	13.9	51.3	48.7
Large Corporate Headquarters	29.5	10.6	20.6	60.6	39.4
Reserve Currency	63	8	23	93	7
Military	46	6	10	62	38

Billionaire data obtained from Forbes website[1]; Population data from Wikipedia[2]; Large corporate headquarters from McKinsey (2013, 22); Reserve currency from the IMF[3]; and Military spending from *Trends in World Military Expenditure*, 2013.[4] Military spending is the proportional share of the top 15 countries.

The disproportionate concentration of oligarchic power reflected above is rife with the potential for conflict. While political leaders routinely use calls to national patriotism to gain popular support, the causes of war and political tension almost never involve a true conflict between populations.[5] It's almost

---

[1] Mapping the Wealth of the World's Billionaires, online accessed March 9, 2013.
   www.forbes.com/sites/luisakroll/2013/03/09/mapping-the-wealth-of-the-worlds-billionaires/,accessed September 17, 2014
[2] Online accessed August 26, 2015.
   www.en.wikipedia.org/wiki/List_of_countries_and_dependencies_by_population
[3] Online accessed August 26, 2015.
   http://data.imf.org/?sk=E6A5F467-C14B-4AA8-9F6D-5A09EC4E62A4
[4] Sam Perlo-Freeman and Carina Solmirano, Stockholm International Peace Institute. Online accessed September 18, 2014:
   http://books.sipri.org/product_info?c_product_id=476
[5] Here's German Nazi leader Hermann Goering at the Nuremberg trials: "Why, of course, the people don't want war. Why would some poor slob on a farm want to risk his life in a war when the best that he can get out of it is to come back to his farm in one piece. Naturally, the common people don't want war; neither in Russia nor in England nor in America, nor for that matter in Germany. That is understood. But, after all, it is the leaders of the country who determine the policy and it is always

always a fight between oligarchic groups over the distribution of global power. Inequality is the cause of war and it's not inter-national but intra-class. The motive of wealth defense* ensures that oligarchs will perpetually seek to extend their share of power and the current arrangement happens to be the historically specific balance. We have no idea how long it will last for while history tells us that oligarchy itself is stable, the balances of power within it are always changing. Global governance today reflects the existing power relations between the global oligarchy and the global population and between oligarchic groups. Despite the disproportionate strength of oligarchs hailing from the core, the rules take into account the global distribution of power and offer benefits to all in accordance with their relative standing. They're therefore widely, if grudgingly, accepted.

The world of many nation-states can appear anarchic but that's not its essence for oligarchy is rarely anarchy; its normal condition is almost by definition the exact opposite—severe governance. We live in such a system today and it can be illuminating to think of it in terms of a global 'state.' A state, after all, isn't a 'thing' but a condensation of power relations; if production and ownership are transnational, then so must relations of power. *The transnational state* is a term coined by sociologist William Robinson who has applied it to "those institutions and practices in global society that maintain, defend, and advance the emergent hegemony of this global bourgeoisie and its project of constructing a new global capitalist historic bloc." The national state in this perspective "does not 'wither away' but becomes transformed with respect to its functions and becomes a functional component of a larger TNS."[6]

Regardless what it's called and despite ever-present intra-class tensions, the power structure expresses itself today through a collection of formal and

---

a simple matter to drag the people along, whether it is a democracy or a fascist dictatorship or a Parliament or a Communist dictatorship...Voice or no voice, the people can always be brought to the bidding of the leaders. That is easy. All you have to do is tell them they are being attacked and denounce the pacifists for lack of patriotism and exposing the country to danger. It works the same way in any country." As quoted in elise.com accessed July 28, 2016.

http://www.elise.com/quotes/hermann_goering_-_the_people_can_always_be_brought_to_the_bidding_of_the_leaders

[6] Robinson (2014: 68)

informal institutions, agencies, and practices. Its prime mission is wealth defense* and like the nation-state, its key job is "to maintain an order of stratification."[7] Stratification requires suppression, indeed it is suppression, and we'll devote the rest of the chapter to a cursory look at some of the ways it's been implemented.

I begin at the dawn of the postwar era when it became clear the US envisioned an oligarchic governance that would span the globe. One of its first key actions was the 1947 Marshall Plan which, while often praised for its supposed humanitarianism, was in actuality an instrument of suppression. The economies of Western Europe, observed historians Joyce and Gabriel Kolko, "were intentionally manipulated to lower living standards, create unemployment, and sharpen inequality."[8] To receive Marshall Plan aid, the US required European nations, with full support of local oligarchs, to balance their budgets, maintain low wages, and restrict state expenditures on social welfare. In standard fashion, "American administrators believed that it was essential to keep internal mass living standards at a low level in order to have a surplus for export and to limit imports so as not to upset further the balance of payments."[9] This set the pattern for future IMF macroeconomic adjustment programs as the first head of the ECB approvingly noted on the Marshall Plan's fiftieth anniversary in 1997.[10]

The IMF has been the primary postwar institution for managing balance of payment shortfalls and by the 1960s it had developed "a remarkably consistent recipe" for countries in financial trouble—ceilings on domestic credit, elimination of budget deficits, and higher interest rates. Added to the menu in the 1980s were "structural" elements like privatization, deregulation, trade liberalization, and the downsizing of the public sector.[11] The IMF and its sister agency the World Bank have consistently imposed austerity on poor countries throughout Latin America, Asia, and Africa and tens of thousands upward to perhaps a hundred thousand have been killed in anti-austerity protests. [12] Many more have undoubtedly died because of the policies

---

[7] Fried, M. (1967: 235) As originally quoted in chapter four. Fried is referring to the nation-state.

[8] Kolko (1972: 382)

[9] Kolko (1972: 429)

[10] Panitch & Gindin (2012: 96)

[11] Peet (2009: 12-14)

[12] Peet (2009: 104)

themselves. (Appendix four takes a further look at these programs.) The motivations driving these actions are often presented in terms of "First World control over Third World economic policy"[13] but this is misleading given that the local oligarchs have almost always supported the interventions. Imperialist power grabs have undoubtedly been part of it but the driving force seems less that than vertical oligarchic control over populations.

The IMF and World Bank are overseen by the US Treasury Department. Their policies are meant to apply globally and have been enforced domestically in the US with the same gusto as abroad. The near bankruptcy of New York City in 1975 is a case in point. The US Treasury extended loans to the poverty ravished city but provided them on terms described by Treasury Secretary Simon as "so punitive, the overall experience so painful, that no city, no political subdivision would ever be tempted to go down the same road." Committees "dominated by bankers framed the loan conditions on the basis of the policies that later became widely identified with neo-liberalism—a concept of fiscal rectitude that rejected higher taxes and instead cut social programs, froze wages, and privatized public services and assets."[14] The people of New Orleans, Detroit , Flint, Michigan, and Puerto Rico are among the most visible US recipients of such treatment in more recent years but it's manifested everywhere in the ready recognition by public officials that it's fruitless to oppose in any meaningful way the logic of financial governance.

The basic suppressionary package was famously coined *The Washington Consensus* in 1990 by economist John Williamson.[15] While his well-known article dealt with Latin America, it has a much broader application as an enumeration of the basic rules of sound public finance within the 'transnational state' of modern oligarchy. Fiscal deficits over one or two percent of GDP are a "policy failure," the national tax base should be broad with "moderate" marginal tax rates, interest rates should exceed inflation, national borders should be kept open with an "outward orientation" to imports and foreign direct investment, privatizations of public assets are encouraged, and property rights enforced. There has been talk over recent years of a kinder, gentler *post-Washington Consensus* but it differs only at the

---

[13] Peet (2009: 82)

[14] Panitch & Gindin (2012: 165)

[15] Williamson (1990)

margins, and its break from laissez-faire neoclassical economics "can only be exaggerated."[16]

The "outward orientation" aspect is codified today by the World Trade Organization (WTO) to which almost all nations belong. Like all global oligarchic institutions, the WTO is "anti-labor" and, despite its central mission of trade, "has no worker-oriented policies, despite a vague commitment to 'observe' core labor standards, or even a mechanism for discussing workers' rights and employment standards or any interest in doing anything to help desperate people in export-oriented plants."[17] "It is a nasty organization run by directors and a secretariat that propagate rightist elitism in the guise of consumer populism."[18] Like other agencies, it generates reviews of member countries and the results "always follow the same model, using a nearly identical language": "good" being "openness, liberalization, export orientation, structural reform, deregulation, privatization, competiveness, macroeconomic soundness, stability, flexibility, simplification, prudence and, best of all, 'rationalization'—that is, determination of the direction taken by an economy by purely market processes."[19]

Property rights are sacrosanct throughout the transnational system. It's settled international law, notes law professors Christian Tietje and Freya Baetens, that the state may not expropriate an alien's property without adequate compensation. What's subject to debate is only the meaning of "indirect expropriation"[20] and this is argued on firmly Lockean ground with the presumption in favor of the natural right to property. International law as it exists today, according to Tietje and Baetens, permits the state to regulate for the public interest only "so long as the regulation serves a legitimate purpose, strikes a proportionate balance between the protection of the investor's investment and the public interest, and does not substantially interfere with a specific investor's property rights."[21]

---

[16] Fine, Lapavitsas, & Pincus (2001: 6)

[17] Peet (2009: 221-222)

[18] Peet (2009: 259)

[19] Peet (2009: 202)

[20] Tietje & Baetens (2014: 49-50)

[21] Tietje & Baetens (2014: 56)

These globally enforceable rights have been solidified over the past few decades through a couple thousand bilateral investment treaties (BIT's) which guarantee oligarchs the right to transfer property and proceeds out of host countries, to protection against expropriation, and to sue host governments in private arbitration panels if they feel their rights have been violated.[22] The latter is referred to as *Investor State Dispute Settlement* (ISDS) and it's included in 93 percent of all BIT's[23] and in such multilateral treaties as the North American Free Trade Agreement between Canada, the US, and Mexico (NAFTA), the Comprehensive Economic and Trade Agreement between Canada and the EU (CETA), the Central American Free Trade Agreement which expands NAFTA to Guatemala, Honduras, El Salvador, Costa Rica, Nicaragua, and the Dominican Republic (CAFTA), and the yet to be ratified Transatlantic Trade and Investment Partnership between the US and EU (TTIP) and the Trans-Pacific Partnership between the US, Australia, Brunei Darussalam, Canada, Chile, Japan, Malaysia, Mexico, New Zealand, Peru, Singapore, and Vietnam (TPP).

The transnational rights of property are the rights of oligarchy and they're the foundation of a postwar international law that owes its creation to the US state. Finding itself with a near monopoly of power at the end of World War II, it sought to "restructure the world so that American business could trade, operate, and profit without restrictions everywhere."[24] Its role, though, has gone far beyond a narrow nationalist vision. The US defends the greater transnational system and it's in this role that it has gained the support of oligarchs almost everywhere.

While the global position of the US state is new, its basic agenda of defending oligarchic power long predates the war. Consider for example this description of US intervention in Latin America in the early twentieth century made by Congressional Medal of Honor winner, Major General Smedley D. Butler in 1935.

I spent thirty-three years and four months in active service in the country's most agile military force, the Marines. I served in all ranks from second Lieutenant to Major General. And during that period I spent most of my

---

[22] Yackee (2014: 491)
[23] Tietje & Baetens (2014: 25)
[24] Kolko (1972: 2)

time being a high-class muscle man for Big Business, for Wall Street and the bankers. In short, I was a racketeer, a gangster for capitalism.

I suspected I was just part of a racket at the time. Now I am sure of it. Like all members of the military profession I never had an original thought until I left the service. My mental faculties remained in suspended animation while I obeyed the orders of the higher-ups. This is typical with everyone in the military service. Thus I helped make Mexico, and especially Tampico, safe for American oil interests in 1914. I helped make Haiti and Cuba a decent place for the National City Bank boys to collect revenue in. I helped in the raping of half-a-dozen Central American republics for the benefit of Wall Street. The record of racketeering is long. I helped purify Nicaragua for the international banking house of Brown Brothers and Co. in 1909-1912. I brought light to the Dominican Republic for the sugar interests in 1916. I helped make Honduras 'right' for American fruit companies in 1903. In China in 1927 I helped see to it that Standard Oil went its way unmolested.[25]

Violence has always been synonymous with oligarchy and it has played a significant role in the global racket that's today's version of it. "The US state houses the ministry of war in a much divided global elite cabinet,"[26] observes Robinson, and its violent actions, direct and indirect, overt and covert, since World War II have encompassed the entire planet. I summarize some better known ones in Table 11 below.[27] The common denominator is that they were attacks against regimes which were posing threats to the global oligarchic project. Untold millions have been killed.

---

[25] Common Sense Magazine 1935. Taken from the *School of Cooperative Individualism* website.
     www.cooperativeindividualism.org/butler-smedley_i-was-a-gangster-for-
     capitalism-1935.html, accessed December 8, 2014
[26] Robinson (2014: 122)
[27] A very helpful compilation of US interventions is Blum (2004)

Table 11: Well-known Postwar US Interventions

1940s

China	Greece		

1950s

Cambodia	Cuba	Guatemala	Indonesia
Iran	Korea	Laos	Syria
Vietnam			

1960s

Bolivia	Brazil	Cambodia	Chile
Congo	Cuba	Dom. Rep.	Ecuador
Ghana	Greece	Guatemala	Haiti
Indonesia	Laos	Panama	Peru
Uruguay	Vietnam		

1970s

Afghanistan	Angola	Bolivia	Cambodia
Chile	Cuba	E. Timor	Greece
Grenada	Guatemala	Jamaica	Laos
Nicaragua	Panama	Uruguay	Vietnam

1980s

Afghanistan	Angola	Cuba	El Salvador
Grenada	Guatemala	Haiti	Jamaica
Nicaragua	Panama		

1990s

Afghanistan	El Salvador	Haiti	Iraq
Kosovo	Nicaragua	Panama	

Post 2000

Afghanistan	Iraq	Mid-East	

The threat is internal as well and one of the state's most important duties is the ongoing surveillance and control of its population. These tasks are normally kept secret since they run counter to democratic notions of popular sovereignty, but a rare peek inside this dark world was provided in the mid-seventies by the so-called *Church Committee*.[28] Forced by the popular pressures of the time, this committee of the Senate investigated US intelligence

---

[28] The formal name was the *Senate Select Committee to Study Governmental Operations with Respect to Intelligence Activities*.

practices and ended up issuing fourteen separate reports that documented widespread government surveillance of the population through secret informants, wiretaps, mail openings, and break-ins. Among many disclosures, it revealed that the CIA and FBI opened hundreds of thousands of first class letters, the National Security Agency (NSA) intercepted millions of private telegrams, and the US Army carried out domestic surveillance. [29] The committee reported that the FBI engaged in a wide assortment of "unsavory and vicious tactics" against civil rights groups, an undefined "New Left,"[30] and others that included attempts to break marriages, disrupt meetings, ostracize individuals from their professions, and provoke rivalries within groups. [31] The FBI's infamous COINTELPRO (Counter Intelligence Program) that began in 1956 and lasted until its public disclosure in 1971, wasn't in fact a counter intelligence program, but rather a "covert action" program[32] having "The unexpressed major premise [that] a law enforcement agency has the duty to do whatever is necessary to combat perceived threats to the existing social and political order."[33] Federal law enforcement looked upon themselves, the report concludes, as "guardians of the status quo."[34]

State security agencies throughout the world have been similarly diligent in opposing all elements that could pose a threat to the oligarchic order. Latin America has had a particularly energetic left and covert action there has thus been more violent. Political murder carried out by the state or its proxies has been one of the prime weapons throughout the region and it has been brandished against anyone seen as sufficiently subversive—against "popular leaders of mass political movements, politically minded former

---

[29] *Senate Select Committee to Study Governmental Operations with Respect to Intelligence Activities*, Book II, "Intelligence Activities and the Rights of Americans", p. 6. All reports can be found online at the Mary Ferrell Foundation, accessed September 2, 2015:

http://www.maryferrell.org/archive/docsets/1014/index.html

[30] According to the FBI agent in charge of New Left intelligence, "It has never been strictly defined, as far as I know. . . . It's more or less an attitude, I would think." (Book II, p. 72)

[31] Book II, p. 5

[32] *Senate Select Committee to Study Governmental Operations with Respect to Intelligence Activities*, Book III, "Supplementary Detailed Staff Reports on Intelligence Activities and the Rights of Americans", p. 4.

[33] Book III, p. 3

[34] Book III, p. 7

revolutionaries and demobilized guerillas, pesky agitators, intellectuals, artists, journalists, academics, subversive activists and ambitious labor organizers, troublesome lawyers, prosecutors and judges, and even crusading priests and nuns."[35]

Especially infamous was Operation Condor, a top secret assassination program against the left from the mid-seventies through the early eighties that originated in Pinochet's Chile and included the military regimes of Argentina, Uruguay, Brazil, Paraguay, Peru, and Bolivia. With US backing, these governments coordinated their intelligence using the latest technology and ended up murdering tens of thousands.[36] Argentina was seen as the expert in death squads and the techniques it refined during its Dirty War of the same period were exported and adopted throughout Central America, again with US support.[37]

Historian W. John Green observes that political murder is a valuable tool of power and that the main reason the last couple of decades in Latin America have been quieter is that the key goals have been achieved.[38] The real metric in judging its effectiveness, he states, isn't the number killed but whether the resulting terror has dampened the democratic spirit.[39] He notes that military and paramilitary death squads have been and still are "nowhere and everywhere,"[40] a point strikingly like the one made by Karen Ho about finance as quoted in chapter six—that part of the power of finance is its "seeking to be everywhere and claiming to be nowhere." We're indeed dealing with the same underlying phenomenon.

While many in the US and Europe believe their resident oligarchs are innately more peaceful than those in Latin America, it's a difficult assumption to sustain. Formal democracy is more established in the core regions but the motives of power are the same everywhere and the American and European oligarchs are surely not lacking in zeal. They have had less need to use violence in suppressing their populations since methods like restrictive laws,

---

[35] Green (2015: 2)

[36] The exact number killed is unknown. Some estimate at least 60,000. https://en.wikipedia.org/wiki/Operation_Condor#cite_note-8, accessed July 28, 2016

[37] Green (2015: 172)

[38] Green (2015: 186)

[39] Green (2015: 178)

[40] Green (2015: 181)

electoral manipulation, propaganda, surveillance, and covert action have been effective. The US and European states have supported political murder throughout the world, though, and undoubtedly stand ready to defend property rights within their borders with at least the same enthusiasm they have exhibited outside them.[41]

We've recently discovered, thanks to the brave disclosures of US government contractor Edward Snowden, that the state's surveillance power has reached unprecedented proportions. As the German magazine Der Spiegel has noted, the possibility now exists for "the absolute surveillance of a country's people." The magazine observes that what's most important about these revelations is that there's a "division of duties and at times extensive cooperation" between national spy agencies with each aiding the others in spying on their citizens.[42] Like everything in modern oligarchy surveillance is transnational.

Massive surveillance makes little sense outside the paranoid logic of oligarchy. The fear of communism was the claimed driver during the Cold War but the real threat was never that of attack but rather of a radically anti-oligarchic philosophy.[43] The great surveillance and military expansion since September 11 is opportunistic and reasonably explainable only through a combination of the oligarchic drive to dominate the resources of the Middle East and a reflexive fear of populations everywhere.

We have barely touched the surface of global governance in this chapter but the evidence is overwhelming that it's of a kind that can produce only one result—a planet of widespread poverty, insecurity, and violence. In the face of massive productive capacity, this is the horrid actuality of our world. We've grown so accustomed to the systemic logic of finance, diversion, suppression, violence, surveillance, speculation, bubbles, crashes, fraud and

---

[41] See Green (2015: 204-207)

[42] July 1, 2013, "How the NSA Targets Germany and Europe", *Speigel Online International*, p. 1. Online accessed September 2, 2015:
http://www.spiegel.de/international/world/secret-documents-nsa-targeted-germany-and-eu-buildings-a-908609.html

[43] J. Edgar Hoover, the "Founding Father of American intelligence and architect of the modern surveillance state," seems to have admitted as much. "Communists and most subversive activities are always attached to labor situations. It's a practical impossibility to divorce Communism from labor situations." Weiner (2012: xv,52-53)

corruption that it all seems part of the natural order. But these have nothing to do with nature, they're all manifestations of the drive for unequal power.

The Adams Maxim tells us that power resides in ownership and our real rulers, therefore, aren't the politicians but the oligarchy. How easily we ignore the key significance of this timeless fact, though, for if we took it to heart, we'd quickly arrive at the realization we live in a very unnatural tyranny not so very different from that of the Roman emperors of old and we wouldn't be so sanguine about being governed by what amounts to an armed band of thugs who devote their luxury soaked days to our suppression and dreams of grandeur via war, idle speculation, and fraud. We're not dealing with a 'thing' called capitalism here; the system is inequality and its essentials have remained constant throughout all of civilization.

Conclusion

This book is founded on the proposition that our socioeconomic system is fundamentally simple. Its simplicity derives from a stark civilization spanning asymmetry of material power in which tiny minorities have possessed virtually everything and the vast majorities almost nothing. We're dealing with raw power and it's been concentrated to such a degree it renders all else superfluous. When it comes to the essence of our social world, there's really nothing more to say—the system, plain and simple, is oligarchy.

It's remarkable how much clarity is gained once we accept this simple definitional starting point. The hostile logic of oligarchy flows necessarily out of the mere existence of inequality and this is so regardless of the means by which the minority obtains power. Even if done in some 'meritorious' way, it would still in the end be a structure of rule in which an empowered minority reigns in accord with the dynamics of diversion and suppression and thereby subjugates the majority. Inequality, however formed, is always tyranny.

A tyranny, though, that in a democratic culture must be ideologically camouflaged behind a suitable world-picture. Capitalism's function within it is to present in an acceptable light the operating details of modern oligarchy. It speaks mostly in the language of money and finance, expressing the key rules of the game in terms of tokens and financial efficiency. It's rooted in an individualistic ideology in which each person is conceived as a self-contained atom concerned with personal rather than collective goals and free to claim whatever his or her powers can obtain in the unfettered jungle of competition. He or she has a "natural" right to whatever property is thus accumulated and the propertyless population has no standing to interfere. By this sleight of hand, extraordinarily concentrated power becomes synonymous with liberty and democracy reduced to the "tyranny of the majority."

The goal of this book has been to explain capitalism as oligarchy and not to present a vision of a post-oligarchic world. To lay out a blue print would be an immense and probably fruitless undertaking given that no such system has existed in the entire history of civilization. We can, however, get a sense of an egalitarian democracy's basic nature by simply reversing the key logic brought out in the preceding chapters. I do this in Figure 6 below.

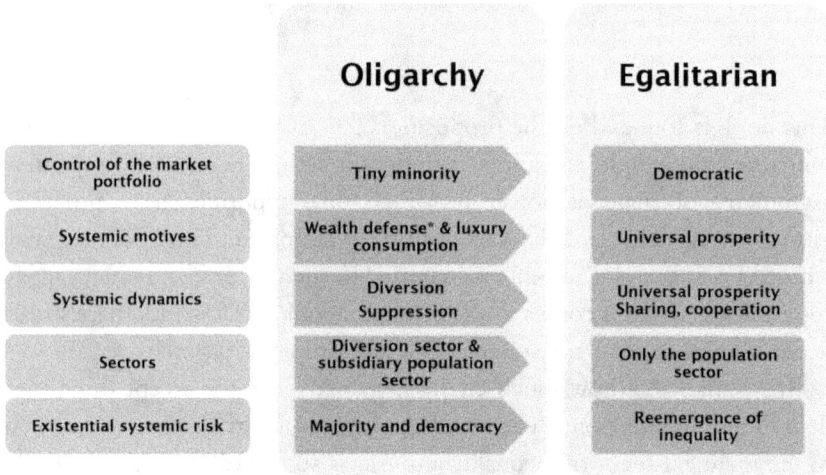

	Oligarchy	**Egalitarian**
Control of the market portfolio	Tiny minority	Democratic
Systemic motives	Wealth defense* & luxury consumption	Universal prosperity
Systemic dynamics	Diversion Suppression	Universal prosperity Sharing, cooperation
Sectors	Diversion sector & subsidiary population sector	Only the population sector
Existential systemic risk	Majority and democracy	Reemergence of inequality

Figure 6: Transition from Oligarchy to an Egalitarian System

Starting with the control of the market portfolio, it's likely that transferring it to democratic hands would be far simpler than we might expect since corporations are tightly consolidated and their ownership widely disbursed. The market portfolio consists of a relative handful of firms and the owners are mostly absentee stockholders playing no role in management. Corporations aren't dependent on the technical owners and it would be a virtual non-event if the current crop of stockholders were magically replaced overnight by some random selection of the population. Stock shares, after all, are traded every day as part of the routine operation of the financial market and mergers and acquisitions occur with minimal effect. In a similar fashion, the state has a great deal of experience taking over failed banks and it's a routine process in which most employees continue their work as if nothing had happened. There would be a myriad of details but it's reasonable to conclude that the act of taking possession of the firms inside the market portfolio wouldn't be a major disruption to anyone but the oligarchs.

Absent the minority's ownership of the market portfolio, everything that supports oligarchy collapses. Wealth loses all meaning and the motives of wealth defense* and luxury consumption, along with the dynamics of diversion and suppression, become nothing but shameful relics of a brutal past. The diversion sector would be eliminated and in its place would rise an expanded population sector designed to assure sustainable prosperity for all.

The existential risk to an egalitarian system would of course not be the propertyless majority as it has always been in oligarchy, it would rather be that inequality would reemerge. To prevent this will require we re-learn what our ancestors knew throughout most of our history and what current hunter-gatherers still do know—that the accumulative urge of the aggrandizer must continuously be brought "back to earth."[1] This applies not only at the societal level but to each of us personally. The state must be altered as well. Traditional representative forms of democracy have proven inadequate (and were designed that way) and would have to be replaced by transparent, locally responsible institutions providing strong protections that secure the public interest. The military/surveillance state is an exceptional danger and will need to be dismantled.

The disease is inequality and almost every single social problem that exists—war, racism, poverty, environmental degradation, crime, exploitation, political corruption, fraud, insecurity, lack of freedom—can be traced to it. The only possible cure is equality. This has to be the guiding principle for a just society, not only because true freedom and prosperity demand it, but because the history of our species has shown how dangerous inequality has been. There's little open ground here, for to allow oligarchy to survive in a somewhat reformed state only guarantees its eventual resurgence in a more virulent form.

---

[1] Erdal & Whiten (1996: 145)

Aristotle wrote 2,500 years ago that "if the members of an oligarchy agree among themselves the state isn't very easily destroyed without some external force."[2] This truth is amplified when we define oligarchy not in terms of a government, as did Aristotle, but as material inequality itself, the central structural constant spanning all of civilization. It most certainly won't be easily destroyed. The oligarchy today possesses the totality of the means of production through its ownership of the market portfolio and controls the key institutions of the state. It exercises power over individual careers and life chances and thus imposes an immense pressure to conform. Its reach oozes into every corner of society to the point where much of the population reflexively supports its ideologies. Any hope of destroying such an immense structural force depends on undermining its world-picture and thereby forming an anti-oligarchic majority.

Is it possible that peaceful democratic means could euthanize a power as ancient as oligarchy? We're in unchartered territory here as the ungainly liberal creation that's democratic oligarchy has never been put to such a test. Its central landmark is the great wall between 'politics' and 'economics' and we don't know if it could peacefully be torn down. Does capitalism (oligarchy) exist today by democratic consent or coercion? The answer is both but it's impossible to find the dividing line. Majorities probably consent, but it has to a very large degree been ideologically manufactured, i.e. coerced, through the many powers inherent to inequality. If majorities in the core West came to no longer consent, would more violent forms of coercion then ensue? We don't know. It seems most unreasonable to believe, however, that democracy could easily be expanded into the territory reserved for oligarchy given the ancient power involved and the near-religious character it takes. The fight isn't about policy but about incompatible versions of freedom; for those opposing it, egalitarianism (democracy) isn't only wrong, it's an elementary violation of natural law, a law that trumps the collective will. The people in this view have no legitimacy and are therefore always feared and loathed. The loss of a power once had is a form of death unlikely to be accepted absent the force of an overwhelming and determined majority.

Should a realistic threat of an unfriendly majority ever arise, and I believe it must, we should expect the foundations to tremble. The oligarchy has an unlimited ability to spend and its power for overt and covert violence and

---

[2] Aristotle (2012: book V, ch VI, 1306a)

propaganda is immense. I hope I'm wrong, but a great civil war seems a real possibility, one in which each side sees the other as intrinsically evil. The battle lines wouldn't be between nations but would rather be internal to each of them. The system is global and so also would be the war.

Three possibilities seem to exist here: i) we never achieve a majority and thereby endlessly submit to oligarchic domination; ii) we assemble a majority and attempt peaceful democratic change with the knowledge we may need to deal with violent resistance; or iii) we form an overwhelming majority and dethrone oligarchy in a peaceful manner. I reject the possibility of the first, would accept the second, and hope for the third. The fight is ultimately about the meaning of freedom and few causes could be nobler.

Freedom is a favored word in the oligarchic vocabulary but the question is always "freedom for whom?" The freedom of wealth to advance its power is a radical one that permits it to rule tyrannically over large majorities. It's the logic of the jungle and for most it's not freedom but oppression. As nineteenth century ecclesiastic Jean-Baptiste Lacordaire put it—"Between the strong and the weak, between the rich and the poor, between the lord and the slave, it is freedom which oppresses and the law which sets free." Everywhere we look today we find freedom—in business we have *free trade*, *free enterprise*, and *freedom of contract*; in politics, we have *free speech*, *free elections*, and a *free press*; in finance we have *free capital mobility*, and to economists, we have *free markets*. The world is bursting with freedom yet so many aren't free in any significant sense of the word. Lacordaire is an important reminder that the fight is about differing versions of it and that between oligarchy and democracy, one side's freedom is the other's oppression. Where we place ourselves in this essential divide is the key political and moral decision each of us must make.

Oligarchy is a staggeringly powerful force; a massive castle built and solidified over thousands of years. We the population have been made subhuman and ignoble, living not in and for ourselves but as the unprofitable scaffolding serving the higher goals of an alien-like elite. We in our ignorance look up to this parasitic power with respect and even love; we adore our monarchs, marvel at the ornate presidential palaces, worship undemocratic constitutions, accept poverty and insecurity as inevitable, parrot rudimentary economics as if it were the pinnacle of wisdom, study the philosophers who despise us, fight in oligarchic wars, work for oligarchic businesses, and incorporate within ourselves the unequal values of oligarchy. We've become what the structure demands.

I ended the intermission on page 137 with a reference to the view that the state's only legitimate role revolves around protecting the Lockean natural right to life and ownership. The final dozen words were taken from the finale of Robert Nozick's influential magnum opus *Anarchy, State, and Utopia* and I bring them back again here:

"How *dare* any state or group of individuals do more. Or less."[3]

Nozick is offering us a defiant philosophic display of the root animosity and fundamental incompatibility between minority ownership and democracy. One can only marvel at the gaping and unbridgeable chasm. He, in full company with the right-libertarian and conservative traditions, denies the right of the people to choose in these matters. "How *dare* they!" he says, bearing his 5,000 year fangs. This ancient assertion of untouchable power is aggressively antisocial and utterly undemocratic. It can't be reasoned with for it appeals not to human consensus but to a divine-like natural law. It can only be accepted or confronted.

I close this book by choosing confrontation. How *dare* these modern day lords assert ownership of our planet; how *dare* they use their fellow man for their self-aggrandizement; how *dare* they impose poverty and insecurity to protect and advance their power.

How *dare* they!

---

[3] Nozick (1974: 334) Italics in original.

Appendices

Appendix 1: Profit and Diversion Equations

I present in this appendix the derivation of the condensed version of Kalecki's profit equation and show also that the "diversion equation" can be derived in the same way. The complete Kalecki equation is:

Gross Profit Net of Tax = Gross Investment + Export Surplus + Budget Deficit - Worker Savings + Capitalist Consumption[1]

The condensed version is:

Profit = Capitalist Consumption + Investment

It flows from the complete equation when we assume a closed economy with no foreign trade, taxes, or state spending, that the sole income of workers is the wage, and they are unable to save. Gross profit is defined as the sum of profit, depreciation, rent, and interest. The derivation of this condensed version along with that of the diversion equation is presented in Table 12 below.

---

[1] Kalecki (1971: 82)

Table 12: Derivation of Profit and Diversion Equations

Kalecki Equation	Diversion Equation
Profit = Capitalist Consumption + Investment	*Profit = Diversion*
Applicable time period for an investment: Specified accounting period, commonly a year.	Applicable time period for an investment: Its entire life.
Purpose: To understand how profit is generated in an accounting period.	Purpose: To highlight the essential class nature of the modern system and to show that the population sector isn't profitable.
1. GNP can be thought of as the sum of consumption and gross investment: *GNP = Consumption + Investment*	1. GNP can be thought of as the sum of consumption and gross investment: *GNP = Consumption + Investment*
2. We can expand consumption into 2 components: *Capitalist Consumption and Worker Consumption.*	2. We can expand consumption into 2 components: *Oligarchic Consumption and Population Consumption.*
3. We then rewrite equation 1 as: *GNP = Capitalist Consumption + Worker Consumption + Investment*	3. We then rewrite equation 1 as: *GNP = Oligarchic Consumption + Population Consumption + Investment*
	3a. We can expand investment into 2 components depending on the ultimate beneficiary: *Oligarchic Investment + Population Investment*
	3b. We rewrite equation 3 as: *GNP = Oligarchic Consumption + Oligarchic Investment + Population Consumption + Population Investment*
4. GNP can also be considered the sum of capitalist gross profit plus the worker wage so that: *GNP = Profit + Wage*	4. GNP can also be considered the sum of oligarchic gross profit plus the population wage so that: *GNP = Profit + Wage*

5. We link 4 and 3 and get: *Profit + Wage = Capitalist Consumption + Worker Consumption + Investment*	5. We link 4 and 3b and get: *Profit + Wage = Oligarchic Consumption + Oligarchic Investment + Population Consumption + Population Investment*
	5a. Since population investment, by definition, will eventually be consumed by the population, we merge it with population consumption. We restate equation 5 as: *Profit + Wage = Oligarchic Consumption + Oligarchic Investment + Population Consumption*
	5b Since diversion is the sum of oligarchic consumption plus oligarchic investment, we restate equation 5a as: *Profit + Wage = Diversion + Population Consumption*
6. Since the wage is assumed identical to worker consumption, we eliminate it on both sides and get the Kalecki Profit Equation: *Profit = Capitalist Consumption + Investment*	6. Since the wage is assumed identical to population consumption, we eliminate it on both sides and end up with: *Profit = Diversion*

Appendix 2: Productivity Growth and Prosperity

I discuss here the proposition that productivity growth is a viable solution to poverty and unemployment in modern oligarchy. This would seem most improbable given our productivity is already immense yet the problem is endemic. How, one may ask, can productivity growth be a solution when hundreds of millions are unemployed and underemployed? Quite simply, it can't. But rather than stopping here, let's take a brief look at this common theme using our two sector model.

Suppose productivity suddenly doubled. To maintain preexisting levels of employment in the diversion sector, the oligarchy would need to double its acquisitions of luxury and wealth defense* goods; to buy, in other words, twice the mansions, yachts, jets, and fine wines just because they could now be produced by half the number of workers. This defies common sense given that if it had wished, the oligarchy could have ordered their production before the productivity rise. It can buy all it needs with a fraction of the world's workforce and productivity has little to do with it at this stage of the game. The likely result, then, of a productivity rise would be a drop of employment in the diversion sector as fewer workers would be needed to produce the desired level of diversion.

Perhaps it could be argued that the lower tier of oligarchs who previously couldn't afford some of the oligarchic luxuries would be incented to step up their acquisitions once they could be produced more cheaply and employment would thereby be maintained in this way. It's a reasonable sounding proposition but it's problematic given that the stability of oligarchic diversion is a collective affair.

Suppose we had two tiers of oligarchs with the wealthiest one owning 75 percent of the market portfolio and the less wealthy 25 percent. Regardless of productivity, the consumption ability of members in both tiers is determined by what has been diverted by the oligarchy as a collective whole. Whatever is spent returns as profit, but each oligarch may spend only up to his applicable ownership percentage of the total. Those in the less wealthy tier may wish to divert more goods but if they sought to keep their relative rank within the oligarchy, they wouldn't be able to spend more than one-third of the richer tier as that's the ratio of ownership (25:75); anything beyond that would reduce their relative wealth. If we assume oligarchs in both tiers seek to maintain their position in the hierarchy, then the spending at the top sets the pattern. If it doesn't increase its acquisitions after the productivity rise, then the lower tier can't do so either without drawing down its relative power. We must therefore conclude it's unlikely the oligarchy would expand its diversionary orders in full line with productivity advances.

Unemployment would then increase in the diversion sector and profit in the population sector would correspondingly decline. The latter would then reduce employment as well. But that isn't all; another hurdle would be the manner in which the population sector reacts to its own increased productivity. The best case scenario for the population would be that production would be expanded in line with increased productivity. Wages would thereby increase for the workers lucky enough to still be employed. But absent strong population pressure, there would be no reason to expect the oligarchy to go along. The logic of wealth defense* would demand that the population sector reduce staff not only in line with the smaller diversion sector but in line also with its own improved productivity. Wages would then stay constant, unemployment would rise even further, and the profit margin would increase as production in the population sector declined. A simple example will help illustrate this.

Table 13: Productivity, Employment, and Wages

	(1) Base Scenario	(2) Pop Prod Passed On	(3) Pop Prod Withheld	(4) Full Prod Passed On
Units/Worker	2	4	4	4
Diversion:				
# Workers	50	37.5	37.5	37.5
Output	100	150	150	150
Population:				
# Workers	50	37.5	12.5	62.5
Output	100	150	50	250
Unemployment	0	25%	50%	0
Wage Level	1.00	2.00	1.00	2.50
Profit Margin	50%	50%	75%	37.5%

Assume in Table 13 above that there is full employment in the base scenario presented in column one. We consider the effects of a doubling of productivity in columns two through four. This is measured in units produced per worker as shown in the first row. Let's suppose the oligarchy doesn't double its diversion purchases but increases them by 50 percent (from 100 to 150 per the third row). In such a case, it would then need just 37.5 workers (row two) versus the original 50 (new purchases of 150 / new productivity of 4). Column two shows the situation if the population sector reduced its employment to account for the fewer diversion workers but otherwise passed on in full the benefits of the productivity rise. We see that unemployment would rise to 25% (row six) because of the reduced number of workers in both sectors but wages for those still employed would double (row seven) because of the higher productivity. (Wages are calculated as population sector output / total workers in both sectors.) The profit margin (row eight) would remain the same (calculated as diversion sector output / total output).

Column three reflects the situation if the population sector didn't pass on the benefits of productivity but instead maintained wages at a constant level. Unemployment then would rise to 50 percent and the profit margin to 75 percent. Finally, column four shows what would be required for the population to reap an unequivocal benefit from a rise in productivity. The fired workers from the diversion sector would need to be rehired in the population sector and the oligarchy would be forced to accept a 250 percent rise in wages along with a slashing of the profit margin to 37.5 percent.

Column three presents what appears to be the normal path whenever the population is weak and it's the one we've seen since the 1970s. The population sector is subservient, we recall, and exists only to support the diversion sector workforce. It would be a 'natural' outcome that its production would fall when both the number of diversion sector employees falls and the productivity of the population sector rises. It's part and parcel of the definition of financial efficiency.

Unemployment along with marginal employment would therefore almost certainly rise with advancing productivity and whether wages rose would depend on the relative strength of the two classes. A weak oligarchy is required for the population to do well in a period of rising productivity.

It boils down to a simple trade off: profit margins aren't likely to be maintained in the face of advancing productivity without higher unemployment and marginal employment. If the population were ever successful in forcing the full utilization of productivity advances, then population benefiting output would surge, the overwhelming monetary trend would be deflationary, and profit margins would be slashed.

These basic forces can be seen in the history of the past two hundred years. The oligarchy was relatively weak from the nineteenth century until the 1970s. In the nineteenth, it was burdened by both 'excessive' competition between numerous independent firms and the rapid expansion in the New World and the result was advancing wages and reduced profit margins in the face of strong deflationary pressures. Its response was the great consolidation around the turn of the twentieth century but it then faced the burdens of two World Wars, the Great Depression, the fear of communism, the advancing power of unions, social democracy, and rising democratic pressures. It was forced into sharing productivity gains with the population. By the mid-seventies, though, the unions had lost most of their power and communism and social democracy were in retreat. The oligarchy became emboldened and wages and living standards have been declining ever since in the face of rising productivity. The profit margin has correspondingly soared and employment has been propped up primarily through consumer debt.

I conclude that productivity growth isn't a solution to poverty and unemployment in modern oligarchy.

Appendix 3: Tax Burden Analysis of the 2015 US Federal Budget

I analyze in this appendix the 2015 US federal budget[2] to gain a more concrete intuition into the dynamics of state spending, how it's financed, and who is bearing the burden.

The budget shows total projected outlays of $3,901 billion of which I identify $1,058.4 billion going to departments which have a straightforward oligarchic purpose. These departments are listed in Table 14 below.

Table 14: US 2015 Budget—Oligarchy Related Spending

Department	Budget
Defense	495.6
National Intelligence	45.6
Department of Energy	27.9
Homeland Security	38.2
Department of State & Other International	40.3
Overseas Contingency	85.0
NASA	17.5
National Science Foundation	7.3
Department of Commerce	8.8
Department of Justice	27.4
Treasury	13.8
Interest on Federal Debt	251.0
Total	1058.4

In Billions of USD

Tax receipts are projected at $3,337 billion of which $1,928 billion represent income or estate and gift taxation. Using estimates provided by the Tax Foundation,[3] we can derive a rough approximation of the portion of the latter

---

[2] Fiscal Year 2015 Budget of the US Government, Office of Management and Budget. Online accessed August 29, 2015
     www.whitehouse.gov/sites/default/files/omb/budget/fy2015/assets/bu
     dget.pdf
[3] The Tax Foundation is a conservative Washington 'think tank' devoted to low taxes. The estimates are taken from their website accessed August 29, 2015.
     www.taxfoundation.org/article/summary-latest-federal-income-tax-
     data#_ftn1

paid by the oligarchy. The foundation calculates that the top 1 percent and top 5 percent of US taxpayers account for 35 percent and 57 percent of total income taxes. If we assume the oligarchy consists of the top 5 percent, we can then summarize spending, financing, and true cost by beneficiary as follows:

Table 15: US Spending by Beneficiary & Financing Source

	Oligarchy	Population	Total
State Spending by Beneficiary (1)	1058.4	2842.6	3901.0
Financed by:			
Taxes on Oligarchy (2)	1058.4	40.6	1099.0
Taxes on Population (3)		2238.0	2238.0
Deficit	0.0	564.0	564.0
Total	1058.4	2842.6	3901.0

In Billions of USD

(1) The spending shown for the oligarchy is from Table 14. Population benefiting output almost entirely consists of Social Security, Medicare, Medicaid, and other social programs which total $2415 billion. The remainder is attributable to various other federal departments.

(2) I use here the percentage of total income and estate tax that's paid by the top 5 percent according to the Tax Foundation which totals $1099.0 billion (.57 x $1928). It covers the output benefitting the oligarchy with a small remainder going toward population benefiting output.

(3) Represents the balance of taxes beyond the income tax attributable to the oligarchy.

These are rough estimates but they show how the federal budget tracks what we should expect. The income taxes of the top 5 percent almost exactly cover the main oligarchic purposes of the state with a paltry $40.6 billion left over (row two above). The population is budgeted to pay $2,238 billion toward its programs (row three) with the rest financed by the $40.6 billion from the oligarchy and a $564 billion deficit (row four). The deficit is presented as benefiting the population and fits the storyline that excessive population spending is forcing the country into unsustainable debt. The population is budgeted to pay almost 80 percent of the cost of its benefits through taxation (2238/2842.6) but will suffer 100 percent of the true tax burden. As discussed in chapter nine, the taxes paid by the oligarchy don't represent a cost since they're returned via the diversion-profit loop. The oligarchy, will get its diversion for free and will incur no effective tax. I note that the same basic pattern holds in Europe and worldwide. Consumption taxes are the primary means of financing the welfare state[4] and the population is thereby forced into paying its 'cost.'

---

[4] Piketty (2014: 496)

Appendix 4: A Review of IMF & World Bank Structural Adjustment Programs

I take a brief look in this appendix at some of the ways global governance is affecting a sample group of 'peripheral' countries. I turn to a rather unique tripartite effort completed in 2002 entitled the *Structural Adjustment Participatory Review Initiative* (SAPRI) involving the World Bank, various national networks of civil society organizations, and national governments.[5] It was formed to provide an independent assessment of IMF and World Bank structural adjustment policies on the following nations: Ghana, Uganda, Zimbabwe, Ecuador, El Salvador, Bangladesh, Hungary, Mexico and the Philippines.

According to the final report,[6] the joint project included meetings with a broad cross-section of local populations; joint meetings with national governments, World Bank officials, and local civil society committees; research carried out jointly with the World Bank, SAPRIN[7] teams, and research consultants; and public review of report drafts by all concerned. While agreeing to participate, the World Bank ended up not fully cooperating and officially withdrew at the time the draft report was submitted in 2001.

The final report was issued by SAPRIN and it identified four basic ways by which adjustment policies have "contributed to the further impoverishment and marginalization of local populations, while increasing economic inequality."[8]

1) "The demise of domestic manufacturing sectors and the loss of gainful employment by laid-off workers and small producers due to the nature of trade and financial-sector reforms."

---

[5] I became aware of this report through Peet (2009).

[6] *The Policy Roots of Economic Crisis and Poverty: a multi-country participatory assessment of structural adjustment*, Prepared by the Structural Adjustment Participatory Review International Network (SAPRIN), First Edition, April, 2002

[7] Structural Adjustment Participatory Review Network, a group of civil society organizations working on this project.

[8] The quotes and discussion which follows are taken from pages 173 to 185 of the SAPRIN Report.

While the report notes that industrialization has faltered in all countries examined, nowhere was the resulting impoverishment worse than in Ecuador where industry's share in the national economy declined by half and the jobless rate in urban areas doubled. Manufacturing in Bangladesh was also halved after the structural adjustment programs were implemented. As many as 20,000 small businesses in Mexico were forced into bankruptcy and in Hungary, tens of thousands of small shops lost their viability because of open trade policies. Overall employment in export industries was limited since they generally operated in "foreign-owned enclaves without forward or backward production linkages." The benefits of export growth have accrued primarily to foreign corporations.

2) "The contribution that agricultural, trade and mining reforms have made to the declining viability and incomes of small farms and poor rural communities, as well as to declining food security, particularly in rural areas."

The adjustment policies, according to the report, "have served to marginalize the poor in rural areas, to reduce the availability of productive farmland for cultivation for the local market and to undermine food security." They've favored export industries at the cost of the domestic market and increased inequalities. The cost of inputs has risen to a point that in some countries farmers have been forced to reduce output, convert to non-food crops, or exit farming altogether. In Mexico, many small producers have been pushed off their land by large export projects in agriculture and mining. Private mining companies in Ghana have staked claims to newly privatized mineral-rich land, have forced families to mine their own land, and have destroyed farmland with open-pit mining methods. Ghana and other countries have lost community control over land to major mining interests. The cost of living throughout the countries has risen along with food insecurity. "The reality is that the poor often lack the means to pay for the imported food, on which of necessity they must now rely, and consequently have suffered from inadequate food intake and increasing malnourishment." Open-pit mining and the relaxation of environmental controls have created extensive health problems including respiratory-tract illnesses. The social and family disintegration has been marked by increased drug use and prostitution and rising incidences of HIV/AIDS.

3) "The retrenchment of workers through privatizations and budget cuts, in conjunction with labor-market flexibilization measures has resulted in less secure employment, lower wages, fewer benefits and an erosion of workers' rights and bargaining power."

> The report observes that privatization and other labor policies have led to more precarious and less remunerative employment in a growing number of countries. "Employees have lost much of their bargaining power and protections" and the working hours required to sustain the household have increased. Real wages have decreased especially among the lowest income groups, income inequality has increased, and wage levels "frequently do not cover a family's basic needs." The share of wages in GDP has fallen. Two-thirds of the population in Zimbabwe survive on less than two dollars per day. In Mexico, the minimum wage has lost about 70 percent of its purchasing power since adjustment measures were first introduced in 1982 and the number living in extreme poverty has risen from six to 30 million between 1994 and 2000. Two thirds in El Salvador earn less than the minimum wage and the average real income of those employed in urban Ecuador is now less than $200 per month. In Bangladesh, 40 percent of workers in the previously state-owned companies have lost their jobs and temporary employment is growing. Newly privatized firms in Hungary commonly hire workers for only one to three months at a time. Throughout the countries, labor laws "have been shaped to provide employers with maximum leverage in their relations with workers, as reflected in the increased use of hourly labor and temporary, fixed-term and part-time contracts." Workers are insecure and unlikely to insist on their labor rights or form unions. "Labor-market reforms and privatization have increased inequality and decreased family incomes, generating an increase in child labor, other survival strategies and social dislocations and problems."

4) "Poverty has been increased through privatization programs, the application of user fees, budget cuts and other adjustment measures that have reduced the role of the state in providing or guaranteeing affordable access to essential quality services."

The report observes that privatizations of public water and electric utilities has led to significant rate hikes while offering little improvement. Rates for electricity, heat, water, and gas increased at twice average wages to provide profit returns to private investors. Public spending on social services have deteriorated while debt obligations are paid. "In fact, controls on social spending, related policies and the theoretical framework in which they fit have been implemented precisely so that debt obligations could be met." The "poor pay the external debt several times over despite having had little or no role in creating it, especially private-sector debts that have often been assumed by the governments." "Furthermore, as civil-society participants in Ecuador have emphasized, the foreign debt has provided a mechanism by which the international financial institutions have applied external pressure for the adoption of their often poverty-inducing policy prescriptions." Health care quality has generally declined because of pressures to reduce social spending leaving countries with insufficient funding levels to meet health needs. Education is also hit. "School infrastructure is often lacking, shortages of educational supplies are widespread and teachers' incomes have declined, as have student-teacher ratios."

The report concludes that the adjustment policies of the IMF and World Bank have resulted in

increased current-account and trade deficits and debt; disappointing levels of economic growth, efficiency and competitiveness; the misallocation of financial and other productive resources; the 'disarticulation' of national economies; the destruction of national productive capacity; and extensive environmental damage. Poverty and inequality are now far more intense and pervasive than they were 20 years ago, wealth is more highly concentrated, and opportunities are far fewer for the many who have been left behind by adjustment.[9]

They have, in other words, been a resounding success.

---

[9] SAPRIN Report p. 185

Appendix 5: The Founding Fathers and the US Constitution

The Founding Fathers of the US feared the population and wrote the 1787 Constitution with the primary goal being to protect the propertied minority. Most members of the Constitutional Convention, observes historian Woody Holton, sought to create a national government "substantially immune to popular influence," while still being capable of being ratified.[10] According to historian Charles Beard, the Constitution is "essentially an economic document based upon the concept that the fundamental private rights of property are anterior to government and morally beyond the reach of popular majorities."[11] Political philosopher Sheldon Wolin notes that the document's elaborate checks and balances "were designed to make it next to impossible for popular majorities to institute policies actually in the interests of the majority."[12]

The fear of democracy that always accompanies inequality is evident throughout the records of the Constitutional Convention. The "origin" of the "evils under which the US laboured," said wealthy Virginia delegate and first US attorney general Edmund Randolph, was "the turbulences and follies of democracy."[13] "Our chief danger arises from the democratic parts of our [state] constitutions" and none of them "have provided sufficient checks against democracy."[14]

Connecticut delegate Roger Sherman asserted that "The people [immediately] should have as little to do as may be about the government."[15] Wealthy Massachusetts delegate and future Vice President Elbridge Gerry tells us that "The evils we experience flow from the excess of democracy."[16] Wealthy Virginia delegate George Mason observed that "one important

---

[10] Holton (2007: 211)

[11] Beard (1921: 324)

[12] Wolin (2008: 155)

[13] Farrand (1911: 1,51)

[14] Farrand (1911: 1, 26-27)

[15] Farrand (1911: 1, 48)

[16] Farrand (1911: 1, 48) The undemocratic manipulation of electoral districts was coined *gerrymandering* after Gerry. As governor of Massachusetts in 1812 he signed a bill that contorted the shape of a district to such an extent that newspaper editors and others likened it to that of a salamander. Thus the gerrymander.

object for constituting the senate was to rescue the rights of property."[17] To which wealthy Delaware delegate John Dickenson argued it should bear "as strong a likeness to the British House of Lords as possible" and be populated only by those "distinguished for their rank in life and their weight of property."[18] Many Americans, according to New York delegate and future Treasury Secretary Alexander Hamilton, were growing "tired of an excess of democracy."[19]

> All communities divide themselves into the few and the many. The first are the rich and well born, the other the mass of the people. The voice of the people has been said to be the voice of God; and however generally this maxim has been quoted and believed, it is not true in fact. The people are turbulent and changing; they seldom judge or determine right. Give therefore to the first class a distinct, permanent share in the government. . . . Can a democratic assembly who annually revolve in the mass of the people, be supposed steadily to pursue the public good? Nothing but a permanent body can check the imprudence of democracy. . . . It is admitted that you cannot have a good executive upon a democratic plan.[20]

In arguing for ratification, he declared that the Constitution should earn "the goodwill of most men of property" by protecting them "against democratic violence and the depredations which the democratic spirit is apt to make on property."[21]

The federal government, according to wealthy Virginia delegate, "father of the Constitution" and future president James Madison, ought "to protect the minority of the opulent against the majority."[22] Following Locke, he asserted that "The personal right to acquire property, which is a natural right,

---

[17] Farrand (1911: 1, 428)
[18] Farrand (1911: 1, 150)
[19] Farrand (1911: 1, 301)
[20] Farrand (1911: 1, 299)
[21] As quoted in Holton (2007: 228)
[22] Farrand (1911: 1, 431)

gives to property, when acquired, a right to protection, which is a social right."[23]

---

[23] James Madison: Speech on the Virginia Constitutional Convention, December 2, 1829.

http://www.thefederalistpapers.org/founders/madison/james-madison-speech-on-the-virginia-constitutional-convention

References

Albrecht, W. (2005) "Business Fraud (The Enron Problem)", Brigham Young University, AICPA, Power Point Presentation, online, accessed June 12, 2015

> http://www.scribd.com/doc/24385256/Business-Fraud-the-Enron-Problem#scribd

Anderson, P. (2013) "Imperium", *New Left Review*, 83, Sept-Oct 2013

Anderson, P. (2014) "The Italian Disaster", *London Review of Books*, Vol 36, No. 10, May 2014, pp 3-16

Anderson, R., Duru, A. & Reeb, D. (2009) "Founders, Heirs, and Corporate Opacity in the U.S.", *Journal of Financial Economics*, Vol 92, Issue 2, pp 205-22

Aquinas (2006) *Summa Theologiae Volume 6, The Trinity: 1a.27-32*, Cambridge: Cambridge University Press

Aristotle (2012) *Politics: a treatise on government*, Kindle Edition, translated by William Ellis, May 5, 2012, New York: J.M. Dent & Sons

Ascher, B. (2012) "Global Beer: The road to monopoly", The American Antitrust Institute, online accessed January 19, 2015

> www.antitrustinstitute.org/~antitrust/sites/default/files/Global Beer Road to Monopoly_O.pdf

Bacevich, A. (2002) *American Empire: the realities and consequences of US diplomacy*, Cambridge, MA: Harvard University Press

Baran, P. & Sweezy, P. (1966) *Monopoly Capital: an essay on the American economic and social order*, New York: Monthly Review Press

Baum, S., Haqq-Misra, J. & Domagal-Goldman, S. (2011) "Would Contact with Extraterrestrials Benefit or Harm Humanity? A scenario analysis", *Acta Astronautica*, 68(11-12): 2114-2149, file version pp 1-33, online accessed April 22, 2011

http://arxiv.org/ftp/arxiv/papers/1104/1104.4462.pdf

Beard, C.A. (1921) *An Economic Interpretation of the Constitution of the United States*, New York: MacMillan Co

Bell, S. (1998) "Can Taxes and Bonds Finance Government Spending?", Working Paper No. 244, Jerome Levy Economics Institute, July, 1998

Berle, A. & Means, G. (1932) *The Modern Corporation and Private Property*, New York: Commerce Clearing House

Blum, W. (2004) *Killing Hope: US Military and CIA Interventions since World War II, updated edition*, Monroe, Maine: Common Courage Press

Boehm, C. (2000) "Forager Hierarchies, Innate Dispositions, and the Behavioral Reconstruction of Prehistory" in M. Diehl (ed.) *Hierarchies in Action: Cui Bono?*, pp 31-58, Center for Archaeological Studies, Southern Illinois University, Carbondale, Occasional Paper No 27

Boesche, R. (1996) *Theories of Tyranny: from Plato to Arendt*, University Park, PA: Pennsylvania State University Press

Boron, A. (2006) "The Truth about Capitalist Democracy", *Socialist Register*, Vol 42

Braudel, F. (1982) *The Wheels of Commerce: Civilization and Capitalism 15th to 18th Century*, Volume II, New York: Harper & Row

Braudel, F. (1984) *The Perspectives of the World: Civilization and Capitalism 15th to 18th Century*, Volume III, New York: Harper & Row

Braudel, F. (1992) *The Structures of Everyday Life: Civilization and Capitalism 15th to 18th Century*, Volume I, Oakland: University of California Press

Brecher, J. (1997) *Strike!*, revised and updated edition, Cambridge, MA: South End Press

Brynjolfsson, E. & McAfee, A. (2011) *Race Against the Machine, how the digital revolution is accelerating innovation, driving productivity, and irreversibly transforming employment and the economy*, Digital Frontier Press: Kindle Edition, October 17, 2011

Burke, E. (2012) *The Works of the Right Honourable Edmund Burke*, Vol. 3, Kindle Edition

Cerny, P. (1994) "The Infrastructure of the Infrastructure? toward 'embedded financial orthodoxy' in the international political economy", in R. Palan & B. Gills (eds.) *Transcending the State-Global Divide: a neo-structuralist agenda in international relations*, Boulder: Lynne Rienner Publishers

Childe, V.G. (1951) *Man Makes Himself*, New York New: American Library

Cicero, M. T. (2010) *The Republic and The Laws*, Kindle Edition, June 24, 2010: Neeland Media LLC

Claessens, S., Djankov, S. & Lang, L. (2000) *The Separation of Ownership and Control in East Asian Corporations*, World Bank

Clark, J. & Blake, M. (1994) "The Power of Prestige: Competitive generosity and the emergence of rank societies in lowland Mesoamerica", in E. Brumfiel & J. Fox (eds.) *Factional Competition and Political Development in the New World*, pp 17-30, Cambridge: Cambridge University Press

Clausewitz, C. von (1873) *On War, 3 Volumes*, Third German Edition, London: N. Trubner & Co

Coeurdacier, N. (2009) "Theoretical Perspectives on Financial Globalization: trade costs and equity home bias", *Hal Archives Ouvertes.fr*, hal-01063456, online accessed May 22, 2015

> https://hal.archives-ouvertes.fr/file/index/docid/1063456/filename/tradecosts-homebias-encyclopedia-1.pdf

Congressional Budget Office (2013) "The Distribution of Household Income and Federal Taxes, 2010", online accessed April 2, 2015

> http://www.cbo.gov/sites/default/files/cbofiles/attachments/44604-AverageTaxRates.pdf

Crozier, M., Huntington, S. & Watanuki, J. (1975) *The Crisis of Democracy: report on the governability of the democracies to the Trilateral Commission*, New York: NY University Press

Cypher, J. & Wise, R. (2010) *Mexico's Economic Dilemma: the development failure of neo-liberalism*, Lanham, Md: Rowman & Littlefield

Davis, M. (2006) *Planet of Slums*, New York: Verso

De Ste Croix, G.E.M (1981) *The Class Struggle in the Ancient Greek World: from the archaic age to the Arab conquests*, London: Duchworth

Diehl, M. (2000) "Some Thoughts in the Study of Hierarchies", in M. Diehl (ed.) *Hierarchies in Action: Cui Bono?*, Center for Archaeological Studies, Occasional Paper No 27, pp 11-30, Carbondale: Southern Illinois University

Diggins, J.P. (1981) "Power and Authority in American History: The case of Charles A. Beard and his critics", *The American Historical Review*, Vol 86, No 4, Oct 1981, pp 701-30

Domhoff, G.W. (2006) *Who Rules America?: power, politics, and social change*, New York: McGraw Hill

Dostoevsky, F. (2009) *The Brothers Karamazov: A Novel in Four Parts With Epilogue*, translated by Constance Garnett, New York: The Lowell Press

Douglass, F. (2012) *The Frederick Douglass Papers: series two: autobiographical writings, volume three: life and times of Frederick Douglass, Book 1: The Text and Editorial Apparatus*, J. McKivigan (ed.), New Haven, Yale University Press

Duménil, G. & Lévy, D. (2007) "Finance and Management in the Dynamics of Social Change: contrasting two trajectories—US and France" in L. Assassi, A. Nesvetailova, & D. Wigan, (eds.) *Global Finance in the New Century: beyond regulation*, Houndmills: MacMillan

Easterlin, R., et al. (2010) "The Happiness - Income Paradox Revisited", *PNAS*, Vol 107, No. 52, December 28, 2010, online accessed December 12, 2014

> http://www.pnas.org/content/107/52/22463.full

ECLAC (2014) *Social Panorama of Latin America 2013*, online accessed Februrary 2, 2015

> http://www.cepal.org/en/publications/social-panorama-latin-america-2013

Erdal, D. & Whiten, A. (1996) "Egalitarianism and Machiavellian Intelligence in Human Evolution" in P. Mellars & K. Gibson (eds.) *Modelling the Early Human Mind*, pp 139-50, Cambridge: McDonald Institute for Archaeological Research

Erturk, I., Leaver, A. & Williams, K. (2010) "Hedge Funds as War Machine: making the positions work", *New Political Economy*, Vol 15, No 1, March 2010, pp 9-28

Ewen, S. (1996) *PR!: A social history of spin*, New York: Basic Books

Farrand, M. (1911) *The Records of the Federal Convention of 1787*, Volume 1, New Haven

Feinman, G. (1995) "The Emergence of Inequality: A Focus on Strategies and Process in Foundations of Social Inequality", in D. Price & G. Feinman *Foundations of Social Inequality*, pp 255-79, New York: Plenum Press

Feynman, R. (1985) *The Character of Physical Law*, Cambridge, MA: MIT Press

Fine, B., Lapavitsas, C., & Pincus, J. (2001) *Development Policy in the Twenty-first Century: beyond the post-Washington Consensus*, London: Routledge

Frank, A.G. (1991) "Transitional Ideological Modes: Feudalism, Capitalism, Socialism" in S. Chew & P. Lauderdale (eds.) *Theory and Methodology of World Development: the writings of Andre Gunder Frank*, New York: Palgrave, 2010

Frank, A.G. (1992) "The 5,000 Year World System: an interdisciplinary" in S. Chew & P. Lauderdale (eds) *Theory and Methodology of World Development: the writings of Andre Gunder Frank*, New York: Palgrave, 2010

Frank, A.G. (2014) *ReOrienting the Nineteenth Century: global economy in the continuing Asian age*, R. Denemark (ed.), Boulder: Paradigm Publishers

Frank, R. (1997) "The Frame of Reference as a Public Good", *Economic Journal*, Vol 107 (Nov 1997), pp 1832-47

Freud, S. (2001) *Civilization and its Discontents* in "The Standard Edition of the Complete Psychological Works of Sigmund Freud", Volume xxi, London: Vintage

Fried, B. (2004) "Left-Libertarianism: a review essay", *Philosophy and Public Affairs*, Vol 32 No 1, pp 66-92

Fried, M. (1967) *The Evolution of Political Society: an essay in political anthropology*, New York: Random House

Galbraith, J.K. (1984) *The Affluent Society 4th Edition*, Boston: Houghton Mifflin Co

Gannssmann, H. (2012) *Doing Money: elementary monetary theory from a sociological standpoint*, New York: Routledge

Geuss, R. (1981) *The Idea of a Critical Theory: Habermas and the Frankfurt School*, Cambridge: Cambridge University Press

Gindin, S. & Panitch, L. (2012) *The Making of Global Capitalism: The Political Economy of American Empire*, London: Verso

Glattfelder, J. (2010) *Ownership Networks and Corporate Control: mapping economic power in a globalized world*, Doctoral Dissertation to the ETH Zurich, No. 19274

Goldstein, F. (2008) *Low-Wage Capitalism: Colossus with feet of clay - what the new globalized, high tech imperialism means for the class struggle in the US*, New York: World View Forum

Graeber, D. (2011) *Debt: The First 5,000 Years*, Brooklyn, New York: Melville House

Green, W. (2015) *A History of Political Murder in Latin America: killing the messengers of change*, New York: Suny Press

Haas, J. (2001) "Warfare and the Evolution of Culture", in T.D. Price & G. Feinman (eds.) *Foundations of Social Inequality*, pp 329-50, New York: Plenum Press

Hayden, B. (1995) "Pathways to Power: principles for creating socioeconomic inequalities" in T.D. Price & G. Feinman (eds.) *Foundations of Social Inequality*, pp 15-86, New York, Plenum Press

Hayden, B. (2001) "Richman, Poorman, Beggarman, Chief", in T.D. Price & G. Feinman (eds.) *The Dynamics of Social Inequality in Archaeology at the Millennium: a sourcebook*, pp 231-72, New York: Kluwar Academic/Plenum Publishers

Hayek, F. (1944) *The Road to Serfdom*, Chicago: University of Chicago Press

Hayek, F. (2009) *Individualism and Economic Order*, Auburn, Alabama: Ludwig Von Mises Institute

Heilbroner, R. (1985) *The Nature and Logic of Capitalism*, New York: W.W. Norton

Henry, J. (2012) "The Price of Offshore Revisited: New estimates for 'missing' global private wealth, income, inequality, and lost taxes", Tax Justice Network, July, 2012, online accessed October 12, 2013
http://www.taxjustice.net/cms/upload/pdf/Price_of_Offshore_Revisited_120722.pdf

Hilferding, R. (1981) *Finance Capital: A study of the latest phase of capitalist development*, translated by M. Watnick and S. Gordon, London: Routledge & Kegan Paul

Ho, K. (2009) *Liquidated: An Ethnography of Wall Street*, Durham: Duke University Press

Hobbes, T. (2012) *Leviathan*, Kindle Edition, May 16, 2012

Hobgood, M. (1991) *Catholic Social Teaching and Economic Theory: Paradigms in conflict*, Philadelphia: Temple University Press

Hobsbawm, E. (1962) *The Age of Capital: 1848-1875*, London: Weidenfeld & Nicolson

Holton, W. (2007) *Unruly Americans and the Origins of the Constitution*, New York: Hill & Wong

Hoshino, T. (2010) "Business Groups in Mexico" in A. Colpan, T. Hikino, & J. Lincoln (eds) *The Oxford Handbook of Business Groups*, Oxford: Oxford University Press, pp 424-455

Huemer, M. (2013) *The Problem of Political Authority: an examination of the right to coerce and the duty to obey*, New York: Palgrave Macmillan

ILO(2013) *Global Wage Report 2012/13: Wages and equitable growth*, online accessed August 19, 2015
> http://www.ilo.org/global/research/global-reports/global-wage-report/2012/WCMS_194843/lang--en/index.htm

ILO (2014) Global Employment Trends 2014: Risk of a Jobless Recovery?, online accessed August 19, 2015
> http://www.ilo.org/global/research/global-reports/global-employment-trends/2014/lang--en/index.htm

Innes, A.M. (1914) "The Credit Theory of Money", *The Banking Law Journal*, Vol 31, Dec/Jan 1914

Jessop, B. (1978) "Capitalism and Democracy: the best possible shell?" in G. Littlejohn, B. Smart, J. Waleford & N. Yuval-Davis (eds.) *Power and the State*, pp 10-51, New York: St Martin Press

Kalecki, M. (1969) *Theory of Economic Dynamics: an essay on cyclical and long-run changes in capitalist economy*, New York: Augustus M. Kelley

Kalecki, M. (1971) "The Determinants of Profits" in *Selected Essays on the Dynamics of the Capitalist Economy - 1933 to 1970*, London: Cambridge University Press

Kalecki, M. (1971a) "The Problem of Effective Demand with Tugan-Barnovski and Rosa Luxemburg" in *Selected Essays on the Dynamics of the Capitalist Economy - 1933 to 1970*, London: Cambridge University Press

Kalecki, M. (1971b) "A Theory of Commodity, Income, and Capitalist Taxation", in *Selected Essays on the Dynamics of the Capitalist Economy - 1933 to 1970*, London: Cambridge University Press

Kalecki, M. (1971c) "Determination of National Income and Consumption", in *Selected Essays on the Dynamics of the Capitalist Economy - 1933 to 1970*, London: Cambridge University Press

Keen, Steve (2011) *Debunking Economics - Revised and Expanded Edition: The Naked Emperor Dethroned?*, London: Zed Books

Keynes, J.M. (1930) *A Treatise on Money v.1 The Pure Theory of Money*, New York: Harcourt, Brace & Co

Keynes, J.M. (1964) *The General Theory of Employment, Interest, and Money*, New York: Harcourt, Brace, & World

Kim, H. (2010) "Business Groups in South Korea" in A. Colpan, T. Hikino, & J. Lincoln (eds) *The Oxford Handbook of Business Groups*, Oxford: Oxford University Press, pp 157-179

Kindleberger, C. & Aliber, R. *Manias, Panics, and Crashes: a history of Financial Crises*, 5th Edition, Hoboken, NJ: Wiley

Kolko, Joyce & Gabriel (1972) *The Limits of Power: the world and United States Foreign Policy, 1945-1954*, New York: Harper & Row

Kron, G. (2011) "The Distribution of Wealth at Athens in Comparative Perspective", *Zeitschrift für Papyrologie und Epigraphik* 179 (2011) pp 129-38, online accessed August 19, 2015

> http://www.academia.edu/1198885/The_Distribution_of_Wealth_at_Athens_in_Comparative_Perspective

Landa, I. (2010) *The Apprentice's Sorcerer: Liberal Tradition and Fascism*, Leiden, Netherlands: Brill

Layard, R., Clark, A. & Senik, C. (2012) "The Causes of Happiness and Misery" in J. Helliwell, R. Layard, & J. Sachs (eds) *The World Happiness Report 2012*, New York: The Earth Institute, Columbia University, online accessed August 19, 2015

> http://www.earth.columbia.edu/sitefiles/file/Sachs%20Writing/2012/World%20Happiness%20Report.pdf

Lefort, F. (2010) "Business Groups in Chile" in A. Colpan, T. Hikino, & J. Lincoln (eds) *The Oxford Handbook of Business Groups*, Oxford: Oxford University Press, pp 387-423

Leibovitz, C. & Finkel, A. (1998) *In Our Time: the Chamberlain—Hitler collusion*, New York: Monthly Review Press

Lerner, A. (1943) "Functional Finance and the Federal Debt", *Social Research*, Vol 10 No 1, Feb 1943, pp 38-51

Lerner, A. (1951) *Economics of Employment*, New York: McGraw Hill,

Lincoln, J. & Shimotani, M. (2010) "Business Networks in Postwar Japan: whither the Keiretsu?" in A. Colpan, T. Hikino, & J. Lincoln (eds) *The Oxford Handbook of Business Groups*, Oxford: Oxford University Press, pp 127-156

Locke, J. (2011) *Second Treatise of Government*, Kindle Edition, March 30, 2011

Luxemburg, R. (1972) *The Accumulation of Capital - An Anti-critique*, New York: Monthly Review Press

Luxemburg, R. (2003) *The Accumulation of Capital*, London: Routledge

Mann, M. (1997) *The Sources of Social Power: A history of power beginning to AD 1760*, Volume 1, Cambridge: Cambridge University Press

Marglin, S. (2010) "Keynes in the Long Run", unpublished, online accessed August 25, 2015

      www.boeckler.de/pdf/v_2010_10_25_marglin.pdf

Marx, K. (1847) *The Poverty of Philosophy*, The Marxists Internet Archive, online accessed August 19, 2015

      https://www.marxists.org/archive/marx/works/1847/poverty-philosophy/

Marx, K. (1978a) "Economic and Philosophic Manuscripts of 1844" in R. Tucker (ed.) *The Marx-Engels Reader*, second edition, New York: W.W. Norton

Marx, K. (1978b) "The German Ideology: Part I" in R. Tucker (ed.) *The Marx-Engels Reader*, second edition, New York: W.W. Norton

Marx, K. (1978c) "Wage Labour and Capital" in R. Tucker (ed.) *The Marx-Engels Reader*, second edition, New York: W.W. Norton

Marx, K. (1978d) "The Grundrisse" in R. Tucker (ed.) *The Marx-Engels Reader*, second edition, New York: W.W. Norton

Marx, K. & Engels, F. (1964) *The Communist Manifesto*, New York: Washington Square Press

McKinsey (2013) "Urban World: The shifting global business landscape", online accessed June 23, 2014

      http://www.mckinsey.com/insights/urbanization/urban_world _the_shifting_global_business_landscape

Mészáros, I. (1989) *The Power of Ideology*, New York: NY University Press

Minsky, H. (1986) *Stabilizing an Unstable Economy*, New Haven: Yale University Press

Minsky, H. (1992) "The Financial Instability Hypothesis", *Levy Economics Institute of Bard College*, Working Paper No. 74, May 1992, online accessed August 19, 2015

      http://www.levyinstitute.org/pubs/wp74.pdf

Monks, R. & Minow, N. (2011) *Corporate Governance, 5th Edition*, Chichester, UK: John Wiley & Sons

Morck, R. (2010) "The Riddle of the Great Pyramids" in A. Colpan, T. Hikino, & J. Lincoln (eds) *The Oxford Handbook of Business Groups*, Oxford: Oxford University Press, pp 602-628

Mosler, W. (2012) *Soft Currency Economics II: What everyone thinks they know about monetary policy is wrong*, Christiansted, US Virgin Islands: Valance Company

Nitzan, J. (1998) "Differential Accumulation: towards a new political economy of capital", *Review of International Political Economy* 5:2, summer 1998, pp 169-216

Nolan, P., Zhang, J. & Liu, C. (2008) "The Global Business Revolution, the Cascade Effect, and the Challenge for Firms from Developing Countries", *Cambridge Journal of Economics*, 32 (1), pp 29-47

Nolan, P. & Zhang, J. (2010) "Global Competition after the Financial Crisis", *New Left Review*, 64, July/Aug, 2010

Nozick, R. (1974) *Anarchy, State, and Utopia*, Oxford: Blackwell

O'Connor, J. (1987) *The Meaning of Crisis: a theoretical introduction*, Oxford: Basil Blackwell

OECD (2014) *Society at a Glance 2014: OECD social indicators*, online accessed August 19, 2015

http://www.oecd.org/social/societyataglance.htm

Palan, R. (2013) "New Trends in Global Political Economy" in R. Palan (ed.) *Global Political Economy: contemporary theories*, 2nd edition, pp 1-14, London: Routledge

Palan, R., Murphy, R., & Chavagneux, C. (2010) *Tax Havens: How Globalization Really Works*, Ithaca, NY: Cornell Univ Press

Panitch, L. & Gindin, S. (2004) "Global Capitalism and American Empire", *Socialist Register*, Vol 40

Peet, R. (2009) *Unholy Trinity: the IMF, World Bank and WTO*, 2nd edition, London, Zed Books

Piketty, T. (2014) *Capital in the Twenty-first Century*, Cambridge, MA: Belknap Press of Harvard University

Plato (2006) *The Republic*, translated by R.E. Allen, New Haven: Yale University Press

Pogge, T. (2005) "Real World Justice", *The Journal of Ethics*, Vol 9, No. 1/2, Current Debates in Global Justice, pp 29-53

Pogge, T. (2008) *World Poverty and Human Rights*, 2nd Edition, Cambridge: Polity Press

Pogge, T. (2010) "How Many Poor People should there be? a rejoinder to Ravallion", in S. Anand, P. Segal, & J. Stiglitz (eds.) *Debates on the Measurement of Global Poverty*, Oxford: Oxford Univ Press

Poulantzas, N. (1975) *Classes in Contemporary Capitalism*, Translated by David Feinbach, London: NLB

Rawls, J. (1999) *A Theory of Justice*, Revised Edition, Cambridge, MA: Belknap Press

Reisman, G. (1998) *Capitalism: A Treatise on Economics*, Laguna Hills, CA: TJS Books

Renger, J. (2011) "The Role and the Place of Money and Credit in the Economy of Ancient Mesopotamia" in H. Ganssmann (ed.) *New Approaches to Monetary Theory: interdisciplinary perspectives*, New York: Routledge

Robin, C. (2011) *The Reactionary Mind: conservatism from Edmund Burke to Sarah Palin*, New York: Oxford University Press

Robinson, W. (2014) *Global Capitalism and the Crisis of Humanity*, New York: Cambridge University Press

Rothkopf, D. (2008) *Superclass: the global power elite and the world they are making*, New York: Farrar, Strauss, & Giroux

Sachs, J. (2012) "Introduction to the Happiness Report", in J. Helliwell, R. Layard, & J. Sachs (eds) *The World Happiness Report 2012*, New York: The Earth Institute, Columbia University, online accessed August 19, 2015
http://www.earth.columbia.edu/sitefiles/file/Sachs%20Writing/2012/World%20Happiness%20Report.pdf

Scheffler, S. (2004) "Choice, Circumstance, and the Value of Equality", *Center for the Study of Law and Society Jurisprudence and Social Policy Program*, presented in the Center for the Study of Law and Society Bag Lunch Speaker Series, University of California, Berkeley, Paper 17, online accessed August 19, 2015
http://philosophyfaculty.ucsd.edu/faculty/rarneson/schefflersamuelvalueofequality.pdf

Schumacher, R. (2013) "Deconstructing the Theory of Comparative Advantage", *World Economic Review*, 2: pp 83-105, online accessed August 19, 2015
http://werdiscussion.worldeconomicsassociation.org/?post=deconstructing-the-theory-of-comparative-advantage

Schumpeter, J. (1947) *Capitalism, Socialism, and Democracy*, 2nd Edition, New York: Harper & Brothers

Smith, A. (2011) *The Wealth of Nations*, Kindle Edition, December 12, 2011: Seedbox Press, LLC

Soros, G. (2000) *Open Society: reforming global capitalism*, New York: Public Affairs

Stanford Center on Poverty & Inequality (2014) "State of the Union: The poverty and inequality report", online accessed August 19, 2015
>   http://web.stanford.edu/group/scspi/sotu/SOTU_2014_CPI.pdf

Stiglitz, J. (2003) *Globalization and its Discontents*, New York: W.W. Norton & Co

Stiglitz, J. (2010) *Freefall: America, free markets, and the sinking of the world economy*, New York: W.W. Norton & Co

Suskind, R. (2011) *Confidence Men: Wall Street, Washington, and the education of a president*, Harper Collins e-books

Thompson, E.P. (1966) *The Making of the English Working Class*, New York: Vintage Books

Tietje, C. & Baetens, F. (2014) *The Impact of Investor-State-Dispute-Settlement (ISDS) in the Transatlantic Trade and Investment Partnership: study*, Report prepared for the Minister for Foreign Trade and Development Corporation and the Ministry of Foreign Affairs, The Netherlands

Tolstoy, L. (1942) *What then Must We Do?*, Translated by A. Maude, online accessed August 19, 2015
>   http://arvindguptatoys.com/arvindgupta/whatthenmustwedo.pdf

Trigger, B. (2003) *Understanding Early Civilizations: a comparative study*, Cambridge: Cambridge University Press

van der Pijl, K. (2009) *A Survey of Global Political Economy*, version 2.1, October 2009, Center for Global Political Economy, University of Sussex, online accessed July 20, 2014
>   www.ps://libcom.org/files/A%20survey%20of%20global%20political%20economy.pdf

Veblen, T. (1908) "On the Nature of Capital, Investment, Intangible Assets, and the Pecuniary Magnate", *Quarterly Journal of Economics*, Vol 23, Issue 1, Nov, 1908, pp 104-136

Veblen, T. (1999) *The Theory of Business Enterprise*, Blackmark Online

Veblen, T. (2001) *The Engineers and the Price System*, Kitchener, Ontario: Batoche Books

Veblen, T. (2003) *The Instinct of Workmanship and the State of the Industrial Arts*, Blackmark Online

Veblen, T. (2012) *Theory of the Leisure Class*, Kindle Edition, May 16, 2012

Vitali, S., Glattfelder, J.B., and Battraton, S. (2011) "The Network of Global Corporate Control", online accessed April 27, 2014
    arxiv.org/pdf/1107.5728v2.pdf

von Mises, L. (1998) *Human Action: a treatise on economics*, Auburn, Alabama: Ludwig von Mises Institute

Wade, R. (2009) "Beware what you wish for: lessons for international political economy from the transformation of economics", *Review of International Political Economy* 16:1 Feb 2009, pp 106-121

Wallerstein, I. (1995) *Historical Capitalism*, Guilford: UK Verso

Weber, M. (2011) "Objectivity in Social Science and Social Policy" in E. Shils & H. Finch (eds.) *Methodology of Social Sciences*, pp 49-112, New Brunswick, NJ: Transaction Publishers

Weiner, T. (2012) *Enemies: a history of the FBI*, New York: Random House

Widerquist, K. (2009) "Libertarianism" in P. O'Hara (ed.) *International Encyclopedia of Public Policy, Volume 3—Public Policy and Political Economy*, Global Political Economy Research Unit, Curtin University, Perth

Widerquist, K. (2010) "Lockean Theories of Property: Justifications for unilateral appropriation", *Public Reason*, 2(1) pp 3-26

Wilkinson, D. (2004) "The Power Configuration Sequence of the Central World System 1500—700 BC", *Journal of World-Systems Research*, X, 3, Fall 2004, pp. 655-720

Wilkinson, D. (2006) "Globalizations: the first ten, hundred, five thousand and million years", in B. Gills & W. Thompson (eds.) *Globalization and Global History*, pp 62-70, New York: Routledge

Williams, W. (1964) *The Great Expansion*, Chicago: Quadrangle Books

Williams, W. (1972) *The Tragedy of American Diplomacy*, New York: Dell Publishing

Williamson, J. (1990) "What Washington Means by Policy Reform", in J. Williamson (ed.) *Latin American Adjustment: how much has happened*, Washington: Peterson Institute for International Economics

Windolf, P. (2002) *Corporate Networks in Europe and the United States*, Oxford: Oxford University Press

Winters, J. (2011) *Oligarchy*, Cambridge University Press, Kindle Edition, May 4, 2011

Wolff, E. (2010) "Recent Trends in Household Wealth in the United States: Rising debt and the middle class squeeze - an update to 2007", *Levy Economics Institute of Bard College*, March 2010, Working Paper No. 589, accessed August 19, 2015

> http://papers.ssrn.com/sol3/papers.cfm?abstract_id=1585409

Wolin, S. (2004) *Politics and Vision: Continuity and innovation in western political thought*, expanded edition, Princeton: Princeton University Press

Wolin, S. (2008) *Democracy Incorporated: Managed democracy and the specter of inverted totalitarianism*, Princeton: Princeton University Press

Wood, E.M. (1995) *Democracy against Capitalism: Renewing historical materialism*, Cambridge: Cambridge University Press

Wood, E.M. (1999) *The Origin of Capitalism*, New York: Monthly Review Press

Wood, E.M. (2003) *Empire of Capital*, London: Verso

Wood, E.M. (2008) *Citizens to Lords: a social history of western political thought from antiquity to the Middle Ages*, London: Verso

Wood, E.M. (2012) *Liberty and Property: a social history of western political thought from Renaissance to Enlightenment*, London: Verso

World Bank (2014) *World Development Report 2014: Risk and Opportunity - managing risk for development*, online accessed August 19, 2015

> http://econ.worldbank.org/WBSITE/EXTERNAL/EXTDE
> C/EXTRESEARCH/EXTWDRS/EXTNWDR2013/0,,conte
> ntMDK:23459971~pagePK:8261309~piPK:8258028~theSiteP
> K:8258025,00.html

Wray, L.R. (1998) *Understanding Modern Money: The key to full employment and price stability*, Cheltenham, UK: Edward Elgar

Wray, L.R. (2014) "From the State Theory of Money to Modern Money Theory: an alternative to economic orthodoxy", *Levy Institute of Bard College*, March 2014, Working Paper No. 792

Yackee, J. (2014) "Political Risk and International Investment Law", *Duke Journal of Comparative and International Law*, Vol 24:477

Young, M. (1996) *The Rise of the Meritocracy*, New Brunswick, NJ: Transaction Publishers

Index

egalitarian nature of, 37–38, 179
transition to inequality, 37–38
productive capacity, 25, 33–34, 108–9
productivity growth & unemployment, 188-91
profit, 90–92, 156-157
timing differences, 101-2, 156
profit equation, 10, 91–93, 98-99, 102-3, 113, 124, 130, 144, 187
derivation of, 186-87
Proudhon, Pierre-Joseph, 70
Rand, Ayn, 56, 58
Randolph, Edmund, 199
Rawls, John, 46-47
Reisman, George, 70-72
revolution of 1848, 53–62
Robin, Corey, 56-58
Robinson, Joan, 95
Robinson, William, 165, 170
Rome, 21-22, 52, 87, 175
Rothkopf, David, 15-16, 18
Russia, 52
Sachs, Jeffrey, 26-27
Samsung Electronics, 83
Schumpeter, Joseph, 114–16
Sharpe, William, 86
Sherman, Roger, 199
Shimotani, Masahiro, 83
simplicity, 5–6
Slim Helú, Carlos, 18-19, 83
Smith, Adam 23
Snowden, Edward, 174
Soros, George, 154
Spain, 32, 54, 63, 82, 129
speculation, 5, 52, 102, 153-61
Stanford Center on Poverty and Inequality, 30
Stanford Encyclopedia of Philosophy, 5

state. *See also* money
debt, 128–32, 147–49, 192-194
ideology of the, 119–20, 123, 134
interest rate, 131, 133–34
money management, 122–23
nature of, 63–65, 119
political murder, 172–74
surveillance, 171–75
taxation, 123–28, 147, 149, 192–194
Steward, Ira, 34
Stiglitz, Joseph, 25, 30, 108, 122
stock markets, 80–81
Structural Adjustment Review Initiative, 195-198
suppression. *See also* trade balance
definition of, 2, 53–54, 107
diversion margin, 109
oligarchic competition, 110–16
private market, 109–18
profit margin, 110–11, 117–18
state spending. *See* state
worker collectivization, 116
Suskind, Ron, 64
Sweden, 83
Sweezy, Paul, 6, 115
Tax Foundation, 193-94
tax havens, 13–14, 17, 30, 147, 161
Taylor, Frederick, 56
Thailand, 82
Thatcher, Margaret, 116
Thompson, E.P., 59
Tietje, Christian, 168
trade balance, 144–46
transnational state, 167
transnational system, 79–81, 83, 108, 139–51, 163–75
Treynor, Jack, 86
Trigger, Bruce, 21, 37-40
Trilateral Commission, 59-61

About the Author

Jim O'Reilly retired in 2003 from a career in banking and mortgage banking. He has an MA in Global Political Economy from the University of Sussex. He lives in Boulder, Colorado and maintains a blog at www.capitalismasoligarchy.com.

www.ingramcontent.com/pod-product-compliance
Lightning Source LLC
Chambersburg PA
CBHW072125270326
41931CB00010B/1676